The Expatriate Myth

The
Expatriate Myth

New Zealand writers
and the
colonial world

Helen Bones

OTAGO

Published by Otago University Press
Level 1, 398 Cumberland Street
Dunedin, New Zealand
university.press@otago.ac.nz
www.otago.ac.nz/press

First published 2018
Copyright © Helen Bones
The moral rights of the author have been asserted.

ISBN 978-1-98-853117-5

Editor: Caren Wilton
Indexer: Diane Lowther

Cover photograph: Jill Battaglia/Arcangel

Printed in Christchurch by Caxton.

CONTENTS

Acknowledgements

I undertook the bulk of the research for this book while writing my PhD thesis in history at the University of Canterbury, with the invaluable financial assistance of a University of Canterbury doctoral scholarship. I was also able to spend a year living and researching in England as a visiting graduate student at Christ Church, Oxford. This was due to the generosity of the Canterbury Association and the Wakefield Trust, who awarded me the Edward Gibbon Wakefield Doctoral Scholarship (I was the inaugural recipient in 2008). This scholarship was endowed to honour the memory of Edward Gibbon Wakefield and his descendants and their role in the founding of the Canterbury Settlement. The scholarship also recognises the ties between Christ Church, Oxford, and Christchurch, New Zealand.

Most vital to the successful completion of the thesis and therefore the book was the extensive and tireless help of my supervisors, Dr Chris Connolly and Professor Patrick Evans of the University of Canterbury. I continue to benefit from their expert guidance and advice today.

I consulted the archives and books in a number of collections throughout this enterprise, from the British Library to the Hocken Collection, and encountered many helpful librarians and archivists. In particular I would like to acknowledge the assistance of the staff of the Macmillan Brown Library, who cheerfully continued to supply my many obscure requests throughout job uncertainties and the aftermath of earthquakes.

In the years since completing my doctorate I have revised and updated my thesis work into the book you see before you. Thank you to Rachel Scott and the team at Otago University Press (particularly Caren Wilton for her very thorough copyediting) for their patient encouragement and efficiency in the last few months.

Sections of my thesis have appeared as journal articles. "'A book is a book, all the world over": New Zealand and the colonial writing world 1890–1945', *Journal of Imperial and Commonwealth History*, 43:5 (2015), pp. 861–81 is based on a condensed version of the first half; and 'New Zealand and the Tasman writing world, 1890–1945', *History Australia*, 10:3 (2013) is based on Chapter Three.

A lost generation?

The 'literary expatriate' is a character familiar to anyone versed in literary history, particularly the literary histories of the countries of the New World. Writers are given this label if they choose to live and write somewhere other than their country of origin, a common occurrence that tends to either be romanticised as a flight from an unpromising artistic environment or criticised as a rejection of national origins. The American writers who went to Paris in the 1920s (Gertrude Stein, Ernest Hemingway, Ezra Pound and so on) are commonly referred to as the 'Lost Generation'[1] – an appellation that manages at once to imply that their travel had a permanent and negative effect on American writing, and that this phenomenon involved pretty much everybody at that time (or at least everyone who claimed to be a writer).

The model of literary expatriatism generally goes as follows: firstly, a would-be writer must grow up in (or be taken against their will to live in) a small town, ideologically challenged society or colonial outpost (and some places are more than capable of fulfilling all three categories) that is vastly inadequate to nurture such a talent. Consequently the only possible course of action is to leave for somewhere more promising – as the Australian writer Henry Lawson put it, to 'go steerage, stow away, swim and seek London, Yankeeland or Timbuktoo'[2] – with great haste. Secondly, this regrettable withdrawal from one's native country results in the creation of an 'expatriate': a special category that implies that the writers and their potential contributions have been permanently lost, even though in most cases expatriatism was not permanent. In the *Oxford History of New Zealand Literature*, Lawrence Jones writes that the only realistic outcomes for aspiring New Zealand novelists between 1890 and 1934 were withdrawal into 'silence' or 'expatriation'.[3] He implies that expatriation was really another kind of silence, because it signalled a loss of literary talent for the country: the expatriate would no longer be contributing to the national canon. Jones also gives voice to a common binary division imposed on the literary past, between authors with a national focus and those with international interests: a division that did not exist in reality. This myth of necessary literary expatriatism, leading in most cases to 'voluntary exile', is an accepted and lamented part of many ex-colonial cultural nationalisms.[4]

This book questions the place of literary expatriatism in the New Zealand national imagination and fills a gap in scholarship made noticeable recently by the publication of several books dealing with Australian examples.[5] Taking a deliberately contrary position, this study questions fundamentally the usefulness of the category of 'expatriate' to explain or evaluate writers' experiences in any meaningful way. An uninterrogated division between disadvantaged 'stayers' and lost 'leavers' does not account for the spaces occupied by many early-twentieth-century writers who lived in New Zealand, and/or thought of themselves as New Zealanders, but did not fit easily into national categorisations. Because of the extensive networks resulting from British colonial expansions into the South Pacific, many authors had multiple attachments to different places and thus fell outside of national canons, or were included in several. A later insistence on narrow parameters of local 'authenticity' in writing had an effect on the literary reputations, careers and reception of authors who operated in the interconnected world of the early twentieth century: the 'colonial writing world'.[6] Terry Sturm's biography of the widely travelled and immensely successful novelist Edith Lyttleton – who generally published under the name G.B. Lancaster – describes a literary life that spanned continents. From the late 1930s onwards Lyttleton virtually disappeared from conversations about New Zealand literature, and Sturm blames her lack of recognition on literary critics with a national focus.[7] The obscuration of such a mode of existence has led to blank spaces and sparsity in literary history, where in fact there was vitality and mobility and creativity.

I also join with an increasing number of literary historians whose work raises questions about the supposedly desperate situation of New Zealand artists and writers in the first place. This book aims to provide an accurate depiction of the international nature of New Zealand writing at this time.

As a result, it includes the stories of authors who did not physically leave the country, but still led international lives through the networks of the colonial writing world. Eileen Duggan, for example, was at one time 'the best-known and most widely admired of New Zealand poets'.[8] She earned her living solely from full-time writing for almost 50 years by publishing her work in magazines and newspapers in Ireland, the United Kingdom, Australia and the United States, and received favourable reviews all over the world. All of this was achieved without ever setting foot outside of New Zealand; Ireland was the inspiration for a number of her poems, but she never visited it. This was largely due to a fear of travel, or at least unwillingness to do so, as she feared that she would 'never see Karori hills again'.[9] In 1926 she wrote to the Australian writer and critic Nettie Palmer: 'I wish indeed I could drop in on you but I'm the worst traveller in the three islands.'[10] Despite this apparent handicap, her five books of verse were published in multiple countries and editions.

Eileen Duggan's story could seem unusual to those only superficially acquainted with recent literary historiography, because nationalist frameworks have so successfully obscured transnational operations. This book will examine the expatriate myth from two main angles. The first is the widely accepted idea that expatriation was necessary for New Zealand writers in the late nineteenth and early twentieth centuries because of the country's supposed dearth of opportunities, a result of both the perceived lack of publishing outlets and the absence of a community of like-minded artistic people. Katherine Mansfield, New Zealand's most famous literary expatriate, is usually the first example who comes to mind. Mansfield applied her talents with the most success after leaving Wellington for England and Europe. She herself did plenty to add to the evidence that it was necessary to flee from New Zealand at the earliest available opportunity. She wrote from Wellington in 1907 that 'life here is impossible – I can't see how it can drag on'.[11] That same year she wrote in a poem: 'It's London ever calling me / the live long day.'[12] At around the same time the budding novelist Jane Mander was living in the Northland town of Whāngārei and working as a subeditor for the local newspaper. In 1909 she wrote to the editors of the *Triad* magazine that her subscription was the only thing that kept her going in the 'brain-benumbing, stimulus-stifling, sense-stultifying, soul-searing silence'.[13] Anecdotes and uncontextualised quotations such as these often-cited outbursts from Mander and Mansfield have until quite recently stood in for concerted attempts to document the actual opportunities available to authors.

Happily, work by scholars such as Chris Hilliard, Lydia Wevers, Jane Stafford and Mark Williams has done much lately to broaden understanding and more accurately depict the literary life and possibilities of early-twentieth-century New Zealand. All of this reveals that literary expatriatism was less necessary and less common than generally assumed. Studies such as Jane Stafford and Mark Williams' *Maoriland* give a nuanced depiction of New Zealand literary life, and what emerges is a very different story to one of cultural deprivation. Even Katherine Mansfield, according to Stafford and Williams, might have remained in New Zealand and still have been a success.[14] Chris Hilliard has contributed considerably to this as well: *The Bookmen's Dominion* describes the 'respectable bohemia' that existed between the two world wars, at least in the major cities, and acknowledges the publishing opportunities on offer outside of the book industry (such as in newspapers and magazines).[15] Michele Leggott refers to a 'lost matrix of women poets' and, along with Heather Murray, describes the literary communities obscured by 'a cultural nationalism inimical to previous competencies'.[16] A trend towards transnational and empirical approaches has reinvigorated topics that had been assumed exhausted of novel interpretations. These studies often refer to the importance of colonial or international networks to their subjects. Lydia Wevers has shown in *Reading on the Farm* that literary culture can be found in the remotest of places, and that rural New Zealanders remained connected to a colonial world of reading.[17] This book draws on these approaches and others to argue that there was more to pre-1930s New Zealand literary life than deprivation and oppression.

The second focus of the book is an investigation into the nature and effects of New Zealand literary expatriatism when it did occur. This requires some definitions. An immediate obstacle to writing a comprehensive account of literary expatriatism is the ill-defined and slippery nature of a term that is simultaneously loaded with meaning. It carries many assumptions along with it, including an inherent negativity and the implication of loss. An expatriate, broadly speaking, is anyone living somewhere other than their country of origin for any length of time. The term has been distorted to mean something specific in terms of artists and intellectuals: it is often used to signify the renunciation of one's country of birth by removing oneself overseas to live

– 'throwing up the sponge', in the words of writer and critic Isabel Maud Peacocke.[18] The second part of this book examines the more loaded use of the term 'expatriate' when used to refer to writers (as well as artists and intellectuals).

'Expatriate' is a ubiquitous term, but often those using it make no attempt to define it. When definitions are provided there is little consensus, and it is difficult to compare studies based on vastly different parameters. The Australian studies dealing with this subject are variable in their approach. Stephen Alomes' *When London Calls* discusses the issues associated with the term 'expatriate' and focuses on the post-World War II period, saying that in this time the journey to Britain became 'increasingly common' for writers and artists.[19] In the 2009 *Cambridge History of Australian Literature* Peter Pierce states that in the period following World War I 'so many artists and writers – far from turning away from Europe – took themselves to live there'.[20] For 'so many' we are referred to a 'long list' in Geoffrey Serle's *From Deserts the Prophets Come* (1973). Serle's exact words were: '[T]he only possibility of becoming a serious professional writer was by migrating. The list of expatriate Australian writers is long and impressive', followed by a list of 23 writers, ending with 'and others'.[21] He gives no indication as to what qualifies these writers as expatriates. Peter Morton directly discusses the problems of definition in *Lusting for London*, asking questions about who qualifies as an Australian writer, and how long and in what fashion someone needs to stay away in order to qualify as an expatriate. He decides that strong initial Australian associations and a lengthy period abroad leading to disassociation from Australia are required to qualify for inclusion.[22] The most recent addition to the field is Bruce Bennett and Anne Pender's *From a Distant Shore*. Their expatriate criteria are 'someone who was born in Australia and who spent substantial or formative periods of their writing careers in Britain … [and] for whom the expatriate years made a difference, and in some way inspired or enabled their literary careers'.[23]

These last two examples at least provide a definition, but as they base their inclusion criteria on expatriatism having a significant impact or resulting in disassociation from Australia, their sample groups are biased in a certain direction. John Arnold has attempted to measure the impact of Australian writers on the English literary scene, concluding that 'over one hundred Australians had at least one book of creative writing published in London while they were in England at some time between 1900–1940'. He also gives the total number of books by Australian authors published in Britain during the same period: 1923.[24] Arnold uses data from bibliographic work that does not include a clear explanation of how an 'Australian' is defined,[25] and without comparative figures for writers who stayed in Australia while publishing in Britain it is difficult to draw any conclusions from this information. Given the variety of approaches, it is impossible to accurately gauge the prevalence and significance of expatriatism for Australian writers from the available sources.

The term 'expatriate' is often commingled with the category of 'exile', a character or idea that occurs frequently within the field of literary criticism. Such criticism represents literary exiles as grappling with dislocation and loss, focusing on the creative inspiration or hindrance that this provides. A common assumption arising from the perceived necessity of expatriation is that expatriate writers were overseas *against their will*: they were compelled to leave their 'home' place, resulting in dislocation and exile. 'Exile' implies inability to return and dislocation from home, resulting from the need to distance oneself from it both physically and intellectually. The study of exile and writing is almost always concerned with readings of literary texts from this angle – as, for example, 'stories and histories that recuperate losses incurred in migration, dislocation and translation'.[26] Although expatriates are often called exiles, the exiles of this category of criticism are usually involuntary exiles crossing linguistic boundaries (for example Joseph Conrad, Vladimir Nabokov and Salman Rushdie). This suggests a whole range of issues that simply do not apply to New Zealanders who voluntarily journeyed to Australia or London.

As a result, while often used interchangeably with 'expatriate', 'exile' is an equally pervasive and ill-defined term used to describe travelling writers. In an article about Godfrey Blunden, an Australian 'exile' in Paris, Patrick Buckridge attempts to clear up the confusion caused by 'fuzzy' terminology:

> I suppose that 'expatriation', strictly speaking, means going and/or staying away from one's homeland, whether voluntarily or involuntarily; whereas 'exile' (strictly speaking) means being forced to go and/or stay away, but is metaphorically used to refer to an expatriate condition where some kind of inner compulsion not to return is present. There seems little point, however, in speaking too strictly, imposing an artificial stability where none exists in common usage ...[27]

He is correct that the categories of 'exile' and 'expatriate' are not clearly defined. This is not a good excuse for avoiding the issue, however. These terms should not be used interchangeably, but they often are. This kind of 'expatriatism' does not describe the experiences of the majority of writers who went abroad, though this use of the term might have had its political uses for those concerned with cultural nationalism.

Critic and literary historian Eric McCormick and other cultural nationalists were influential in creating the image of the archetypal New Zealand writer as exiled expatriate. Monte Holcroft later echoed this sentiment when he wrote that talented New Zealand writers were compelled to 'escape' from an 'unpromising environment'.[28] These assumptions continued to resonate throughout the rest of the twentieth century, with Riemke Ensing speaking in 1974 of the 'exile theme which had dominated New Zealand literature'.[29] For example, the unchallenged Wikipedia page on 'Culture of New Zealand' states that 'New Zealand's most successful early writers were expatriates such as Katherine Mansfield'.[30] The page expresses a popular belief that is also a staple of literary historiography, and yet there is little interrogation of the nature of this expatriate status – for some it represents the regrettable necessity for writers to distance themselves from their roots in order to be successful, and for others it describes the fate of New Zealand writers forced to leave but remaining 'outsiders' overseas. Either of these options could result in silence as New Zealand writers. Unlike many other assumptions made in the course of the search for New Zealand national identity, the assumed importance of expatriatism has not been thoroughly examined. I focus on the experiences of New Zealand writers overseas to describe the nature of literary expatriatism and its effects.

While Australian investigations into literary exoduses have severe limitations, no surveys exist at all about this topic for New Zealand writers. As a result, for New Zealand this question has been entirely neglected (although Felicity Barnes has utilised a nuanced view of the role of literary expatriation to London to bolster her argument about the city functioning as an extension of New Zealand in the imagination of New Zealanders).[31] To properly quantify the significance of literary expatriatism, I have compiled statistical information about the movements and publications of New Zealand writers, to determine the number who managed to conduct literary careers without leaving New Zealand. I have also examined the lives and careers of writers who did leave, to determine if their experiences fit the model of exile and disconnection assumed to be the fate of literary expatriates. The stories and arguments presented in this book have a statistical underpinning that has allowed me to model the international workings of New Zealand writing in the first half of the twentieth century. For simplicity, I have defined a 'New Zealand writer' as someone who spent at least 10 years living in New Zealand, and who published a book in English between 1890 and 1945. My figures are based on a dataset of publications by New Zealand writers during this time period, comprising 717 works (first editions only) by 322 authors.[32] 'Overseas writers' are New Zealand writers who were out of the country at the point in time being discussed. A smaller subset of 118 traceable writers about whom adequate biographical information could be collected – in my thesis I refer to them as 'prominent writers' – was used to derive statistics pertaining to location and movement of authors.

Literary empirical techniques and book history have in recent decades brought new light to subjects previously left to literary critics and scholars with different aims (such as a focus on content rather than the historical context in which a literary work was created). This gap is increasingly being bridged by historians and literary scholars with historical sympathies, using techniques that have been dubbed the 'new empiricism', and others interested in the structures and networks behind book production. The work of Franco Moretti has emphasised the importance of looking at the whole system of book production rather than the 'minimal fraction' of published works that make it into a national canon.[33] David Carter, influenced by Pierre Bourdieu's idea of the 'cultural field', has argued that texts 'are produced within a system, an economy, a field, a network, a circuit, a culture, a community' and cannot be separated from their environment, and that the focus on 'remarkable texts' that are held up as national archetypes reinforces the fixation on nationalism in writing.[34]

These approaches naturally intersect with the idea of 'colonial networks': the system or field within which New Zealand writers were creating literature in the early twentieth century. The vital role of these networks has been emphasised by a number of recent scholars such as Alan Lester in his work on the communication of humanitarian ideas between Cape Town, New South Wales and New Zealand through trans-colonial systems. Lester presents the British Empire as 'bundles of networks, often overlapping and intersecting, but never unitary, never stable, always contested'.[35] Tony Ballantyne prefers the metaphor of a web for the set of networks through which ideas could be easily transmitted.[36] The 'colonial writing world' was made up of these networks, which were available to anyone with connections to the British Empire (which was the majority of people in New Zealand in the early twentieth century), although they were most easily accessed by those of British descent.

When a combination of these ideas and techniques is applied to the history of New Zealand writing, the results show that not as many writers left New Zealand as is often assumed: just under half did not leave the country at all between 1890 and 1945, but did not let this hinder their attempts to publish their work. Of those who did leave, the majority undertook journeys of different lengths but then returned.[37] Within the context of colonial networks, mobility was unremarkable. As Peter Morton points out with regard to Australian writers, 'In the early days many saw shifting from Melbourne to London as intrinsically no more noteworthy to shifting from any English provincial town to London ... rarely was it seen as a matter of conflicting allegiances, of being a matter worthy of public concern or condemnation.'[38] Very few writers left without ever returning. The life of Nelle Scanlan provides a more representative story. Scanlan was a New Zealand novelist who travelled widely throughout her life and was immensely successful (she has been called 'New Zealand's most widely read popular novelist of the 1930s and 40s').[39] She returned to New Zealand a number of times and supported the founding of the PEN (Poets, Essayists, Novelists) New Zealand Centre and the New Zealand Women Writers' and Artists' Society. She settled permanently in Paraparaumu Beach in 1948.

Such mobility was common within the colonial world, and did not only involve migration either to or away from the colonies. Studies of broad population trends have tended in the past to focus on large-scale, one-way, permanent emigration flows in the British diaspora, or in postcolonial terms on the impact of colonies on the centre of empire and the expatriation of colonial prodigies back to the metropolitan centre. Much colonial world mobility fell outside of these categories, however. As Lester and Lambert have argued, the colonial world involved multi-directional mobility, and many mobile Britons occupied a third category outside of 'those who settled in or those who travelled through the empire'.[40] Sofia Eriksson has noted in her thesis on travel writing about Australia that a significant group of people did not have a permanent base and 'perambulated the Empire back and forth as business and inclination dictated', meaning that 'a definite distinction between migrants and travellers becomes tenuous, certainly in the very mobile Victorian era, but also in the later Edwardian years'.[41] There was much more to this story than two-way traffic – as Angela Woollacott describes, communication and networks 'extended beyond England ... to many global points'.[42] The multi-faceted British Empire reinforced this, as did the nature of travel: traversing the empire involved calling at several ports in diverse countries in Africa, South Asia or South America, ideally places controlled by Britain.

Scanlan and a host of other writers who were well travelled (or at least who published their books overseas) are under-represented in the history of New Zealand literature and in attempts to compile a 'national canon', because of the distorting influence of nationalism and the centrality of 'the nation' to New Zealand literary criticism and history until the late twentieth century. An early anxiety about New Zealand literature and the questions of its creation and composition resulted in a preoccupation with the project of creating 'authentic' New Zealand artistic expressions in the late 1930s and 1940s (as espoused by Allen Curnow in the introduction to *A Book of New Zealand Verse* in 1945).[43] Curnow and his associates' occasional preoccupations became literary orthodoxy, and these conditions were anachronistically applied to earlier times in which colonial mobility was actually viewed unproblematically. The cultural nationalists' vision of New Zealand national identity and culture has since been extensively deconstructed and exposed as narrowly defined and based on a Pākehā, male, rural and pioneering 'ideal'.[44] While transnational approaches have become virtually standard in recent years, there is still much work to be done to restore a number of early-twentieth-century New Zealand writers to their place in literary history, and to do so in a way that questions rather than cements 'the analytical primacy of the nation'.[45] Often the focus is still on contributions to national literature, even if transnational aspects of this are accepted.

Foreign publication and overseas practitioners have not sat well with the drive to create and describe a national canon. Foreign publication has often been disparaged by authors and those in the industry because of the perceived damage to local production, and because the need to pander to foreign markets and audiences is thought to interfere with the 'authenticity' of the writing. If the writers' experiences or preferred subject matter fell outside of nationalist frameworks, they risked being either deliberately or accidentally ignored, leading to a much reduced picture of what was possible for New Zealand writers, as well as a widespread belief in the mutual exclusivity of nationalism and expatriatism. This is still the underlying attitude in discussions of expatriatism and foreign publishing, even if the existence of broader options is becoming more widely acknowledged.

A further division that became more marked from the 1930s onwards was between 'high' and 'low' art. In the early part of the century the arbiters of literary production were newspaper editors, as many careers were fostered or supplemented by publication in newspapers. From the 1930s, those in positions of literary power were increasingly based in the universities and concerned with a modernist aesthetic (including the idea of expressing the essence of locality and nation). The focus on fostering a canon which would express quintessential 'New Zealandness' obscured other approaches. The earlier writers who interacted with the colonial writing world were concerned with many genres, including various forms of popular writing. As well as this, many were not interested in modernism and despaired of the absence of beauty in art for its own sake. Eileen Duggan asked in 1951: 'Where are the words that broke the heart with beauty? / This is the age of the merely clever.'[46] Ironically, despite the importance of locality, landscape and nation to the cultural nationalists, the models that they followed were from Britain and Europe, particularly from the new group of young English poets of the 1930s, which included W.H. Auden and Cecil Day Lewis. Their foundational publication *Phoenix* in fact 'looked a lot like' John Middleton Murry's *New Adelphi*, produced in London.[47] As well as ignoring the clear international influences on New Zealand writing and the transnational origins of modernism, insistence on this particular approach to art and literature obscured the work of many writers not engaged with this very narrow genre.

If anxiety about New Zealand's depth of culture and place in the world is an aspect of the 'national character', it is certainly not unique. The idea that many writers and artists have regrettably been forced to leave their inadequate colonial starting points can be found commonly in the British settler colonies. Traditional Australian literary history describes a nationalist flowering in the 1890s followed by a 'cultural desert' in the 1920s and 30s, leading to a mass exodus continuing into the second half of the century. Settler colonialism was not confined to the British Empire, and Paris functioned in a similar way to London as the centre of the francophone colonial writing world. A book with similar conclusions could have been written about one of the other British settler colonies, as indeed they too were important parts of the colonial writing world. New Zealand makes a useful case study as an entry point into this field of enquiry because the number of proponents is relatively small, making comprehensive data collection feasible.

The first half of the book questions entrenched ideas about New Zealand's unsuitability for writers and the resultant need for them to leave. These ideas all contribute to a relatively widely held notion that would-be writers in New Zealand were disadvantaged if they remained so far from the origins of culture. Chapter One takes issue with the idea that late-nineteenth- and early-twentieth-century New Zealanders lacked an interest in culture or, indeed, their own culture, while Chapter Two questions the proposition that local literary opportunities were lacking. Chapters Three and Four reveal that the availability or otherwise of local opportunities was far from the end of the story, as the connections of the colonial writing world extended far beyond the physical constraints of New Zealand shores, removing the need to leave to participate in overseas literary networks.

The mobile, modern world produced both the colonial writing world and the reaction against it that was literary nationalism. The disruption of old certainties might have caused some 'discomposure',[48] but it also meant that New Zealanders were world-minded, and opened up opportunities for writing wherever they were. Chapter Five investigates the origins of the myth of expatriate exiles with reference to modernism and the cultural nationalists' efforts to replace lost traditions. Chapter Six discusses the lives of writers largely outside this paradigm in the modern world. Writers' success did not hinge on either their location or the location of their works' publication. Chapters Seven and Eight make the point that writers gained no great advantage by going to London because they already had access to Britain's literary infrastructure through the networks of the colonial writing world. At the same time, they were at no greater disadvantage, as New Zealanders, than any other writers struggling to be recognised in the milieu, and they continued to be assisted by colonial world networks.

Terry Sturm's work on Edith Lyttleton gives a detailed picture of the possibilities that existed outside of national categorisations.[49] This book joins

Sturm and others in helping to reposition the lives of New Zealand writers in the context of the colonial writing world. It furthers this argument by describing the New Zealand literary field's part in the colonial world system, and in doing so acknowledges the blurred lines that existed in practice between nations and nationalities, and between 'home' and 'abroad'.

CHAPTER ONE

Literary culture in
New Zealand

Jane Mander's first novel, *The Story of a New Zealand River*, tells the story of a young mother brought out from England to live in the wilds of the Northland kauri-harvesting region. Initially bewildered by the rough and ready ways of the settlement, she encounters a fellow Englishwoman who immediately senses her despair: "'I know just how you feel," cried Mrs. Brayton impulsively. "You've been here one week, and you think it's the end of everything, and that you'll die, and that there's no God. I know.""[1] It is not hard to imagine that this was a common reaction to being stranded in such a far-flung place with a relatively short history of European inhabitation. Others have reacted similarly, leading James Belich to write in 2002 that '[v]isions of New Zealand as a cultural wasteland stretch back from the 1900s to the whole nineteenth century, and forward into the twentieth century'.[2]

Early European inhabitants of New Zealand had a reputation for having no culture of their own and few cultural interests. The usual explanation is that the settlers were initially overwhelmed by the immediate task of forging an existence from an unforgiving land, so had little interest in the trivialities of art and literature. Contemporaries and later commentators alike, up until the very present, have assumed that the realities of a rural-based economy left little time for such pursuits. In 1936 Alan Mulgan said that New Zealand was a young country, preoccupied with 'taming a land of mountain, forest and flood',[3] and its inhabitants could not be expected to have the extra energy required to produce literature as well. The most recent version of the *Oxford History of New Zealand Literature in English* includes Terry Sturm's endorsement of this idea: while practical, non-fiction topics might have had some appeal, the vital forms of literature at this time were '[c]ertainly not poetry and fiction'.[4] Later on in that volume MacDonald P. Jackson makes the same assumption, arguing that '[m]igration and the setting up of a home at the other end of the world exhausted the creative impulse.'[5] Lydia Wevers, in accounting for the lack of stand-out nineteenth-century novels, finds the answer in the 'energy expended on the heart of the bush … You can only write the novel after you have built the hut to write it in.'[6]

New Zealand's early colonists were, in fact, surprisingly quick to create cultural institutions, although there were natural limitations due to the remoteness and small population. Of course, there were those who complained that New Zealand was a dreadful place for anyone interested in anything beyond the material basis of life – but such complaints continue in the present. In 1860, writing from high-country Canterbury only 12 years after the settlement was founded, Samuel Butler noted wryly that a mountain was thought beautiful only if it were good for sheep. 'But it does not do,' he said, 'to speak about John Sebastian Bach's "Fugues", or pre-Raphaelite pictures.'[7] Katherine Mansfield left for London in 1908 purportedly to escape the country's 'suffocating materialism'.[8] Other writers resented the lack of importance attached to their art compared to more materialist activities. R.A.K. Mason described New Zealand after World War I as a society run by '[m]en who consider the world was made and the stars ranged in order to facilitate the transport of pigs between Taupiri and Wairoa'.[9] Winnie Gonley wrote in 1932: 'Our remoteness and our preoccupation with the task of subduing a new country have given us little interest in or time for acquiring literary technique.'[10] Comments like these have been used to suggest that New Zealand was not a place that provided intellectual nutriment or support for literary-minded inhabitants, forcing them to leave or languish. However, this is not the end of the story, as indicated by a more thorough investigation of the underlying evidence.

Ideas about New Zealand's unsuitability to support writers often hinge on anachronistic and impossible requirements of local 'authenticity'. New Zealand was believed to lack culture, meaning an interest in cultural pursuits, but also its own unique New Zealand culture as expressed in art and literature. Even today, questions about whether New Zealand can claim to have a unique national character at all are not uncommon. These issues were all the more pertinent when British and New Zealand culture were harder to separate. Such unanswerable questions were the focus of much of New Zealand's literary history and criticism in the twentieth century, including an endless search for the 'great New Zealand novel' – an accolade which the hundreds of candidates already on offer never seemed to deserve.

In fact, many cultural amenities were well established by the turn of the twentieth century. Many New Zealanders were deeply interested in art and literature, and it was not necessary to leave the country to encounter European high culture. Cultural artefacts were imported from Britain to the colonies along with the immigrants, in both tangible and intangible forms. Eric McCormick himself attests that the suitcases of British immigrants were stuffed with books, including the works of Tennyson, the Brownings and Dickens, to name a few.[11] The settlers had, apparently, followed the literary advice of immigration publicists like E.J. Wakefield, who in 1848 told every colonist 'to supply himself with a good collection of these cheerful companions'.[12]

Adding to this, in the last few decades a number of scholarly works have appeared making it clear that the deprived picture of New Zealand's intellectual offerings is the result of narrow definitions of culture. Jane Stafford and Mark Williams, for example, have described in detail the 'Maoriland' school of writing, which was the name given to a prolific output of verse and prose between the 1880s and late 1910s.[13] Dismissed as derivatively British with embarrassing attempts to include 'local colour', 'Maoriland' writing was rejected by the cultural nationalists of the 1930s as 'largely provincial, imitative and undistinguished', as opposed to the desired 'native or distinctive'.[14] This insistence on a somewhat meaningless distinction between 'imported' and 'native' culture led to the perception of a cultural vacuum in the early twentieth century. The hugely damaging effects of the spread of British culture at the expense of indigenous culture (whether inadvertently or in the form of deliberate eradication or appropriation) increased the aversion to the study of colonial culture in the later twentieth century. While colonial culture is widely studied today, and books like *Maoriland* approach it on its own terms, some of this postcolonial embarrassment remains (and it is important not to ignore the role of colonial culture in the oppression of indigenous cultures). This lingering discomfort, along with a stronger focus on cultural expressions that relate to New Zealand specifically, has slowed the uncovering of the rich cultural milieu that people enjoyed due to connections with the colonial world. What follows continues to build up the picture of cultural life in New Zealand from 1890 to 1945, focusing on the fruitful and neglected interwar period. Because of the blind spot towards so-called 'imported' culture created by cultural nationalism, the depth and pervasiveness of artistic pursuits in New Zealand has rarely been acknowledged.

It is evident that New Zealanders, from the very beginning of British settlement, built up a contemporary reputation for being unusually keen on cultural pursuits when compared to their compatriots from Britain and the British Empire – something that has not been widely recognised in recent times.[15] Whether or not it was truly exceptional compared to other colonies, by the turn of the twentieth century New Zealand was quite well-provided with books. According to the literary collector T.M. Hocken, books imported from Britain stocked the 'good supply of bookshops ... and were eagerly borrowed from the many public libraries'.[16] William Pember Reeves wrote in 1898 that 'music, reading, and flower gardening' were the three chief colonial pastimes.[17]

Howard McNaughton opens his survey of New Zealand by claiming that New Zealand's European settlers were 'antagonistic to the arts', but this is quickly tempered by his own evidence regarding the enthusiastic instigation of drama groups and theatres in the colony in ways that have been obscured from historical view. He claims that early New Zealand drama was 'initially a labouring-class phenomenon' and the bulk of its audience was 'totally illiterate', meaning such pursuits were seldom mentioned in the newspapers. By 1843, he continues, 'regular theatrical performances were established' in Auckland, Wellington and Nelson, which is rather astounding considering official settlement had only begun three years earlier.[18] There were well-established amateur dramatic societies by the turn of the twentieth century,[19] and theatrical performances were provided in abundance by touring English, American and European companies. Maurice Hurst wrote in 1944:

> Young people of to-day can hardly conceive of the 'good old days' when outstanding stage artists and theatrical companies, singers and musicians, came to New Zealand from abroad in an almost continuous procession, bringing with them something of the glamour and excitement of the great theatres of London and other cities of Europe and sometimes of New York.[20]

In Dunedin, even in the late nineteenth century, there were 'few nights of the year' when something theatrical was not on offer.[21] Alan Mulgan also related that 'it was astonishing how much drama and music came to this very remote colony with its tiny population'.[22] There was certainly a great deal of enthusiasm for these performances, with demand outstripping supply. Ngaio Marsh remembered how 'colonial audiences were elated at the sight of advance notices of theatre companies, how they formed long patient queues for tickets, and rushed for seats at performances'.[23] These troupes were not discouraged from visiting even during World War I, though they were fewer in number. Attendance then improved again during the 1920s.[24] Although performances were not of the quality or quantity that could be found in a place like London, there was still plenty on offer. When moving pictures threatened to divert audiences, private theatre companies diminished but local amateur organisations rose to take their place, bolstered by the Workers' Educational Association, universities and repertory theatres, and the establishment of a New Zealand branch of the British Drama League in 1932.[25]

Music was another cultural fixture the colonists were loath to leave behind. According to the official statistics quoted by Elizabeth Plumridge, 'musical activity was widespread in the colonial community', and '[m]usical instruments of all kinds were available and in demand as soon as British settlers arrived'.[26] Census records confirm the wide availability of music in the colonies: by 1911 there were 1939 New Zealanders whose recorded occupation was musician, vocalist, or student or teacher/professor of music.[27] In 1905 some laudatory comments from a visiting English piano manufacturer were published in the Christchurch *Star* about New Zealanders' enthusiasm for musical pursuits:

> *The colonials generally, he stated, are very large purchasers of pianos, but New Zealand is in this respect far ahead of the other colonies. 'It is an undoubted fact,' he added 'that in proportion to population the people of New Zealand are the greatest purchasers of pianos in the world. There is no other country where the sales reach such a relatively large figure.' The standard of musical culture in the colony, in our visitor's opinion, is ahead of that in any of the other colonies.*[28]

Charles Baeyertz presided over elocutionary and musical competitions in Christchurch, and these proved popular. Hurst records that there were also many performances by visiting musicians. Musical entertainments included opera performances, and brass and pipe bands existed in most towns. The Woolston Brass Band, for example, was formed in 1891 and is still well-known in Christchurch. Orchestras and choirs were formed in every sizeable town. Hurst lists major and well-established musical societies in the 1940s, many of which had existed for decades. Christchurch alone could offer the Royal Christchurch Musical Society, the Christchurch Harmonic Society, the Christchurch Liedertafel (male voice choir), the Laurian Club (chamber music), the Eroica Club (piano music), the Christchurch Orchestral Society, the Christchurch Liederkranchen (ladies' choir), and the Christchurch Operatic Society.

New Zealanders were also highly literate. Guy Scholefield conducted a study of the readership of local newspapers and concluded that they were widely read because of the high levels of literacy of the New Zealand people, 'all of whom by virtue of the national education act of 1877 will have been taught to read and write.'[29] The literacy rate was close to 100 per cent by the time Scholefield wrote this in 1958; Anna and Max Rogers claim that in 1886, only nine years after the act was passed, 'over 73 per cent of the population could both read and write.'[30] James Belich has used census reports to estimate that the overall illiteracy rate was 25 per cent in 1858, which was 'probably not dissimilar to that of Britain', and this is echoed by Lydia Wevers as well as other sources.[31] As noted earlier, reading was one of the three favoured colonial activities in 1898. Reeves mentioned the abundance of 'booksellers' shops and free libraries'.[32] A.G. Stephens (editor of the Sydney *Bulletin*) went so far as to hint (somewhat unflatteringly) that New Zealanders were *over*educated, commenting that 'Maoriland is a curiously "educated" country. There are "high schools" and "colleges" and "universities" galore.'[33]

Colonists in New Zealand showed an interest in enhancing the educational opportunities on offer from the very beginning. Many libraries began their lives as Mechanics' Institutes, which were educational establishments formed to provide adult education to working men: the Auckland public library is an example (as a Mechanics' Institute Library it dates back to 1842). A 'proliferation of libraries' and varied educational institutions were created by colonists concerned with self-improvement.[34] This was not confined to the cities: some sheep stations boasted libraries that were available for staff to use for the benefit of their literacy skills.[35] Lydia Wevers' study of Brancepeth Station in the Wairarapa focuses on one such library, which was established in order to 'improve literacy among the workers', as well as to facilitate classes in adult literacy.[36] As a result of these initiatives there is some cause to infer that New Zealanders were unusually well acquainted with literature: in 1872 after visiting the 'Tuapika' Athenaeum (in Tuapeka, Otago) Anthony Trollope reported that 'Carlyle, Macaulay and Dickens are certainly better known to small communities in New Zealand than they are to similar congregations of men and women at home'.[37]

While it might seem logical that a new colony first occupies itself with establishment, and puts aside the task of encouraging cultural pursuits until life is more settled, evidence would suggest that this was not the case, at least in New Zealand. Almost as soon as they arrived, immigrants from Britain set to work recreating the cultural institutions that they remembered and missed from home, including the public library.[38] The British library movement was in its heyday in the 1850s, when British institutions were being transplanted whole to the colonies.[39] The first legislation empowering local authorities to set up public libraries by providing tax support was passed in 1869, along the lines of the Public Libraries Act of 1850 in Britain.[40] Records show that by 1926 there were as many as 435 libraries in New Zealand, ranging from small collections of a few hundred volumes to those in the bigger cities, 'which [could] stand comparison with libraries of towns in England of similar proportions'.[41] Libraries were not professionalised or institutionalised until the 1940s, when the Labour government became involved.[42] As the universities did not have a large role in public life until later in the twentieth century, libraries were centres for research and discussion of ideas.[43] Though the infrastructure was not yet in place to make libraries highly successful, even the smallest towns had some sort of collection, reflecting a high interest in reading throughout the colony.

In fact, J.E. Traue claims that New Zealand was a 'veritable paradise for readers' by the end of the nineteenth century, and that 'New Zealand appears to have achieved, within some fifty years of settlement, the highest density, that is, number of libraries to total population, ever reached in any country or state in the world'.[44] In his article 'The public library explosion in colonial New Zealand', Traue gives figures to back this up, recounting:

> Such libraries were not confined to urban areas; many sparsely populated rural counties were particularly well served. In 1906 the county of Otamatea had six libraries for 2,921 people, Weber, one library for 593, and Cheviot, one library for 1,605.[45]

Traue recorded that the ratio of libraries to people was one for every 2099 people in 1908. This ratio is considerably higher than the figures for Australia or North America. This is possibly because of the late timing of New Zealand's European settlement, coinciding with a time when libraries were more prevalent, combined with overcompensation resulting from a desire not to be culturally disadvantaged.[46]

Like libraries, bookshops were also remarkably common. One commentator reported that in Wellington in 1909 there were 15 good bookshops serving 60,000 people, and that at least three were worthy of a city three times Wellington's size.[47] This was to continue, and an American author wrote in 1954:

> I have never ceased to be amazed at the profusion, the excellence, and the service of New Zealand bookshops. There are three bookshops in the small city of Wellington, two in Christchurch, and three in Auckland which are larger than the largest bookshop in Baltimore, Maryland, a city of a million people.[48]

Where a specialised bookshop was not available, the general store took over this role. In 1890 only 20 per cent of the population lived in the four main centres, and demand for books was catered for by general retail establishments.[49] Readers might not always have been able to get the latest titles, but there was a demand and enthusiasm for books that presents a contrasting picture to the image of cultural deprivation. Stanley Unwin, of the British publishing firm Allen & Unwin, wrote in 1935 that 'New Zealand, with its one and a half million inhabitants, is a wonderfully steady buyer of books – probably, per head of population, one of the best in the world outside Scotland.'[50] A survey conducted in 1906 of the reading habits of colonial girls concluded that they were better read, in general, than their British counterparts. Of New Zealand, it said: 'Some of the New Zealand girls' papers were equal to the very best English or Scotch, and the varied nature of their reading was astonishing.'[51] The survey also credited colonial girls with better spelling and depth of knowledge of different authors.

Another British institution that emigrants recreated enthusiastically in New Zealand was the newspaper. The first newspaper in Canterbury was set up in Lyttelton in early 1851, just 26 days after the first printing presses arrived on board the *Charlotte Jane*. Eric McCormick mentions the many newspapers produced in the earliest days of the colony, 'on one occasion with the aid of a mangle'.[52] According to Dennis McEldowney, 'printing presses were stowed in the first emigrant ships as a matter of course', and the printed items required to establish the new settlements, such as newspapers and official proclamations, were being 'peeled off them within days of landing'.[53] Printing was encouraged by the transnational missionary organisations, which competed to get their catechisms translated into native languages. The Church Missionary Society sent William Colenso to the Bay of Islands in 1834 with a fully equipped press, and by 1835 he had succeeded in printing Māori translations of the epistles of Paul to the Philippians and the Ephesians.[54] Cultural information of all kinds was transmitted through colonial networks, some of which existed prior to official political control.

Once established, newspapers were popular and widely read. By 1885 the population was around half a million and there were already at least 100 newspapers being produced, 30 of them on a daily basis.[55] In 1926 there were 61 daily newspapers in print throughout the country. The *New Zealand Official Yearbook* provides figures for the number of registered newspapers in New Zealand for each year. In 1933 there were 281 registered newspapers: 55 published daily, 64 weekly, and more that were produced fortnightly or monthly.[56] Many people were relatively isolated in rural areas, but this was no great barrier to the consumption of printed information; in fact, it encouraged it. As Ross Harvey says, 'Geographical conditions in New Zealand were particularly conducive to the establishment of small-town newspapers.'[57] Smaller communities often had their own presses, and the weekly newspapers particularly targeted rural areas (although many had to close during World War II due to lack of manpower). Newspapers and the like were an important tool of colonial communication and dominance. According to Patrick Evans, the disproportionate number of small colonial newspapers provided a sense of 'regional community', while also maintaining ties to Home by reproducing information from Britain.[58]

New Zealand's extreme isolation in a far-flung corner of the Pacific has been regarded as a disadvantage for artists and writers. Literary commentators assumed that being so far from the centres of cultural production denied New Zealanders access to art and literature. Some believed that culture had frozen at the point of contact with the new land. According to Monte Holcroft, earlier English writers had worked 'in a new country; their successors, born in New Zealand near the turn of the century, were reared on English literature but were cut off from its self-renewing influences'.[59] Keith Sinclair, who investigated the effects of isolation on New Zealand in his edited work

Distance Looks Our Way, later took a more moderate view. He used the term 'peripheral survival', which he defined as 'the tendency for the periphery to lag behind the centre in cultural change'.[60] More recently, Patrick Evans has also talked of this lack of innovation, saying that 'for Victorian colonials ... literature was a gift received rather than a mechanism to tinker with: the right way of doing things had long been perfected by the great figures of the age'.[61]

However, while there was always going to be some kind of delay, the cultural information to which New Zealanders had access was not frozen at the point when the emigrants left their place of origin, or limited to the artefacts they had brought with them. New Zealand maintained communication with Britain through larger networks based on the wider colonial world, at least until World War II. The legacy of Britain's colonial expansion, and New Zealand's resultant ties to Britain, meant that the business of literary consumption and production could be conducted by means of the family, commercial and political connections which facilitated the colonial writing world. Rather than facing disadvantage due to isolation from the trappings of culture found in Europe, New Zealanders were able to keep relatively up to date through these networks (whether or not they were the product of British immigration themselves).

The Australasian connections to the British colonial world were the result of European involvement in the South Pacific from the eighteenth century, and this was an ongoing process. As Tony Ballantyne has said, 'the Anglo-Celtic colonists of New Zealand were anything but settled', and 'the circulation of people, money, goods and news was the lifeblood of colonial life'.[62] Traffic was not all one way, and various scholars have portrayed the trans-colonial organisations that perpetuated and renewed these connections as people moved about for reasons of employment, family or governance.[63] James Belich has described this as an 'Anglo-world': 'a politically divided but culturally and economically united intercontinental system'.[64] Ideas about governance, humanitarianism, women's suffrage and art and literature flowed through these

> *global networks of family, friends and professional or vocational associates; by the transport and postal systems which disseminated both textual and material forms of culture (such as domestic furniture, textiles, crockery, antiques, books and journals from British publishing houses as well as newspapers from British presses).*[65]

While other networks existed due to connections with countries outside of the British world, the vast majority came from Britain – thus Māori and the descendants of non-British migrants existed in the British world as well (and potentially had access to these same connections to Britain).

New Zealand's place in the colonial world meant that physical distance from Britain was not as great a difficulty as has been widely assumed. It is true that consumers in New Zealand would have experienced a delay in receiving the latest information, but the magnitude of this problem has been greatly exaggerated. The continuing links allowed the constant renewal of cultural information. In the words of Lydia Wevers:

> Books, newspapers and their seductive companions, the illustrated magazines, ensured that readers everywhere stayed connected to Britain, and particularly to London's intellectual culture – and, thanks to the ubiquity of lending libraries, the circulation of ideas and narratives about Britishness and the empire was a normal part of daily life wherever you lived.[66]

Peter Gibbons refers to this interconnectedness in a 2003 article, saying that 'the country's isolation has probably been overemphasized by poets and other commentators, to the extent that the frequency and firmness of links to the rest of the world have been underestimated'.[67] Links were numerous and frequently utilised, encouraging the 'not unreasonable notion of an enduring "Greater Britain" beyond the seas'.[68]

These links actually strengthened over time rather than growing more distant as the colony matured. Rather than relegating New Zealand to the 'colonial periphery', new technologies turned the country into a 'modern member of empire', with even stronger links with Britain and other parts of the world.[69] Felicity Barnes relates that New Zealanders were increasingly able to 'imaginatively overcome' the 18,000-kilometre and six-week journey distance from the centre of the empire.[70] Existing links and communications were greatly improved in the last few decades of the nineteenth century. With the introduction of steamships, says James Belich, 'the length of the voyage from New Zealand to Britain fell by about two-thirds between the 1870s and the 1900s'.[71] The completion of telegraph communications with Britain via Sydney (through 25,358 kilometres of telegraph cable[72]) in 1876 meant that up-to-the-minute news could be printed in local newspapers, and that New Zealanders did not have to wait weeks for the English print version to make its way across the sea.

Most people maintained links with overseas relatives or friends, and the lines of communication stayed open through the exchange of letters, or through visits. Brancepeth Station records state that in 1903 the station sent out '40,000 letters, 140 newspapers, 122 samples (of all kinds of goods) and 102 parcels, books and photos'; the volume of inward mail would have been even greater.[73] Letters were the main form of communication and it was quite possible to conduct a relationship by maintaining a written correspondence. The nature of British colonial service meant that family networks could be spread over many parts of the empire. By regularly writing letters to one another, people in New Zealand gained information about the rest of the world that supplemented what they read in newspapers. As Angela Woollacott argues in *Settler Society in the Australian Colonies*, letter-writing was a 'key form of imperial knowledge' that shaped the mindsets of those in the colonies and thus the nature of colonial society.[74]

There was a regular flow of new literary material into New Zealand through its participation in the colonial world. Fiction by British authors was purchased from agencies like the McClure Newspaper Syndicate and serialised in local newspapers. Many New Zealanders received British publications by subscription in the mail: immigrants were advised to arrange, before leaving Britain, 'to receive a file of some weekly London paper'.[75] This was not limited to the main centres, either. G.R. Gilbert grew up in Westport in the 1920s and wrote about the publications that arrived at his grandfather's shop there:

> *Every month or so the service car ... brought the bundles of periodicals and books from 'overseas'. There were magazines,* Pearson's, The Strand, Windsor, Wide World, Punch, Bystander, Illustrated London News, *and the* Tatler, *as well as bound copies, a month's supply stapled together, of the* Daily Sketch *and the* Daily Mirror, *two popular English tabloid magazines.*[76]

As well as news gleaned and printed from telegraph communications and imported publications, there was also a lively 'cut-and-paste economy', in the words of Sydney Shep. This refers to the widespread practice of reprinting material from other publications and recirculating: 'repurposing snippets of information for domestic consumption, and sending the results out once more into the great sea of textual circulation'.[77]

Books were imported in great numbers as well, as it was usually cheaper to do this than to have them published locally. With the exception of Whitcombe & Tombs, there were no local companies solely responsible for all the stages of book production (publishing, printing and selling), so the product suffered from a mark-up in price between each stage. In order to print overseas books locally, a colonial printer would have to reset all the type: a lengthy and costly task. The small number of sales in New Zealand could not possibly have financed the cost, except in the case of school textbooks. Whitcombe & Tombs came to dominate the market for schoolbooks because they sold as well as produced them and could avoid the mark-up in price.[78] They also had the advantage of local knowledge about the appropriate curricula, as well as lower transport costs for delivery. They published literature as well, but this did not have the guaranteed demand that educational publishing offered. Imported schoolbooks could not compete in price with locally produced ones, but in other cases books from British publishers worked out cheaper.

As London was the centre of the publishing world, British publishers dominated much of the globe in terms of the production and distribution of English-language literature. After the formation of the Association of Booksellers of Great Britain and Ireland in 1895, the Net Book Agreement was signed in 1900, attaching a fixed price to books sold in the British Empire. At the signing of the Berne Convention in 1886 the world was divided into trading 'blocs' with 'breathtaking assurance' by the publishers of Great Britain, according to Nile and Walker.[79] The United States did not sign the convention because they held a different view of copyright laws, and did not necessarily subscribe to the British assertions of dominance (particularly over Canada, where British publishers were gradually pushed out by cheap American editions). Nonetheless, well into the second half of the twentieth century the major British publishing houses retained a dominant hold, described by Nile and Walker as a 'cartel', over English-language book markets in Europe and the colonies and dominions, including Australia and New Zealand.[80]

The introduction of the 'colonial edition' made literature even more accessible to those living in far-flung parts of the empire. Most British publishers brought out a colonial edition of a selection of their books. In terms of content these were the same as editions of the books sold in Britain. Writing on the history of the book in Australia, Martyn Lyons explains:

> *[T]he colonial edition did not usually have a different text from the English*
> *or 'home' edition, but the text was packaged differently. It might have a new*
> *title page announcing the colonial series of which it was a part, and it would*
> *be bound in cheap 'colonial cloth', or 'C.C.' as it was known in the trade.*[81]

The 'colonial edition' was not usually an example of colonial fiction (although many titles by New Zealanders were put out in these series), but rather 'popular British fiction put on the market at one title each fortnight'.[82] Several British publishers (for example Macmillan) had 'colonial libraries', and published lists of the books available in these series. These editions were cheaper than those printed for sale elsewhere.

From this it can be inferred that publishers were trying to redress any perceived imbalance that distance might cause. An advertisement in the *Times of India* stated the aim of Macmillan's Colonial Library, which was to 'give English readers out here the same advantages that are enjoyed at home by those who live close to one of Mudie's agencies, or one of W.H. Smith's bookstalls'.[83] Nineteenth-century novels were usually published in an expensive three-volume format, and were too costly for mass sale in New Zealand or other colonies. According to Luke Trainor, the cheaper single-volume colonial editions gave local booksellers an extra incentive to sell them. Trainor also relates that 'there is some evidence' that the cheaper editions were a response to fear of being undercut by American publishers, as the United States had not consented to agreements designed to protect original work by authors from different countries.[84]

Discussion of the availability of colonial editions in Australia and New Zealand has almost entirely concentrated on the negative aspects: the encouragement of imported literature over local, and the reduced royalty rates for local authors when they were featured. This reflects the prevailing focus of literary criticism on the development of national literature. Luke Trainor suggests that the phenomenon of the colonial edition 'offers a window on the British dominance of book culture in New Zealand until the third quarter of the twentieth century and what that meant for local print culture'.[85] While colonial editions were clearly an attempt by British publishers to compete with American and local publishing rivals, Martyn Lyons says that they were actually good for local bookseller-publishers (such as Angus & Robertson and Whitcombe & Tombs).[86] The royalty that authors received for colonial editions was less than half that of a 'home' edition,[87] but, on the other hand, colonial editions provided New Zealand readers with easier access to cheaper books.

These books were mostly by British authors, but this was not necessarily a problem: it is both difficult and anachronistic to draw a clear dividing line between 'New Zealand culture' and 'British culture' at this time. Immigrants from Britain naturally continued to possess the many centuries' worth of British culture and tradition that was theirs from birth and to pass this cultural legacy on to their children. It was not a borrowed culture; it was simply *their* culture, which was then adapted to suit local circumstances. Cultural information is stored in memories, not in places, so it was not left behind when the colonists sailed from Britain. As Jock Phillips has said, 'the Pakeha of nineteenth-century New Zealand were not cultureless people somehow stripped of all habits and traditions by the voyage out'.[88] It is only a cultural nationalist viewpoint that does not allow for imported British traditions legitimately 'belonging' to the colonial New Zealanders.

Later critics of the continuing British cultural influence in New Zealand dismissed early expressions of culture as lacking authenticity, but this was an anachronistic application of principles that were irrelevant to much of early-twentieth-century New Zealand. New Zealanders, as members of a British world system at this time, were interested in what made them nationally distinctive, but this meant distinctive *within* British culture and the empire rather than distinct *from* it. Keith Sinclair once observed that New Zealanders had their own identity but were also a 'nation of imperialists', and 'the New Zealander never did consider his two loyalties incompatible'.[89] Eddy and Schreuder, in *The Rise of Colonial Nationalism* (about Australia, New Zealand, Canada and South Africa), say: 'Just as "Englishmen" could claim to be both democrats and monarchists, so colonists saw no tension in being nationalists and imperialists'.[90]

These New Zealanders of British descent took pride in being a distinct, potentially superior brand of colonial Briton, measuring themselves against the original version. When Sir John Hall's New Zealand-born son was sent to be educated at Oxford, Hall was proud to see that he compared favourably to his 'British contemporaries', expressing pleasure 'that my boy should be upholding the character of Colonists for strength & manliness'.[91] The same kind of sentiment applied to New Zealanders' pride at the way New Zealand soldiers conducted themselves in the South African War and World War I, as a superior kind of British soldiery. O.E. Burton was a 2nd Lieutenant in the Auckland Regiment in World War I, and in *The New Zealand Division* he described the New Zealanders as 'the children of a splendid pioneer stock ... the very finest of material for the making of a fine army'. Later he recounted that 'the majority were used to a hard, open-air life, and the townsmen were men whose athletic habits had made them as fit as those from the countryside'.[92] These New Zealanders saw themselves as particularly hardy Britons, their physical prowess enhanced by their pioneering history, even when they had not come from a rural environment.

This type of colonial nationalism also manifested itself in cultural creations like the hopeful manifesto of the *New Zealand Illustrated Magazine* in 1899. The magazine's first editorial declared that it was 'the vessel by which the young scion of New Zealand national life has begun to awake to a knowledge of itself'.[93] A 'scion', as a twig or offshoot of a parent plant, conjures the image of New Zealand nationalism as a younger, local version of Britishness, still very much attached to the original. As Jock Phillips has noted, this local version often included the use of appropriated Māori cultural elements to provide a local flavour, and the country itself was often referred to as 'Maoriland'.[94] According to Jane Stafford and Mark Williams, this served to 'provide the descendants of the settlers with a history peculiar to themselves', where perhaps they felt they did not have a history before.[95]

Nationalism is not a fixed concept: it means different things to different people at different times. People were quite happy merging seemingly disparate elements, including international influences. Edith Lyttleton's novel *Promenade* features the young children of English immigrants, brought up first at Russell then in Auckland, who display these relaxed cultural tendencies: 'Tiffany and Roddy (with sometimes Hemi and Eriti Fleete) had a private world where they trafficked gloriously with goats, giants, Maori tohungas, Queen Victoria, and a Chinese god called Pang out of a book of Major Henry's'.[96] The cultural nationalists' particular vision of autochthonous nationalism was foreign to writers of the earlier period, as well as being impossible, given the international origins of settler New Zealand.

As many scholars in recent decades have noted, using a national framework to investigate the past can only lead to inaccurate historical representations and a partial picture of New Zealand life. Miles Fairburn has argued that the only truly all-encompassing 'national' trait of New Zealand is that it is so completely the product of outside influences. What 'made New Zealand distinct', says Fairburn, was 'the abnormal degree to which its people have borrowed from other cultures'.[97] The very inward-looking focus of cultural nationalism served to obscure the literary efforts of a very outward-looking group of people, and the full extent of this has yet to be untangled.

All the dominance of British-origin literature means, then, is that New Zealanders had access to affordable editions of up-to-date literature, and were further able to participate in the colonial writing world. Imported British culture and New Zealand culture were deeply intertwined rather than at odds with one another. Chris Hilliard relates that '[Pat] Lawlor appears to have felt no tension between his love of English literature, including the work of self-consciously *English* writers, and his sense of New Zealandness'.[98] There is no reason why Lawlor should have felt such a tension, and expressions of Britishness within a New Zealand context were just as genuine as deliberate attempts at autochthony. Lawlor's outlook comes as no surprise once we view the period on its own terms and realise that New Zealanders of British descent were both colonials and Britons, unselfconsciously part of the colonial writing world, whether mobile or not. Alice Roland discovers in *The Story of a New Zealand River* that the trappings of culture do not depend on being in Britain or Europe. As Mrs Brayton wisely says: 'No place can bury you, my dear. We bury ourselves.'[99] If writers felt they had to leave, it was not because New Zealand lacked culture.

CHAPTER TWO

Making the Waitematā smoke

Just as the pursuit of literature and culture had reached and occupied this distant outpost of the colonial world, so had the impulse to *create* works of literature. Edith Searle Grossmann's 1910 novel *The Heart of the Bush* paints a picture of a land awash with literary ambition; even Kate, the Borlases' maid in the novel, is in the habit of scribbling down stray poems in the margins of newspapers.[1] Such literary ambition was allegedly thwarted, however, because of the lack of outlets. R.A.K. Mason had his first book of poems, *The Beggar*, privately printed by Whitcombe & Tombs in 1924, and the book received so little interest that he is later supposed to have thrown 200 copies in the Waitematā Harbour.[2] This story is debatable, but *The Beggar* certainly did not receive the recognition it deserved.[3]

The absence of a publishing industry in New Zealand is usually the beginning and end of assessments of the literary opportunities available, and the main reason given to explain why writers were forced to leave. It is true that there were not many options when it came to local book publishing. Until the 1930s Whitcombe & Tombs was New Zealand's single large publishing firm, and they were mostly concerned with history, biography and school textbooks. Fiction was rare, but they did publish many books of verse, nearly always paid for by the authors and sold on commission.[4] This more often than not turned into a costly exercise. Robin Hyde's first book was a collection of poems called *The Desolate Star*, which was published by Whitcombe & Tombs. In 1931, 250 copies had been sold, but Hyde was still getting bills from the publishers for amounts up to £9.[5] Whitcombe & Tombs' monopoly could lead to troubles for authors: Eileen Duggan was promised half of the profits on the publication of *New Zealand Bird Songs*, but she was given no copy of the contract. She wrote to Nettie Palmer: 'In spite of requests I have never had a balance sheet.' Nor had she seen any profits, though she knew the book was selling well.[6] Other companies provided printing services but left the author with the burden of cost, advertising and distribution. Simpson & Williams of Christchurch was one such institution, and it printed several of Jessie Mackay's books of verse. It was not until the mid-1930s that there was any real alternative to Whitcombe & Tombs, with the creation of institutions such as the Caxton and Unicorn presses, which were set up with the intention of publishing local literature. A.H. & A.W. Reed began publishing a 'smattering' of New Zealand fiction and poetry in 1934.[7]

There is much more involved with the cultivation of writing than merely the publication of books, however. Participation in overseas publishing networks would not have been possible if local literary culture had been completely absent from New Zealand. Writers must begin somewhere and receive encouragement at an early stage of their careers. Practice is needed before attempting to create a novel or collection of verse. Indeed, a vigorous literary culture did exist in New Zealand at this time, although those influenced by cultural nationalism have been reluctant to recognise it.

New Zealand's abundant newspapers provided crucial encouragement for writers early in their careers, supplying a useful and fairly easily accessible outlet for aspiring writers' work. Many New Zealand authors began their careers writing for local newspapers and would later credit the editors of these with supporting their fledgling literary ambitions. In his early days, A.R.D. (Rex) Fairburn had poems 'almost weekly' in 'The Bookmen's Corner' of the Auckland Sun.[8] Other significant New Zealand poets also began this way: Ursula Bethell, Robin Hyde, Eileen Duggan and Geoffrey de Montalk all received early encouragement from seeing their names in print in one of the local dailies. The weekly papers also printed poems, and the dailies had occasional supplements which ran literary competitions. Success in these competitions launched the careers of several writers. For example, Alice A. Kenny won second prize in a short-story competition run by the Auckland Star in 1890. Following this, she became a regular contributor of lyrical verse and short stories to many periodicals and went on to write novels.[9] It was also common for longer prose works to be serialised in publications, thus catering for novel writers as well. Various stories written by Monte Holcroft were serialised in New Zealand newspapers, such as 'The Hateful Valley' in 1934 in the Christchurch *Sun*.[10] Upon returning from overseas in 1932, Jane Mander went so far as to say there was too much encouragement by newspapers:

> *I have heard much complaint already since landing that N.Z. papers do not encourage their own authors ... This is nonsense. There is far too much encouragement for would-be authors in this country ... I have been astonished by the amount of it.*[11]

Though the writers did not earn a great deal from their enterprises, perhaps half a day's wages for one poem if anything at all, the newspapers had high circulations and publication in one would guarantee useful exposure and the recognition of influential editors.[12] Such exposure might well have led to the formation of a group of admirers who would be interested in purchasing a book of verse. Writers could already have established a name for themselves before a book was published, as Isabel Maud Peacocke appears to have done. Her book *Songs of the Happy Isles* was published in 1910, and a reviewer wrote: 'Many may think that a better selection might easily have been made from the numerous fine verses which have appeared over Miss Peacocke's signature', suggesting readers were already familiar with her work.[13]

Some newspaper editors were particularly sympathetic to the efforts of local writers and contributed much to the cultivation of literary achievement. For example, Reginald O'Neill compiled a history of the Christchurch *Press* in 1961, in which he praised the contribution of the editors. According to O'Neill, 'under [Michael] Keane's administration, the literary page became an important focus for a generation of New Zealand-grown literary craftsmen'.[14] He also mentioned 'M.C. Keane's literary feast in the 1920s'.[15] O'Neill's book was commissioned for the *Press*'s centenary, and as a result his comments have a celebratory tone, but they do tie in with other evidence.[16] Michael Keane was the editor of the *Press* from 1919 to 1929, and his successor Oliver Duff continued his policy. Together they encouraged and printed local writers, including Ngaio Marsh, Monte Holcroft and D'Arcy Cresswell.[17] John Schroder, literary editor of the Christchurch *Sun* in the 1920s and the *Press* from 1929, had a similarly good reputation. The Auckland *Sun*, an offshoot of the Christchurch *Sun*'s success, also developed a good name as a literary outlet. Percy Crisp was the editor, and the foreword to Eileen Duggan's *New Zealand Bird Songs* states that he was 'always ready to help any national and literary effort in New Zealand.[18] Fairburn commended Crisp's efforts in a letter to Geoffrey de Montalk, exclaiming: 'Compare the "Sun" with the "Herald"!!! My God.'[19] Winifred Tennant, a little-known poet and the writer of the children's page of the Auckland *Sun* for a time, wrote to Pat Lawlor that Crisp's encouraging notes were a 'spur to endeavour'.[20] Charles Marris, Alan Mulgan and Schroder were all variously praised for their efforts in assisting writers. Eileen Duggan said of Marris that he had a 'real devotion to the cause of New Zealand literature',[21] and of Mulgan that he 'used his position as literary editor to inspire and to forward beginners'.[22]

This small group of 'bookmen', as Chris Hilliard has called them, played a vital role in the success of newspapers in assisting New Zealand writers.[23] An indication of the importance of individuals can be seen in the reaction to the publication of Ursula Bethell's second book. The first, *From a Garden in the Antipodes*, was published in London in 1929 and reviewed in the *Press*. Her second collection of verse, *Time and Place*, was published in Christchurch by the Caxton Press but not reviewed in the *Press* because the literary editor, John Schroder, was away and other staff members were not aware of Bethell's significance.[24] It is telling that the absence of one person could have had such a profound effect. Counting pages devoted to literature under different editorships further demonstrates the influence of these individuals. The space taken up by the literary section of the Christchurch *Sun* doubled while Schroder was the editor, and then dropped off markedly after he left for the *Press* in 1929.[25]

These men and others attempted at various times to launch dedicated literary periodicals within New Zealand, but they were few and short-lived, making only a small contribution to literary achievement. *Zealandia* was established in 1889 but failed to last out the year, and the next attempt, the *New Zealand Illustrated Magazine*, in 1899, folded after six years.[26] According to Dennis McEldowney, no other publications emerged between 1906 and 1930, save for student magazines and supplements to newspapers.[27] McEldowney neglects to mention the quarterly *Art in New Zealand*, which was edited by Charles Marris and published by Harry Tombs, and which began in 1928. Though this primarily focused on visual art, it did feature the poems of prominent New Zealand writers such as Eileen Duggan, Robin Hyde, C.R. Allen and Mona Tracy. Pat Lawlor also began two fairly unsuccessful journals, the *New Zealand Artists' Annual* and the New Zealand edition of

Aussie magazine, but dismissed them himself as containing much that was 'ephemeral, if not trivial'.[28]

Only one purely literary periodical was remotely successful before the 1947 launch of Charles Brasch's *Landfall*: the *Triad* fared remarkably well. G.A.K. Baughen estimates that by 1897, only four years after its launch, the journal had a circulation of 10,000, 'enough to supply one copy to every fifteenth New Zealand household'.[29] Jane Mander wrote in 1909 that the *Triad* was the only thing that kept her from 'preaching temperance, or making draughty garments for the superfluous heathen, or marrying a Sunday School teacher'.[30] The *Triad* had an international reputation as well. It came to the attention of Ezra Pound, a major figure in the modernist movement, who was interested in the verse of a regular contributor, Alice A. Kenny. Judith Wild describes the editors of the journal as unimpressed by this attention, as was Kenny.[31] For all the excitement the *Triad* generated, the views expressed by its editors were not shockingly innovative, and their attitude to 'modern' writing was encapsulated in their reaction to Ezra Pound's interest. Baughen attributed the magazine's unusual success to the audacity of Charles Baeyertz, the editor. On the first page of every issue the *Triad* declared itself to be the 'most courageous, conscientious and candid magazine in the Dominion … unique in its style and function'.[32] This seemed to involve Baeyertz being 'rather excitingly rude to almost everyone',[33] as Robin Hyde put it. The editors were not necessarily interested in local writing, and McEldowney says that the *Triad* 'did not discover or nurture any strikingly interesting writers'.[34] However, regardless of its reputation, the *Triad* published writing, and its contribution should not be ignored.

Several other magazines with less highbrow ambitions published the work of local writers and became useful ways to get into print. Because audiences were small, magazines that focused primarily on another subject often fared better financially. Religious publications sometimes offered an outlet and an audience for writing, including the Catholic *New Zealand Tablet*, whose editors encouraged Eileen Duggan. *Art in New Zealand* might well have owed its limited success to the fact that it was mostly devoted to the visual arts, but it published poetry and short stories as well. General-interest magazines such as the *Mirror* often published verse or short fiction.

The *New Zealand Railways Magazine* was launched in 1926, carrying railway news and technical articles, and promoting domestic tourism through travel stories, photo spreads, advertisements and accommodation listings. It soon expanded to include all sorts of literary endeavours, including verse, fiction, historical and biographical stories and book reviews. From 1935 to 1936 Robin Hyde contributed a travel series called 'On the road to anywhere: Adventures of a train tramp', and the magazine published many pieces by New Zealand poets and prose writers that might not have seen the light of day otherwise. Such outlets offered better prospects than purely literary magazines, which were very expensive because of the small market. Jane Mander complained in 1934 that C.R. Allen had asked £1 in advance for his periodical *Golden Fleece*. Mander said: '[W]ho would pay 2/6 regularly for a magazine of such tripe as N.Z. writers get out?'[35] This is from someone who actively sponsored and encouraged emerging writers. A much safer option was to include literary content in another publication already guaranteed of success.

Often overlooked, the editors of children's pages in newspapers and magazines also contributed a great deal to the development of New Zealand's literary culture. Many authors credit their early development to encouragement from one of these individuals. Bill Pearson began writing for Aunt Hilda's children's page in the Christchurch *Star-Sun* in 1935 at the age of 13. Hilda's 'Starlets', of whom Pearson was one, accumulated marks towards certificates for good work.[36] Gloria Rawlinson's early poems appeared on the children's pages of the *New Zealand Herald*, which were edited by Elsie K. Morton. Known as a child prodigy, Rawlinson then received further encouragement from Winifred Tennant of the Auckland *Sun*.[37] Noel Hoggard recalled his early literary endeavours in the children's section of the *Hutt News*, where he was given 'a couple of columns each week'. He also met Alison Grant, editor of the children's page of the *Evening Post*, and had 'fond memories of [her] bright little room on the second floor'. He noted: 'In those days the old "Otago Witness" and the "Weekly Press" (both now defunct) were publishing interesting and helpful criticism pages for the benefit of budding authors.'[38]

Measuring the output of New Zealand writers in terms of published books gives a reduced picture of the amount of writing put into print, making the situation look worse than it actually was. The figures given in this book are based on book publications; counting incidences of story and verse publication of even one author in periodicals would be a mammoth task. If it were possible, however, the acknowledgement of the opportunities afforded by newspapers and magazines would only strengthen my argument. A piece by Lydia Wevers in the *Griffith Review* aims to explain the absence of any 'great' nineteenth-century New Zealand novels in the vein of Australian authors such as Marcus Clarke, Henry Handel Richardson and Joseph Furphy.[39] In answer to this, J.E. Traue investigated those novels serialised in magazines and newspapers, thinking that the focus purely on novels published in monographic form might have obscured a 'goodly taniwha or two'. What he found was more than he expected: at least 114 New Zealand novels were published in serial form but never appeared in monograph form (98 of these were published in New Zealand newspapers and periodicals).[40] Whether or not any of these would have met Wevers' criterion of 'greatness' is another question, but certainly the extent of novel writing has been hugely underestimated.

Despite the limited nature of New Zealand publishing, a surprising number of locally published novels, short-story collections and books of verse survive from the late nineteenth and early twentieth centuries. Even though these generally had small print runs, and were sometimes financed by the author, they attest to a high level of literary activity, and amount to 43 per cent of all the books written by New Zealand authors from 1890 to the late 1930s.[41] Considering there was only one dedicated literary publisher until the mid-1930s, this proportion is high. The figure is 48 per cent for the period 1890 to 1945, when 344 books out of a total of 717 by New Zealand authors were published locally. It must be acknowledged that a high percentage of these publications were small books of poetry with short print runs, published by newspaper subsidiaries or companies like Whitcombe & Tombs. Novels, as we shall see, were more likely to be published in Britain.

Later on more and more small presses were set up with the intention of publishing literature. These included, most notably, the Caxton Press, which was established by Denis Glover and John Drew in 1935 (it had begun as the Caxton Club in 1932). Glover noted that they had been inspired by the efforts of Bob Lowry, who in 1932 had set up the Auckland University College Students' Association Press, which produced the short-lived but influential literary magazine *Phoenix*.[42] Lowry went on to start the Unicorn Press in 1934 and later the Pelorus Press. Noel Hoggard and the Handcraft Press in Wellington also printed a number of original works. These smaller, specialised presses were interested in certain types of writing, and not necessarily concerned with encouraging all kinds of literary pursuits. This did not help all writers, and in some ways the expansion of local publishing actually narrowed the options available to writers outside of 'highbrow' genres.

When investigating New Zealand's literary culture up to 1945, it is easy to document the extensive links between writers and publishers and between writers and editors. Still more links existed between the authors themselves. Yet, according to New Zealand literary legend, before these local presses were established in the 1930s New Zealand writers suffered lonely lives in a land without literary networks. There was little contact between writers, according to Robert Chapman in 1953,[43] and few opportunities for writers to adopt a place outside of society as observers. Eileen Duggan's sorrowful lines in the poem 'Heralds' have all too often been read as the final word on the subject: 'we are but stumblers in the hinterlands, / Too few for linking hands.'[44]

While New Zealand's population was small and fairly well dispersed, postal communication allowed discussion and collaboration. Although numbers were too few to allow a fringe or bohemian subculture to form and encourage avant-garde literary innovation, there were fledgling literary networks. A dispersed population was not an insurmountable obstacle to the formation of literary relationships in a time where corresponding by letter was a common form of communication. Writers could 'link hands' figuratively through the post and form networks that way. Internal postal systems were well developed by this time, and the country boasted '1700 post offices by 1900, handling 70 million post articles'.[45] Enterprising writers could strike up relationships with other writers; it was quite common to write to admired authors without being personally acquainted. Mary Scott, who lived in the backblocks of the King Country, noted:

> *If you write for a number of years, however lightly, you sooner or later acquire a large number of correspondents. My articles in the Dunedin* Star *have, as I have said, brought me many friends; they have also produced some strange contacts. I have had letters from people with all sorts of curious ideas which they have wanted me to air in my column; some of my admirers have been inmates of mental hospitals, and this is perhaps a commentary upon my work.*[46]

Even if living in remote areas or at opposite ends of the country, writers were able to get advice and encouragement from more established practitioners through letters. Eileen Duggan, for example, communicated with fellow poet Jessie Mackay. Mackay lived in Christchurch, Duggan lived in Wellington, but this was no great handicap. Eventually they arranged a meeting, as Duggan informed Nettie Palmer in 1924: 'I met Jessie Mackay last week. She had written to me before, but it was our first meeting.'[47] Mackay acted as one of Duggan's literary mentors, and in turn Duggan sponsored less well-established writers, acting as a go-between with publishers. Duggan also corresponded with many other writers, including A.R.D. Fairburn, who wrote, she said, 'frank, unorthodox epistles.'[48] Fairburn, in turn, struck up a literary correspondence with Geoffrey de Montalk, whom he remembered from primary school. He wrote to de Montalk in 1926, reminding him of 'a little golden-haired, blue-eyed boy ... who used to kick round with you' in Standard One at Remuera School.[49] Even Robin Hyde, who lamented that she had 'no-one in Auckland to whom she could turn for assurance and criticism', talked of 'all [her] scribbling friends ... "the gang"',[50] and corresponded regularly with John Schroder in Christchurch, receiving feedback and literary companionship.[51]

In some cases, usually but not always in the four main centres, small communities of writers did evolve. Fairburn and R.A.K. Mason were two of the most vocal protesters about the lack of support for writers, but were fortunate enough to have each other's company. They met while at Auckland Grammar and were great friends, meeting regularly, walking and having lengthy discussions about, in Mason's words, 'everything under the sun'.[52] James Bertram, Ian Milner and Charles Brasch reportedly had a secret society devoted to 'poetry, D.H. Lawrence, and sun worship' while at Waitaki Boys' High School in Ōamaru in the 1920s.[53] Ursula Bethell and Jane Mander presided over their own little groups. Bethell patronised the artist Toss Woollaston and many writers, leading Charles Brasch to say that she was 'the centre of an astonishingly diverse circle of interesting people'.[54] Woollaston recounts in his autobiography that Bethell employed him as a gardener in his youth so they could 'converse without the strain of continuity, and my income would be happily augmented'.[55] Through her he met many others, including D'Arcy Cresswell, 'a strange author' that Bethell knew of.[56] The care and attention Bethell devoted to young writers and artists has made her the subject of a chapter of Peter Simpson's book *Bloomsbury South: The arts in Christchurch, 1933–1953*, which makes a case for a thriving intellectual community.[57]

Other networks were formed deliberately, as in Auckland in the 1920s. Isabel Maud Peacocke was heavily involved as a founding member of the New Zealand League of Penwomen, a group started by Edna Graham Macky of Texas in 1925, in the style of similar American groups.[58] Hilda Rollett was also a founding member of the League of Penwomen, and ran the literary circle of the Auckland Women's Club. Noel Hoggard's magazine *Spilt Ink*, named after Pat Lawlor's literary gossip column, became 'the hub of a network of clubs in smaller towns such as Gore and Dannevirke as well as Wellington, Auckland and Dunedin'.[59] It is a credit to the quality of support these clubs provided that Rollett, Isobel Andrews (a founding member of the New Zealand Women Writers' and Artists' Society) and Peacocke were all highly successful writers, published overseas, whilst never having left New Zealand for more than a short trip. In 1899 Frederick Rollett (Hilda's husband) was one of the leading figures in the establishment of the Auckland-based New Zealand Literary and Historical Association. Theresia Marshall relates that the association had a 'Criticising Committee', 'a well-meaning if misguided initiative to provide "advice and criticism to young writers" in order to "prevent literary aspirants from sending crude unpolished work to [overseas] publishers"'.[60] It cannot have been entirely misguided: according to a piece in the *New Zealand Illustrated Magazine* from 1903,

> *Miss Edith I. [sic] Lyttleton received her training in literature from the New Zealand Literary and Historical Association. She has since been successful in securing the first prize given by the Association for the best short story of New Zealand life, character and scenery, for which eighty-six competed ...*[61]

Lyttleton, too, was a successful writer while in New Zealand. These groups provided a solid foundation from which to engage with the wider colonial world.

The 'bookmen' (to further use Chris Hilliard's term) often had a role in the formation of these networks. Literary relationships regularly began and revolved around a particular editor. When Robin Hyde's book of verse *The Desolate Star* was published, she referred to John Schroder as its 'literary godfather'.[62] Schroder acted as a mentor for Hyde, Gloria Rawlinson and Ursula Bethell, among others. Through Schroder, Bethell met other writers, scholars and artists such as D'Arcy Cresswell, Eric McCormick and Monte Holcroft, and became a mentor to this younger group in the 1930s and

1940s.[63] The bookmen also set up more formal groups, recognising the need of writers to have the company of their peers. Pat Lawlor created the New Zealand Women Writers' and Artists' Society, and served as the secretary of the New Zealand branch of PEN founded in 1934.[64]

This local literary machinery was significant for the encouragement of writers but came under fire from the next generation of bookmen, who were interested in different aspects of the craft. In a small, sparsely populated country like New Zealand, literary power was in the hands of a few people whose tastes determined the kind of writing that could be published locally. As a result, these editors had considerable control over what was written. Denis Glover commented in 1935 that New Zealand literature was 'to a great extent under the patronage of our daily papers'.[65] He described this journalism-based process as a 'literary mincing machine'.[66] The earlier bookmen were accused by later generations of having a stranglehold over literary production in New Zealand, and subsequently stunting its development. Thus, what had been largely a positive intervention in local literary culture was framed as holding back the development of an independent New Zealand literature.

This earlier group of individuals, largely members of a generation older than the cultural nationalists, propagated the literary ideals of the time. As editors and literary commentators they expressed a dislike for 'modern' techniques, including free verse. They tended to prefer well-established styles within the British tradition, such as Georgian-inspired poetry, and were suspicious of modernism. Their thoughts about literature were shaped by the influence of such standards of literary taste as Palgrave's anthology *The Golden Treasury*, and others like it. According to Hilliard, 'the more immediate models for much New Zealand poetry in the 1920s and 1930s were Rupert Brooke, Walter de la Mare, and the other British poets featured in Edward Marsh's *Georgian Poetry* anthologies between 1912 and 1922'.[67] Georgianism was a 'reaction to the lifeless, vitiated condition of English poetry at the beginning of the twentieth century'.[68] F.W. Neilsen Wright quotes Lord Alfred Douglas, a Georgian poet, as saying that poets wished to 'strike beautiful notes, not new notes',[69] a sentiment with which Alan Mulgan and Charles Marris would no doubt have agreed.

Georgianism, in the eyes of contemporaries, did not negate the possibility of writing 'local' literature. A review of Jessie Mackay's poetry in a 1909 *Dominion* article predicted:

In the New Zealand poetry of the future we shall expect to hear the song of the sea, the wind's sweep over plains of manuka and tussock, the sound of rivers ramping over stony courses, and to feel a zest and beauty and sense of freedom that are akin to these ... Miss Jessie Mackay, in a new selection all too small, lifts a lyric note as sweet as it is rare.[70]

This type of writing fulfilled both the Georgian ideal of beauty and its practitioners' need for a sense of indigeneity. Similarly, Eileen Duggan effortlessly combined the wider literary conventions of the colonial writing world with New Zealand content. Her *New Zealand Bird Songs* was praised widely for its simple lyrical eloquence and local themes.

It was quite possible to develop ideas of 'colonial difference' using traditional forms and conventions, and many writers attempted this. Novelists often played a part in the creation and perseverance of colonial stereotypes such as that of the rugged, pioneering 'outdoors man'. Edith Searle Grossmann's 1910 novel *The Heart of the Bush* exhibits the literary apotheosis of these ideals and probably had a hand in propagating them as well. The story is about a young woman, Adelaide, and ultimately her choice between fashionable England and honest New Zealand. The greatest contrast in the book is between Adelaide's English suitor, Horace, and Dennis, the rough but genuine New Zealander. Horace is the height of 'civilised' fashion – a member of the 'Smart Set'. Cold and detached, he 'liked to have even his emotions prepared for him by unleisured authors and composers'.[71] Showing genuine emotion is dismissed as being 'early Victorian', as when Adelaide nearly faints.[72] The outlook that Grossmann expresses through her work, such as 'the dangers of cosmopolitan sophistication versus the honest worth of rural folk', was not, according to Stafford and Williams, exclusive to her writing, but rather 'part of the cultural climate in which she wrote'.[73] Local character was not just the concern of the cultural nationalists or the 1930s.

Proponents of cultural nationalism like Allen Curnow and his associates dismissed the majority of writing from before the 1930s because it lacked 'authenticity' (meaning a certain kind of expression of essential 'New Zealandness' that they happened to endorse). The contribution of the earlier writers and editors has often been ignored or played down because it was unpopular with the next generation, many of whom were interested in a particular genre of writing. Members of the new generation (referred to by Patrick Evans as the *Phoenix* group, after the publication of the same name)[74] mocked their predecessors and belittled them. 'The gentlemen whose sacred mission it is to direct literary standards in N.Z.', wrote R.A.K. Mason, 'are for the most part old men (or youths prematurely old) who have never even studied literature deeply.'[75] The older generation were accused of having 'imposed on New Zealand writing a worship of the safely dead past and a fear of anything modern', as they led the country down the 'daisied path of pallid good taste' with their preferences for 'leisurely-whimsy, feminine-mimsy' old-fashioned writing.[76] The *Phoenix* group's rejection of the 'derivative' and imported in favour of writing that was, in Curnow's words, 'as immediate in experience as the island soil under his feet',[77] imposed a distinction that was meaningless for a society in which most of the cultural reference points were imported from Britain.

Viewed retrospectively, it is easy to see the older generation of bookmen as old-fashioned, when in fact they were merely reflecting the preoccupations of the time they lived in. The writers they patronised were largely complicit in this. The older editors' dislike of free verse, for example, was shared by many writers; Jessie Mackay described it as 'treason against eternal poesy'.[78] Eileen Duggan said of Mackay that 'she has always stood in this country for the high tradition, the grand manner, and has rejoiced that free verse has not caught New Zealand's heart';[79] she herself disliked the modern tendency toward the 'merely clever'.[80] The newer generation were not as revolutionary as they seemed – they simply adhered to slightly more modern, but also imported, poetic conventions.

The earlier group of bookmen were no more tyrannical than their successors, and had broader interests over several genres. The newspaper-based literary culture was more democratic and accessible, particularly for women, than later literary circles, which tended to be based in universities. This division caused genre to be more of an issue, as the university-based scholars favoured realist and modernist modes of expression (excluding genres like popular writing). The contribution of newspapers to local writing was not acknowledged because they became less popular as a medium for 'serious' writing as time went on: later writers were not so interested in this kind of exposure. Derek Challis mentions the dominance of newspapers in the 1920s and their subsequent decline, described by Robin Hyde as a 'tragedy to New Zealand scribes'.[81] This aligns with the changing nature of book production for New Zealanders, as the more highbrow intentions of the Caxton Press and its ilk were at odds with the egalitarian nature of newspaper publication, which thrived on creating a general audience.[82]

The introduction of the cultural-nationalist paradigm was so successful that later historians looked back at the few nationalist voices in the wilderness and believed New Zealand to have been largely bereft of literary culture. In 1950, reflecting on pre-cultural-nationalist literature, Monte Holcroft wrote that 'most persons feel a kind of blankness in the past'.[83] This subjective nationalist theory remained the orthodoxy until at least the 1990s. It influenced a whole generation of scholars, excited to discover that, starting with Curnow and a few of his predecessors, New Zealand had 'its own history, its own politics, its own literature'.[84] As a result, Ian Wedde's 1985 *Book of New Zealand Verse*, while more inclusive than Curnow's 1945 version, still applies a cultural nationalist test to the included poems. Wedde says that New Zealand poetry truly began with Blanche Baughan, as 'it is with Blanche Baughan that we first sense the beginnings of an internal relation of *where* to the language of the poems'.[85] He also judges Hubert Church by a later paradigm of literary worth and disparages his 'earnest castings at the indigenous'.[86] Although this version of cultural nationalism has been heavily critiqued, the achievements of writers are still often valued for their contribution to 'New Zealand literature', even if the criteria have broadened and the discussion is more nuanced.

Cultural nationalism also marginalised women writers because it presented a largely masculine view of literature and national identity. As the *Phoenix* group criticised previous writing for being 'cut off from local reality', the alternative they sought, according to Kai Jensen, was to 'produce work that might be relevant to ordinary New Zealanders – by whom they often meant the hard-bitten Kiwi bloke'.[87] The 'man alone' figure (as in John Mulgan's novel of the same name) epitomised the pioneering masculine spirit that encountered an 'empty' land. John Newton's article on the 'South Island myth' reports that the cultural nationalists preferred to stay at home and write about their literary surrogates' adventures in the bush and up mountains.[88] Previous writing was generally dismissed as too sentimental and feminine, and famously derided by A.R.D. Fairburn as the 'junketings of the Menstrual School of poetry'.[89] The new literary establishment of the 1940s was as a result bereft of women, where they had been strongly represented in the earlier circles.[90] The genres where the majority of women's contributions could be found, such as novels and popular writing, also fell out of critical favour in the late 1930s, further sidelining female writers.

The earlier bookmen had played a vital role as local agents for the colonial writing world and had helped encourage much literary activity. While their detractors presented their role as somewhat trivial, New Zealand could never have functioned as part of the colonial writing world if it had not been for the ground-level literary encouragement that is described in this chapter, in the form of facilitating publication in newspapers and magazines, introducing writers to each other, or setting up organisations and supporting them. These writers and editors often played a number of roles, which was made necessary by the disorganised nature of the literary infrastructure at this time.[91]

The preoccupation of New Zealand literary history practitioners with identifying 'authentic' New Zealand writing or the 'great New Zealand novel' has blinded commentators to the reality of the literary industry before World War II. Looking back, it appeared that before the cultural nationalists saved the day with the invention of New Zealand literature and the instigation of local publishing initiatives, there were very few opportunities for writers. It was believed that most writers dearly wished to leave New Zealand for societies more sympathetic to literary ambition, and that those who could not leave felt as if they were 'exiled'. This mindset has prevented scholars from seeing New Zealand as a part of the colonial writing world, with its literary operatives working as part of a much bigger picture than the limitations of nationalist histories can possibly allow for. The period was not a 'black hole' for New Zealand writing, as McCormick implied when he wrote of the literary movement of the 1890s 'petering out' and not reviving again until the 1930s.[92]

CHAPTER THREE

The Tasman writing world

I n 1968 Bruce Nesbitt calculated that New Zealanders were responsible for 'about 10 per cent' of the total content of the Sydney *Bulletin* between 1890 and 1900.[1] This is significant considering the *Bulletin*'s reputation as the bastion of Australian literary nationalism, particularly in the 1890s. The *Bulletin* school is famously representative of the flowering of an Australian local, democratic, outback tradition epitomised by writers like Banjo Paterson, Henry Lawson and Joseph Furphy, but Nesbitt's thesis suggests there was more to it. Others have also argued that Australian literary nationalism was only one of the *Bulletin* editors' many preoccupations. Alfred George Stephens, instigator and editor of the all-important literary 'Red Page', had broad interests, reflected in the range of content he published. Peter Kirkpatrick observes that J.F. Archibald, part-founder of the paper and its 'greatest editor', was a particularly devoted Francophile'.[2] Stephens had a particular interest in New Zealand writing, and reading the *Bulletin* at this time, according to Jock Phillips, gives 'the impression of an Australasian cultural world based in Sydney and Melbourne with Queensland and New Zealand as its provinces'.[3]

This points to an earlier connectedness of Australasian literary worlds, which has been widely forgotten because it was replaced by national literary concerns. The limited literary opportunities in New Zealand mattered less than others have claimed because writers viewed both sides of the Tasman as their publishing domain, whether or not they actually travelled between the two. Well into the twentieth century, Australasia retained an interconnectedness created in the very early days of British settlement. For literary people, the *Bulletin* and A.G. Stephens were the centre of this Tasman world. Theresia Marshall calculates that in the 12 years Stephens was literary editor of the Red Page (1894–1906),

> the number of New Zealand entries increased six-fold, producing a total of 818 altogether, averaging close to 100 per year from 1900 onwards. No New Zealand journal during this period ... remotely approached the Bulletin as a venue hospitable to New Zealand creative writing.[4]

Many New Zealand authors used the Bulletin as a 'testing ground', including Edith Lyttleton, who described it as her 'literary father'.[5]

Nowadays the two worlds are not nearly as well connected. In 2001 Lydia Wevers asked whether Australia and New Zealand are part of the same literary community and concluded that the answer is broadly no, because the two countries have a 'resistant relationship over books and readers'.[6] She found that there is very little interest in the literature the other country is producing, and that Australian books are surprisingly hard to come by in New Zealand and vice versa. Terry Sturm blames the publishing and distribution arrangements of Australasian books, saying that decisions about which books appear in each country are made by the British or American publishing companies. This means that the works of big names like Janet Frame and Patrick White are available, but rarely anything published locally in the other country. There is also no easy way to test these theories or discover other reasons for the disconnect, as

> there is no established discourse about Australian–New Zealand literary relations in the literary historiography or criticism of either country: no documentation of the extent or pattern of literary influence, interaction, conflict, movement into or out of each other's culture – let alone any theoretical effort to account for such relations, or for their absence.[7]

Aside from a few small-scale studies relating to trans-Tasman connections, this is still the case today (Chris Hilliard's Bookmen's Dominion frequently refers to it, but this is not the focus of the book). This current lack of trans-Tasman literary dialogue is very different to the way things were organised until the middle of the century.

From the early days of settlement Australia and New Zealand were closely linked, which means that a trans-Tasman model is a necessary part of any assessment of literary culture in New Zealand. This ties in with a wider trend in transnational approaches to Australasia, known as 'Tasman world' history.

In *Remaking the Tasman World*, Peter Hempenstall, Philippa Mein Smith and Shaun Goldfinch argue against the idea that Australia and New Zealand had entirely separate histories after Australian federation in 1901. They suggest instead the existence of continuing 'communities of interest that traverse the Tasman' well into the twentieth century and up to the present.[8] For example, Australia and New Zealand were a single banking community until the formation of the Reserve Bank of New Zealand in 1934.[9] British colonial rulers initially saw Australia's eastern colonies and New Zealand as one combined area to be exploited, with New South Wales as the administrative centre until New Zealand was officially annexed by Britain in 1840. Much of the history of the two countries is the result of collaboration, and this history is lost when it is written solely as the national story of either country. In the same way, it is necessary to consider the area as one site of analysis in order to observe the true nature of the Australasian literary world.

If New Zealanders and Australians tend to ignore each other's books nowadays it is most likely the result of the subsequent triumph of their respective cultural nationalisms. Philippa Mein Smith suggests that the 'persistence' of the Tasman world has been obscured by the pursuit of 'unique national stories and identities'.[10] Some important writers of the early twentieth century, such as Douglas Stewart, Will Lawson and David McKee Wright, have been all but dismissed from the New Zealand literary canon because they left to spend time in Australia, and as a result their national allegiances have been called into question. They remain only half-appreciated by Australia as well. Pat Lawlor complained in a survey from 1962 that 'there is a small but distinctive group of expatriates in Australia' but 'we hear nothing of their work'.[11] Writers who stayed in New Zealand but published overseas also risked not being included.

Mid-century editors and critics concerned with literary nationalism resisted acknowledging the links between the two countries, and thus did their bit to obscure them. Hilliard has talked at length about this, describing the way Eric McCormick

> *edited out the Australasian dimension of the New Zealand scene. [Joseph] Heenan apparently pointed out that* Letters and Art *said nothing about the* Bulletin's *contribution to New Zealand writing. McCormick said, probably half-heartedly, that he would read up on it, 'but I am not in sympathy with the* Bulletin's *jargon – Maoriland, etc – or its desperate aiming at brightness, often at the expense of truth'.*[12]

Curnow, also, was inclined to ignore the literary relationship between New Zealand and Australia. He refused the opportunity to appear in an Australasian anthology proposed by Oxford University Press because he objected to the idea of 'trading our birthright for an Australasian mess with a famous imprint stuck on the outside'.[13] When the title was changed from 'Australasian Verse' to 'Australian and New Zealand Verse', Denis Glover wrote to Alan Mulgan, who was editing the New Zealand section, and said: 'I certainly agreed with Curnow that the anthology had undesirable features … to a certain extent these are removed by the change of title.'[14] In 1947 Curnow referred to the Australian scene as 'the neglected middle distance', and suggested grudgingly that 'we cannot avoid some acquaintance with the literature of our nearest neighbouring country, and we may be interested to improve that acquaintance, to attend occasionally' to it.[15] The younger poets, such as A.R.D. Fairburn, often had a 'blind spot' on Australian writing,[16] and were frequently unaware of the close literary links the two countries had had for so long, as well as the debt owed to their Australian nationalist predecessors. This continued, as Pat Lawlor observed in 1966 when he said that the general literary knowledge of the university men and women dealing with New Zealand literature was 'painfully restricted. They know little of N.Z. literature beyond the Sargeson–Curnow clique. They know little of writers like [Hector Bolitho] or even of Douglas Stewart in Australia who have won celebrity'.[17]

As well as ideological concerns, the gradual introduction of economic nationalism also eroded the ability of the Australasian literary world to operate as one. In the 1930s discussions began about protections for local publishing and printing, which damaged the cross-pollination enabled by publishing relationships that spanned the Tasman. According to Jason Ensor, George Ferguson of Australian publishing firm Angus & Robertson 'found the attitude of New Zealand booksellers towards Australian titles "extremely favourable" but uniformly "hampered by the import licensing system" which was steadily reducing the quota of books they were allowed to sell to New Zealand'.[18] As internal transport and communication facilities improved, national mindsets replaced Australasian and colonial ones. Trans-Tasman connections may also have relied on interest from particular editors to keep them active. People like Pat Lawlor, who actively sought out writers 'here and abroad' to include in publications like the *New Zealand Artists' Annual*,[19] ceased to be influential as time went on and fewer editors were interested in being involved in an Australasian or colonial writing movement. Whatever caused the decline in connectivity, well into the twentieth century New Zealand had a mutually beneficial relationship with Australia which complemented what was available within the local literary culture. New Zealanders could remain in New Zealand but have access to higher-level literary institutions in Australia that they lacked at home (for example, the publishing company Angus & Robertson). They could also enjoy the benefits of a larger audience and fellowship of writers through the Tasman writing world (which was the most immediately available part of the colonial writing world) without leaving the country. Marshall concludes that New Zealand's literary culture at this time had much more 'vigour and variety' than is usually acknowledged, and that 'the *Bulletin* contributed substantially to this'.[20] There was a great deal more material submitted than was printed, indicated by the lengthy list of notes on contributors, including often acerbic comments from the editor, such as: 'Ben S.: It creaks like a cattle truck ... G.A.H.: Your effort is not worth the blow it strikes at the national ink supply'.[21] Nelle Scanlan recalled sending her poems to the Red Page, as the *Triad* seemed too ambitious, and said: 'I think most of us turned our eyes towards the Red Page of the Sydney *Bulletin.*' She received the reply after many weeks: 'As your poem was neatly typewritten we restrain our wrath'.[22]

Although Marshall claims that 'the almost universal pattern of expatriation of New Zealand-born *Bulletin* contributors to Australia' between 1915 and 1926 was 'a sign that it was becoming increasingly difficult for New Zealand writers to maintain a transtasman or "Australasian" connection *without* migrating physically to Australia', the connections were not limited to the *Bulletin* and, outside of this small sample, links were kept up.[23] New Zealanders also submitted work to many other Australian newspapers and magazines, including A.G. Stephens' *Bookfellow*, the *Australian Journal* and *Aussie* magazine. A New Zealand version of *Aussie* was edited and distributed by Pat Lawlor from 1925. The *Australasian* published New Zealand writing, including pieces by Edith Lyttleton, as did the *Lone Hand*. Some of Katherine Mansfield's earliest stories appeared in the *Native Companion* of Melbourne. Stafford and Williams raise the possibility that, because of the availability of such outlets, Mansfield might have remained in New Zealand and still made the same contribution to literary modernism.[24] After being rejected by the

Bulletin, Nelle Scanlan tried again with the Australian *New Idea*, which had a page called "'Literary Gems I Love and Why", short stories, articles, and bits about this and that – the usual kind of mixed-up magazine'. Her poem was published, though at first she thought she had again been rejected, and this imagined rebuke from 'an upstart like *The New Idea* was shattering to [her] pride'.[25]

Some Australian periodicals were produced with the intention of dealing with New Zealand and Australia together. They were circulated in both countries, and became an extension of the literary journals that dealt with New Zealand literature. The *Bookfellow* was an example. It was largely the product of a single-handed effort by A.G. Stephens, but the attempt eventually 'ruined him financially and broke his spirit'.[26] Nonetheless, it contained plenty of New Zealand material and interest, such as articles on New Zealand writers and trade reports from booksellers in Christchurch, Dunedin and Wellington.[27] Other periodicals, like the *Bulletin*, had high circulations in New Zealand, and Arthur H. Adams wrote of an Otago hut papered with old copies of it.[28] New Zealand authors were by no means limited to a New Zealand audience or New Zealand literary outlets.

Likewise, people in Australia could and did publish in New Zealand newspapers and magazines, seeing the cities across the Tasman as an extension of their own literary field. A.G. Stephens wrote a literary column specifically for the *Auckland Star*. This clearly had some influence: in 1910 Isabel Maud Peacocke wrote to him asking if he would review her new book (presumably she is referring to her first book, *Songs of the Happy Isles*, a collection of verse).[29] Madeline Duret, who lived in Sydney from 1893 after moving from England via Wellington and Dunedin in 1883, reported that she still contributed to the *Otago Witness* from Australia.[30] The writings of well-known critics with Australasian interests, such as Nettie Palmer, were reprinted in New Zealand newspapers (if not written specially for them).

Because Australia had a better-developed publishing industry than New Zealand, it was easier to get books published there as well. Thomas C. Lothian of Melbourne (a company formed in 1912) published the works of Jessie Mackay and Hubert Church, among others. Angus & Robertson began publishing in Sydney in 1886 and were particularly significant in Australian publishing history. They added to their list several trans-Tasman authors, including Douglas Stewart, Will Lawson and Eve Langley. Arthur H. Adams had his first book, *Maoriland and Other Verses*, published by the Bulletin Newspaper Company, before making the move to Australia himself. In 1933 the Sydney *Bulletin* set up the Endeavour Press, for which Pat Lawlor acted as a New Zealand agent. The New South Wales Bookstall Company and the New Century Press in Sydney also published New Zealand writers, as did Gordon & Gotch Australasia. Writers who had no obvious connection to Australia had books published there: the Macquarie Head Press published two novels by Alice Kenny in 1934, and Lothian put out Jessie Mackay's *Poems* in 1911.

Australia could offer more freedom than New Zealand in terms of literary content, but this may have had more to do with Australia's increased distance from disapproving locals rather than increased permissiveness. The stories Katherine Mansfield had published in Melbourne most likely appeared there and not in New Zealand by necessity, as they were 'sexually risqué' compared with anything permitted in New Zealand at this time.[31] Australia was still more restrictive than Britain, however. Andrew Nash writes:

> British censorship was certainly excessive in this period, though not, perhaps, as extreme as in Australia where both The Colonel's Daughter *[Aldington, 1929] and Huxley's* Brave New World *were banned by the government, and copies seized and returned by the customs authorities.*[32]

Deana Heath claims that, as the result of rigid control linked to the White Australia policy (which apparently extended to imported literature as well), 'between 1901 and the Second World War, Australia had arguably the severest censorship laws of any democratic country'.[33] Thus it was perhaps proximity to the subject that reduced publishing opportunities in New Zealand as compared to Australia, rather than harsher restrictions.

The most compelling evidence for the existence of a trans-Tasman literary world is that in the early twentieth century people saw themselves as part of wider literary networks, the most immediate focus of these being Australia. Chris Hilliard describes the trans-Tasman outlook of authors. Jessie Mackay, he says, saw herself as part of an Australasian culture, 'like [Pat] Lawlor and many other figures'.[34] Nettie Palmer, poet, critic and wife of the aggressively nationalist Australian writer Vance Palmer, saw Mackay as part of the Australian literary scene as well as her native one, describing her as an 'Austrazealander'.[35] The Palmers regularly reviewed and praised New Zealand writing in the *Bulletin*. *All About Books*, based in Melbourne, was subtitled 'For Australian and New Zealand Readers', and reported on the activities of several New Zealand literary societies along with Australian ones (such as the Fellowship of New Zealand Writers from 1930, and the New Zealand League of Penwomen).[36]

A.G. Stephens showed particular concern for New Zealand writers, and saw his field of interest as 'Australasian' literature as a whole. His papers in the State Library of New South Wales include a scrapbook of New Zealand verse that appeared in the *Bulletin*, and a compilation of biographical notes about Australian and New Zealand writers (including surveys sent out and returned), as well as a list of literary pseudonyms of Australian and New Zealand writers. His correspondence, also preserved, includes a large proportion of letters from New Zealand, and many New Zealand writers had close relationships with him. Jessie Mackay wrote to him in 1910, 'When I see a bold expanse of violet ink [referring presumably to the usual medium with which he wrote] on my desk, I know some kindly idea has been buzzing round on my behalf across the Tasman Sea.'[37]

In the early twentieth century, New Zealand and Australia were seen as one market by publishers in both Australasia and Britain. Graeme Johanson notes that British publishers had little interest in differentiating between the two countries. According to him, the 'large quantity of British books which were re-exported from Australia to New Zealand may explain some of the confusion, [but] there is also much evidence suggesting that British publishers were ignorant of a number of vital aspects of the Australian market'. The words 'Australia' and 'Australasia' were used 'without differentiation'.[38] Australian publishing companies, however, were not at all confused when they saw New Zealand as an extension of their market. Booksellers in New Zealand sometimes worked via an Australian colleague, who would import books and then send them on. Thus within the colonial writing world, cities like Sydney and Melbourne acted as 'provincial capitals' for the Tasman world.[39] Imported books, including colonial editions, usually came to New Zealand via Melbourne.[40] Local New Zealand publishing firms treated Australia as their home ground. As locally produced textbooks 'tailored to the local syllabus' gradually overtook British imports, Whitcombe & Tombs saw Australia as simply an extension of their New Zealand market and kept a Melbourne office. Their Pacific Readers (printed in 1912 mainly for New Zealand schools) utilised Australian and New Zealand material, since a trans-

Tasman role gave the company a bigger pool of authors on whom to draw.[41] Ian F. Maclaren estimates that 'over twelve million copies' of Whitcombe's Story Books 'were printed during the years between 1908 and 1962' and sold throughout Australasia.[42] Similarly, Angus & Robertson maintained an office in New Zealand.

In Chapter Two we saw that a dispersed population was not an insurmountable obstacle to the formation of literary networks. Political borders and 2000 kilometres of sea also proved no great barrier. In the early days of the Australasian colonies, the settlers saw themselves as part of a Tasman world rather than a cohesive continent. This was because of the maritime outlook of the Australian colonies, as the sea was vital to their existence.[43] The interior of Australia, in particular, was difficult to traverse, so trans-Tasman connections could be utilised at least as easily as internal ones. A transcontinental railway was not opened until 1917, and while this had a psychological impact on the way Australians imagined themselves as part of a continent connected by land, in practice the rail remained 'colonial rather than national in conception'.[44] While it was possible to travel from Perth to Brisbane, the journey took five days and passengers were obliged to change trains 'on account of gauge differences no less than eight times'.[45] The journey between Sydney and Auckland, however, took just four days by 1918.[46] Sea-based commercial industries, such as sealing and whaling, which predated political distinctions between the two countries, 'did not distinguish between two sides of the Tasman in their activities, with Bass and Foveaux Straits and the subantarctic islands all being referred to as the "Sealing Islands", in "a joint past historians in both countries seem reluctant to recognise"'.[47] 'Tasman world' historians prefer this label to 'Australasia', because the area of interest really only includes Australia's eastern seaboard and New Zealand. Tasman ties were in many ways stronger than those between New South Wales and Western Australia or the 'Top End'. The vast majority of the literary activity discussed in this chapter took place in Sydney or Melbourne.

As New Zealand literary networks were often by necessity letter-based, they could naturally extend to include Australian writers, and did so. It was no greater effort for someone in Auckland to communicate with someone in Sydney than in Wellington or Christchurch.[48] Links were established through contacts, or when writers initiated a correspondence after seeing a piece they admired in a publication. Some amiable and mutually beneficial relationships were struck up across the Tasman, evolving from initial polite enquiry to informality. One of Eileen Duggan's literary mentors was Nettie Palmer. Their relationship began when Palmer wrote to Duggan after seeing her 'name in the book-lists'.[49] Duggan mentioned to Palmer at one point that she had had to ask Jessie Mackay who A.G. Stephens was, he being the influential editor of the *Bulletin*'s 'Red Page' who had criticised her for not writing 'by ear'. Duggan said: 'She was shocked! Is he a great nob on your side?'[50] In later letters Duggan familiarly referred to Stephens as 'old A.G.S',[51] as he was known to most New Zealand literary types. She told Palmer in 1927 that 'it's been part of God's goodness that you and she [Mackay] were my first mentors'.[52] She went from addressing her as 'Mrs Palmer' to 'Nettie', having obviously been instructed to do so by Palmer, and said she was 'only too pleased for that is what I think of you as'.[53] Such relationships often led to face-to-face meetings, although in this case Duggan said she would like to meet Palmer but was not a good traveller.[54] Literary friendships were not confined by geographical borders but conducted along well-established colonial and trans-Tasman lines of communication.

The Tasman world was a small part of the wider colonial world, and movement between New Zealand and Australia was common for people in many lines of work – those with business interests that spanned the sea, and people like journalists and writers who led trans-Tasman lives. There was a constant flow of people back and forth across the Tasman, as well as letters and literary works. Quite a few New Zealanders headed over to try their luck as journalists in the more varied and competitive environment that could be found in Sydney. They included David McKee Wright, who made the journey in 1910, and Arthur H. Adams, Douglas Stewart, Will Lawson and Pat Lawlor. Some New Zealanders went in pursuit of the enhanced freedom Australian cities were rumoured to offer. Jean Devanny was a committed communist, but could not find the political and intellectual company she craved until she went to Australia.[55] Her novel *The Butcher Shop* had recently been banned in New Zealand, but this was probably not her principal reason for departure: according to the *Dictionary of New Zealand Biography* she moved because of her son Karl's weak heart, which they believed would fare better in a warmer climate.[56] Moreover, *The Butcher Shop* was soon banned in Australia as well, and Devanny disliked the frivolity of the bohemian Sydney scene.[57] Hector

Bolitho moved to Sydney, and later said that the city 'gave me the challenge, and friends with talent, that I had lacked in New Zealand'.[58] It was the enhanced social freedom and the greater variety of opportunities that a larger population could offer that induced writers like Bolitho to go to Australia.

The fact that large numbers of people headed across the Tasman has all too often been seen solely as a negative event, as if New Zealand were being rejected in favour of a superior destination. While relocations might have occurred because of the broader range of opportunities to be found in Australia, or for a range of other reasons, there is little acknowledgement that these moves were often not permanent, and formed part of the general atmosphere of colonial mobility at the time. Terry Sturm's essay on the importance of Tasman literary connections refers to the 'continuing history of expatriatism by New Zealand writers to Australia', and still adheres to the mindset that associates expatriatism with permanence and loss, although he is cognisant that cultural assets are lost if these writers are dismissed.[59] The idea of a 'brain drain' originates from the general idea that too many people of talent have throughout the years been forced to leave New Zealand. Though the exchange of people and ideas with Australia is completely natural and inevitable, it has traditionally been viewed in a bad light, implying a loss of talent overseas.

It is much more accurate to envisage the process as a constant flow backwards and forwards. Peter Hempenstall invokes Rollo Arnold's model of a '"Perennial Interchange" of people and ideas' to portray this, with the relationship between Australia and New Zealand involving an interchange of 'bankers, businessmen, miners, axemen, shearers, clergy and journalists'.[60] This phenomenon has had many positive outcomes, such as the exchange of ideas across the Tasman. Moreover, a 2001 working paper from the New Zealand Treasury takes issue with the idea that New Zealand suffers from a 'brain drain' even today, and concludes that it has been more of a 'brain exchange'. In terms of immigration overall, New Zealand typically has a net increase in population, and these immigrants are usually highly skilled. In relation to Australia, there has generally been more migration to than from Australia, but this group is fairly representative of the general population: the paper calls it a 'same drain'.[61]

The consistent net loss of New Zealanders to Australia is only a fairly recent phenomenon. Since the beginning of European colonisation in Australasia,

New Zealand has had to compete with its larger, wealthier and more populous neighbour for citizens. At times, the outflow to Australia has been less than the inflow, depending on economic circumstances. An early surge of immigration to New Zealand due to the Otago and West Coast gold rushes in the 1850s and the availability of assisted passages in the 1870s ended with the depression of the 1880s, at which time 'marvellous Melbourne' experienced a 'boom'.[62] This outflow was again reversed in the 1890s when Australia was suffering a depression and New Zealand was benefitting from the recent invention of refrigerated shipping. From the mid-1960s onwards, migration to Australia followed a cyclical pattern, with net migration reaching a peak at the end of each decade.[63] A government working paper published in 2012 points out that migration to Australia was much higher in the 1970s than it is today: 1.42 per cent of the New Zealand population moved to Australia in 1979, as compared to 0.73 per cent in 2010 (the 2011 figure is 1.02 per cent, but that year included a spike in departures due to the Canterbury earthquakes).[64] Throughout New Zealand's European history, migration numbers have been subject to ebb and flow, and the general belief that a problematic number of able people are leaving every year is rarely based on solid, long-term statistical evidence. To underline this point, in recent years the flow has reversed for the first time since the 1970s – December 2015 was the third month in a row to show an annual net gain for New Zealand, with 800 more people moving from Australia than to Australia.[65] Longer-term patterns show a decrease in net migration to Australia: there was a 'small net loss of 3500 New Zealand citizens to Australia in 2015/16, the smallest it has been since 1990/91'.[66]

Finally, not all, or even most, of the writers who left New Zealand for Australia did so permanently. Of the 19 New Zealand writers in my dataset who went to Australia between 1890 and 1945, eight returned to New Zealand and two continued on to the United Kingdom.[67] Similarly, the supposed 'exodus' of New Zealanders to Australia in the present day is not an accurate reflection of the facts: those lamenting it do not necessarily differentiate between gross departures and net departures, which would take into account the people who return after only a short visit.

The traffic was certainly not all one way. The most famous example of an Australian writer relocating to New Zealand is of course Henry Lawson, who gained a teaching appointment at Mangamaunu School near Kaikōura. He went to live there in 1897 with his wife Bertha. Lawson made the move because of a shortage of government posts in Australia, and possibly because of the manipulations of Bertha, who wanted to find him a position away from the lure of public houses.[68] The couple intended to settle in New Zealand, but failed because they found it hard to cope as they were in a particularly isolated rural area and had difficulties fitting in with the community.[69]

Anne Glenny Wilson, born Anne Adams in Queensland in 1848, moved to New Zealand at the age of 26 upon marrying a Scottish farmer (later a member of parliament). After this she began publishing widely in literary journals throughout Australasia, and 'continued to identify with her birthplace, which provided the inspiration for much of her writing'.[70] She published two books of verse, and later two novels in London. Other Australian-born writers who relocated to New Zealand were Hubert Church, David W.M. Burn and Edith Lyttleton. Steven Loveridge asserts that 'a strict understanding of the myth of two countries peopled independently by entirely different categories of settler seriously misreads global migration' because it 'ignores the substantial flows of people across the Tasman' and the fact that 'between 1858 and 1915 Australia served as a gateway for migration to New Zealand'.[71] Writers who came to New Zealand via Australia include Dugald Ferguson, who emigrated from Scotland to Otago via Australia in about 1870, and Frank Morton. Morton was a truly a man of the colonial world, in particular the Tasman world. He emigrated to Sydney at the age of 16, worked on ships en route to Hong Kong and Singapore, married and moved to India, then returned to Australia and worked on various newspapers before moving to Dunedin for a post on the *Otago Daily Times*; he 'left abruptly' in 1908 and moved to Wellington. Originally associate editor for the *Triad*, after moving back to Sydney in 1914 he became the 'mainstay' of its Australian edition.[72]

The New Zealand literary scene benefitted from the movement of people backwards and forwards across the Tasman, and was improved by the ideas brought back by Australasian itinerants. For example, when Pat Lawlor decided to create New Zealand Authors' Week in 1936 he was inspired by an Australian precedent: he had previously attended the Australian Authors' Week organised by Will Lawson (another writer who alternated between Australia and New Zealand).[73] Returning or overseas New Zealand bookmen had contacts on both sides of the Tasman as a result of the movement to-and-fro of journalistic staff. Lawlor had worked on the *Daily Telegraph* in Sydney in the 1920s, and worked hard to maintain his contacts and put New Zealand writers in touch with Australian publishers.[74] He was also the New Zealand agent for *Aussie* magazine, the *Bulletin* and the *Australian Women's Mirror*.

Like Will Lawson and Lawlor, there were writers who operated in the Tasman world and who are difficult to classify as either Australian or New Zealanders. Arthur H. Adams is, at different times, referred to as a New Zealander, Australian, Australasian, New Zealand-born Australian and colonial, among other epithets. He was born in New Zealand and moved between Sydney and Wellington for a number of years, as well as spending a few years in London and embarking on a journalistic assignment to China to cover the Boxer Rebellion for Australian and New Zealand papers. He was not partial to Australia at first – his first book of verse, *Maoriland and Other Verses*, was a loving portrait of the land of his birth. Two poems refer to Australia, and in 'Written in Australia' Adams sums up his feelings with the words 'My heart is hot with discontent – / I hate this haggard continent'.[75] Over the next 35 years he used the labels of nationality interchangeably, often depending on his audience.[76] Although Kirstine Moffat claims that 'he always defined himself as a New Zealander', there is little obvious evidence for this.[77]

The literary periodical the *Triad*, which had had unusual success in New Zealand, moved to Australia in 1914, when Charles Baeyertz and Frank Morton relocated to Sydney. The magazine still had an Australasian outlook and a 'reputation for uncompromising honesty of purpose, originality, and general interest', and continued to publish work from New Zealand. The December 1916 issue, according to a newspaper report, included 'some rather scathing criticism of Sydney' from a New Zealand writer named Gladys Kernot and a 'breezy tale' by Alice A. Kenny, a staunch contributor from the New Zealand days.[78] The relocation did not have a marked effect on the journal's contributions and circulation.

Examples of 'in-between' trans-Tasman writers abound. Hubert Church, for example, is usually referred to in New Zealand as a New Zealand poet. His brand of Georgian-inspired poetry, though largely dismissed by later critics (Evans calls him the 'worst poet of the period, although the title was keenly contested')[79] supposedly typified the verse commonly written by New Zealanders at this time. However, Church was in fact an Australian expatriate, born in Hobart in 1857, educated in England and only arriving in New Zealand in 1873 (in Australia, he is known as an Australian poet). Another writer, Eve Langley, was Australian-born and wrote her most successful novel,

The Pea-Pickers, about Australia; but she lived in New Zealand, only returning to Australia when she was 53. Edith Lyttleton is touted as New Zealand's most successful author of the period, yet she was born in Australia and a significant number of her famous novels were written about that country, including *Pageant*, set in Tasmania. Her books are often referred to as 'Dominion' novels, as they are set in Australia, Canada and New Zealand. In a way, that is symptomatic of Lyttleton's extensive participation in the life of the colonial writing world. The 'trans-Tasman writer and journalist'[80] Will Lawson was described by Pat Lawlor as 'the restless poet of Australasia. If he is not leaving or joining the staff of a newspaper, he is embarking or disembarking, on or from, the Sydney boat. In fact, he moves so quickly from one place to another that I have heard him credited with the supernatural gift of omnipresence.'[81] This sort of transient existence was by no means uncommon within Australasian circles.

These writers who fell in between easy national categorisations have frequently been ignored or inadequately acknowledged for their contributions to the world of letters. Douglas Stewart complained about the 'villains of his native land' and the 'Christchurch gang' who had been ignoring him and Eve Langley because of their Australian ties.[82] Terry Sturm notes the ways in which the contributions of trans-Tasman authors have only been partially considered:

> *The New Zealand traces in Douglas Stewart's work, for example – not only in the subject matter and themes of plays like* The Golden Lover *and* Fire on the Snow *and poems like 'Rutherford', but also in the style of his approach to Australian landscape – have remained unexplored, as have the perspectives on Australia carefully built into New Zealand novels like Robin Hyde's* The Godwits Fly.[83]

Arthur H. Adams appears in the literary histories of both countries but only in terms of his contribution to 'national' literature. According to the *Australian Dictionary of Biography* Adams' 'forte' was urban social comedy, when he attempted 'to deal dramatically with Australian conditions viewed from an Australian standpoint by the creation of characters essentially Australian',[84] in novels such as *Grocer Greatheart: A tropical romance* and *Galahad Jones*. Kirstine Moffat, on the other hand, sees his best work in the poems and novels that 'display a distinctively New Zealand sensibility and an unsentimental pride in the nation's cultural identity'. *Tussock Land* fulfils this criterion as 'one of the earliest to give a sense of an authentic New Zealand landscape'.[85] Nationalist influences mean that neither tradition sees Adams' life and work in its entirety. Similarly, Theresia Marshall says that the poetic contribution of Frank Morton 'in the first two decades of the twentieth century has been underestimated, primarily because he never identified himself wholly with either country (and was thus never seen to "belong" to either of them)'.[86]

Rather than spending time and energy trying to differentiate between New Zealand and Australian authors, it may be far better to accept trans-Tasman perspectives and ways of life as the reality for many people. Indeed, it is futile and anachronistic to insist upon clear distinctions between Australian and New Zealand writers based upon later, more rigid conceptions of nationality. Letting nationalism dictate literary history is to be blinded to the reality that writers' lives and work were not yet organised around the nation state (if they ever have been), but took place within a series of networks – global, colonial and trans-Tasman. At this point New Zealand, Australian, colonial, imperial and British identities co-existed and overlapped. As James Belich has said: 'New Zealandness, Australasianism – and Britishness – were not mutually exclusive.'[87] Nationalism does not account for the fact that all writers are unique amalgams of their varied and often transnational cultural and social influences. 'New Zealandness' and its meaning varies from individual to individual, although, as David Carter argues, the fact that people believe in the existence of nationalism means that it has had a 'massive effect'.[88] What it meant to Allen Curnow was different from what it meant to writers a generation later, and even to Curnow's own contemporaries. Concentrating on the writers' nationality makes it impossible to create an accurate picture of the context within which they created literature. To do this, we must acknowledge the role not only of the writers' New Zealand context, but of the wider Tasman and colonial writing worlds.

CHAPTER FOUR

From a Garden in the Antipodes: The colonial writing world

M ary Scott's *The Unwritten Book* features a woman on a remote New Zealand farm who has written for local publications but longs to 'break into the English papers'. This seems like an impossible task, however, and at one point, she asks: '[W]ho would be interested in the New Zealand backblocks?'[1] Scott based these experiences on her own life at Strathallan, a sheep farm on the slopes of Pirongia mountain in the King Country, where she and her husband farmed in primitive and isolated conditions, beset with disasters including two fires that destroyed most of their possessions.[2] Still, she 'decided to start writing' in the 1920s and achieved quite a local following for her stories. In the book, and in Scott's real life, her doubts about international recognition were circumvented by a friend who secretly posted one of Scott's short manuscripts to Alan Monkhouse, literary editor of the *Manchester Guardian*. It was accepted for three guineas, and longer work set locally was suggested.[3] Scott went on to write popular novels about her experiences in New Zealand, and published an impressive amount of material considering her circumstances.

Mary Scott could achieve her publishing ambitions because of the networks of the colonial writing world. The Tasman world system was a small part of a much greater arena of cultural interaction that existed because of the connections forged and reforged by the workings of British colonialism. The most important aspect of participation in the colonial writing world for New Zealand writers was that it allowed them access to London's well-developed publishing infrastructure. New Zealand writers took advantage of this in large numbers, and were often reliant on London publishers to produce their novels and sometimes their books of verse, at least up until the middle of the twentieth century. London remained the indisputable centre of literary production, boasting most of the world's major publishing houses. Many of the most significant literary works written by New Zealanders during this time were published in London, including Eileen Duggan's poetry collections, Robin Hyde's novels and Edith Lyttleton's *Pageant*. Between 1890 and 1935, 491 books written by New Zealand authors were published, 241 of which (49 per cent) were published in the United Kingdom (see Table 4.1).[4] Forty-three per cent were published in New Zealand.

Table 4.1: Place of publication of books by New Zealand authors, 1890–1935

Place of publication	Novels	Poetry	Short fiction	Total
New Zealand	24	172	15	**211**
United Kingdom	157	65	19	**241**
Australia	10	16	2	**28**
United States	8	1	0	**9**
Other	0	1	1	**2**
Total	**199**	**255**	**37**	**491**

New Zealand publishers put out most of the poetry, but British publishers were responsible for over half the short fiction and fully 79 per cent of the novels. The contribution of British publishers to the development of the New Zealand novel was substantial, and the availability of British publishers was very significant for New Zealand literature.

Table 4.2: Place of publication of books by New Zealand authors, 1890–1945

Place of publication	Novels	Poetry	Short fiction	Total
New Zealand	46	263	35	**344**
United Kingdom	219	73	20	**312**
Australia	20	22	4	**46**
United States	11	2	0	**13**
Other	0	1	1	**2**
Total	**296**	**361**	**60**	**717**

If the period is extended to 1945 (see Table 4.2), the percentage of books published in the United Kingdom is slightly lower at 43 per cent, due to the increasing presence of local publishing infrastructure from the mid-1930s. This is somewhat underestimating the role of British publishers, for the books published there were usually longer, with bigger print runs and wider circulation. Many of the books published in New Zealand were small print runs of books of verse. Moreover, because it is the books' presence in New Zealand that determines their inclusion in libraries, New Zealand-published material is over-represented, as some books published in the United Kingdom did not make it into major New Zealand libraries.

Due to the local publishing initiatives in the late 1930s and their reported significance for New Zealand literature, one might expect this British influence to be a phenomenon of an earlier time. It continued until at least 1945: between 1936 and 1945, 64 per cent of novels were still published in Britain, despite the rapid development of New Zealand publishing facilities in this period (only 23 percent were published in New Zealand). Many important New Zealand and Australian books simply would not have appeared were it not for the accessibility of London publishers, and these opportunities greatly enhanced the options available. Because the statistics relate to book publication, as mentioned in Chapter Two, they show only a fraction of the enhanced opportunities. Magazine and newspaper publications made up a huge portion of the published material produced by New Zealanders, and played a significant part in the writing industry.

The importance of London to the New Zealand writing industry has not been widely acknowledged or thoroughly investigated. If noted in literary histories, it is usually as further evidence for the deprived nature of literary life in New Zealand. Very few accounts of New Zealand's publishing or writing history take a broad focus, although at the same time they often discuss work that was published across a broad geographical area. Terry Sturm provides an account of Edith Lyttleton's international publishing life but describes 'the American and British publishing establishments' as the 'villains' of the story.[5] Lyttleton was very successful, and thus was in an unusual position regarding the rights to her work in different countries, but Sturm's stance does not give enough credit for her success to the existence of colonial writing networks which allowed her to succeed in the first place. Dennis McEldowney's 'Publishing, patronage and literary magazines' in the *Oxford History of New*

Zealand Literature contains the most comprehensive description of overseas publishing opportunities, but this short summary of overseas outlets still has a negative tone.[6]

Even those immersed in the industry were not always aware of the importance of overseas publishing, or they chose to ignore it to emphasise later, local advances. Pat Lawlor wrote in 1962:

> *In the 30s and 40s a further impetus was given through the interest shown by visiting London publishers, notably by Stanley Unwin and Hugh Dent. The expatriate writers (Hector Bolitho, Jane Mander and Nelle Scanlan) had already achieved London publication, but when the resident N.Z. writers (John Lee, John Schroder, Gloria Rawlinson and Alan Mulgan) were published overseas other writers worked furiously to achieve similar distinction.*[7]

Lawlor implied that until the 1930s the only New Zealanders published in London were expatriates. In fact, between 1890 and 1929 there were 54 books (33 of them novels) by New Zealand authors published in London while the authors themselves were in New Zealand (probably more, but in the case of some authors there is not enough information to ascertain their whereabouts). These were by a total of 34 different authors. A further 12 books (11 novels) were published in Australia by New Zealand-resident authors. Lawlor was incorrect in implying that before the 1930s publishing in London was only possible upon relocation.

Many important books that are included in the New Zealand literary canon were published overseas, and yet surveys of the state of New Zealand literature at this time generally ignore the option of overseas publishing. For example, *The Story of a New Zealand River* was published in New York and London in 1920, but not in New Zealand until 1938. Edith Searle Grossmann's *The Heart of the Bush* was published in London in 1910 but never in New Zealand. Important works by Jessie Mackay, Jean Devanny, D'Arcy Cresswell, Eileen Duggan, A.R.D. Fairburn and many others were *only* published overseas. Most consider these to be vital works of New Zealand literature. However, most discussions of outlets for New Zealand writers bemoan the dearth of publishing opportunities in the early twentieth century, focusing only on those available locally. This is at least partly due to the influence of local publishers and cultural nationalists who resented the dominance of overseas companies.

Writers themselves did not necessarily have a negative attitude to publishing overseas; in fact, some preferred it. There were obvious advantages. The audience to which British publishers had access was much larger, which gave writers better exposure and the potential for a better financial return. A.G. Stephens supposed that Miles Franklin's *My Brilliant Career* 'could hardly have been published in Australia with a chance of profit: the local audience whom it will interest is too scanty'.[8] Jane Mander noted that the majority of New Zealand prose writers published their books in London and listed some reasons for this in a talk for Authors' Week in 1936:

> *First of all reputable English publishers now almost invariably pay the novelist a cash advance on the expected sales. Thirty pounds is the usual minimum for an ordinary story by an unknown writer, but if the book rises above the ordinary, or has some special selling feature, the publisher may offer a larger sum, according to how much he likes it himself and is disposed to risk on it. The London publisher, who serves an enormous Empire market, can take risks that no New Zealand firm can yet afford to do.*[9]

Thirty pounds (equivalent to around a month and a half of the average wage)[10] was not a huge sum for the amount of work it took to write a novel, but it was far in advance of anything you could get in New Zealand. C.R. Allen's novel *The Ship Beautiful* sold 'between two and three thousand copies' after it was published by Frederick & Warne of London. For this Allen received 'about Forty Pounds in all'.[11]

The cheaper 'colonial editions' sold in the colonies were designed to combat competition, and inevitably had a negative effect on local publishing (unless the publishers were also involved in bookselling). On the other hand, the colonial series put out by British publishing houses like T. Fisher Unwin provided an outlet for colonial writers as well, and the series often contained New Zealand writing. Martyn Lyons says that the arrangement was 'immensely profitable' to Australian booksellers and 'Australian dealers suggested titles to British publishers'.[12] The authors, however, 'suffered', according to Lyons, because they got a lower royalty rate for a colonial edition than a book published for the British market – four pence per copy as opposed to 11 pence for the 'home' edition.[13] There is no reason to assume that the negative aspects outweighed the positive, however, as colonial editions provided a valuable publishing opportunity for colonial writers, and could give books 'a circulation that they might never have secured from local publication'.[14]

Another reason writers might have preferred overseas publication was the prestige attached to having one's manuscript accepted by a respected London publisher. Eileen Duggan had the chance to have a collection of poems published and funded by New Zealand's State Literary Fund in 1947. She declined, and wrote to Stanley Unwin (of George Allen & Unwin) that 'partly from independence, partly from loyalty, I would not like to leave your banner ... I think a writer feels much the same pride in his publishers as a sailor in a ship.'[15]

Others were partial to the higher-quality product that overseas publishers could offer, at least until the introduction of good quality typography in New Zealand in the 1930s. Ursula Bethell, when writing to Frank Sidgwick of Sidgwick & Jackson, who published her first volume of poetry, *From a Garden in the Antipodes*, said of the end result, 'The paper, the print, the size, the arrangement, the colour – as Raven says it's all so superior (I really think I must post you a copy of a little vol. of local verse recently published, to show you what I have escaped).'[16] Geoffrey de Montalk declined to appear in the New Zealand Artists' Annual when invited by Pat Lawlor, writing:

> *I am far too stuck up to appear in such a 'New Zealand' publication. You would have to change the whole thing from typography upwards before I could see my way to write ... I assure you I'd rather starve than appear in company with all the other bandaged moas. This moa won't be bandaged.*[17]

New Zealand writers viewed the whole colonial writing world as their publishing domain, and this allowed many to have successful careers without needing to leave the country. The career of Hilda Rollett is an excellent example of how the colonial world worked for New Zealand-based authors. She was a successful journalist, and began writing for local publications such as the *New Zealand Illustrated Magazine*, the *New Zealand Herald* and the *Auckland Weekly News*. Over time she became a prolific contributor to magazines throughout the world, writing fiction published in English periodicals, the New York *Sun* and Australian journals including the *Bulletin*. Rollett was the New Zealand representative for the London Lyceum Club and won a place in its first overseas literary competition. Such was her success and reputation that when she did travel to London in 1910 she was welcomed and elected as a member of both the Empire Press Union and the Institute of Journalists,

London.[18] By the early 1940s she was the New Zealand representative for *All About Books*, published in Melbourne.

In a similar fashion to Rollett, the popular novelist Edith Lyttleton began her career writing for *Pall Mall* and *Windsor* in the United Kingdom and *Harper's* and *Scribner's* magazines in New York.[19] Eileen Duggan had poems published in Australia, the United States and England. This was partly due to her work as a Catholic poet[20] and also her Irish work, but her New Zealand poems were appreciated overseas as well. Hector Bolitho's international success began in 1919 when he wrote a piece about a friend of Keats who had emigrated to New Zealand. The London *Observer* accepted this with a cheque; Bolitho wrote that 'my name had been printed in one of the noblest of England's newspapers and the world seemed to be in my hands'.[21] To list a few others, Mary Scott, Isabel Maud Peacocke and William Satchell all had successful careers publishing books, serialised novels, poems, articles and short fiction overseas while remaining in New Zealand.

Colonial networks were not entirely confined to connections with London publishing. British immigrants to New Zealand were disproportionately Scottish: at the turn of the century 10 per cent of the British population were Scottish, whereas 23 per cent of British-born New Zealanders came from Scotland.[22] There were quite a number of poets, particularly around Dunedin, who wrote of Scotland or in a Scottish dialect and published in Scotland, as well as in England and New Zealand. Scotland also had important publishing houses operating in the global market, such as Blackwood's, Chambers', and Murray's.[23] The poet Angus Robertson held the title of 'Honourable Bard' of the Gaelic Society of New Zealand, while being a member of the Dunedin Burns Club and the Dunedin Pipe Band. John McGlashan and Robin Blochairn (real name Robert Hogg) were others: Blochairn lived in Wellington and had three books of poetry published in Paisley, Scotland, between 1917 and 1920. W.H. Guthrie-Smith's book *Tutira: The story of a New Zealand sheep station* was published by Blackwood's in Edinburgh. Jessie Mackay was also famous for her Scottish poetry.

The colonial writing world included Canada, and it also facilitated some access to publishers in the United States, a still-emerging giant in English-language publishing that treasured its British literary heritage. Table 4.2 shows that 13 books were published by New Zealanders in the United States between 1890 and 1945. US periodicals were also an important outlet and source of income for prolific writers like Edith Lyttleton, who had many stories placed in American magazines, including *Harper's, Scribner's* and *Putnam's* magazines and the *Cosmopolitan*.[24] More books were published in the United States simultaneously with their London publication, though the official 'first' publisher was the London one.

Several authors made significant trips to the United States. Jane Mander studied at the Columbia School of Journalism and remained in New York for 13 years. Nelle Scanlan was in the United States from 1921 to 1923 and attended the first Limitation of Arms Conference in Washington, DC. Edith Lyttleton travelled extensively in Canada; in 1923 her book *The Law-Bringers*, about two Canadian mounted policemen, was made into a film that starred famous Hollywood actors and had 'impressive international success'.[25] Later, she reflected further on her experiences in the Yukon in *The World is Yours*.

The literary links with North America were nowhere near as strong as those with Australia and Britain, however. As the numbers indicate, though New Zealanders did publish in the United States, they did this less often than in other English-speaking countries. Moreover, while some writers travelled there, many more went to Australia or Britain. Due to the links being more common, and reinforced by the British publishing houses' attempts to control the empire book world and shut out American competition, Britain remained the centre of the colonial writing world. New Zealand cannot be viewed in isolation from its British connections.[26]

The colonial writing world was more than just an informal collection of networks. It had a basis in economic policy as well, and economic links were strengthening during this time. James Belich's theory of 'recolonisation' hinges on the tightening of those links due to advances such as the introduction of refrigerated shipping in 1882, enabling New Zealand to supply most of Britain's meat and dairy products (coupled with the development of steamship technology that sped up the journey). This meant '[t]he town-supply district of London had shifted 12,000 miles to the south'.[27] Felicity Barnes argues for the benefit of viewing the relationship as between 'a city and its hinterland', providing a useful vantage point to examine the continuing links between the two countries.[28] Publishing, like many other things, worked in this shared and reciprocal fashion. If New Zealand was the United Kingdom's supply district for foodstuffs, the United Kingdom was the source of New Zealand writers' metaphorical bread and butter because of a continuing interdependent relationship. British publishers had selling rights over American publishers within the colonies due to the copyright law, as

> *Britain's closed market was protected by copyright legislation which effectively gave British publishers exclusive rights to distribute their titles in Australia.*
>
> *Australia's book trade and readers were therefore part of an imperial cultural space, dominated and defended by London publishers, and shared with Canadians, South Africans, Indians, New Zealanders and other readers of the Empire.*[29]

Australia was the 'single largest off-shore market for British books' and this continued into the 1980s, when British publishers gained access to the American market.[30] By the 1920s, 3.5 million books were sold annually in Australia at a profit of over a million pounds.[31] For British publishers, 'Australia' could mean New Zealand as well. Regardless of whether they made this distinction, the British profits from Australasia as a whole must have been even greater.

Nonetheless, New Zealand's geographical isolation led to the false assumption that New Zealand was detached from the culture of the centre, and the large distances involved in publishing a book in Britain are assumed to have been prohibitive. Australian writers had the same potential problems – A.G. Stephens told Joseph Furphy in 1897: 'To send MS to London is to invite delay, heartburning, and weariness of flesh and soul, with a 90 per cent chance of rejection at the hands of a reader who thinks of his English audience only.'[32] There were, of course, difficulties in negotiating with publishers from a distance of 18,000 kilometres. Firstly there was the lengthy wait between sending a manuscript and receiving a reply: this process could take several months. In times of world war there was the added difficulty of not knowing whether the mail had arrived there at all, as the ships carrying mail were sometimes sunk and correspondence could easily fail to reach its intended destination. Stanley Unwin wrote to Eileen Duggan in 1941 asking if she had received copies of her book, saying that 'most of the mails during one month seem to have gone to the bottom of the ocean.'[33] During times of war, book production suffered in general, due to different priorities, and paper and metal shortages. Any negotiations with publishers took time, and the risks involved were exacerbated by long distances, but there was no easy option even when based close by.[34] Overall, the high number of writers who did manage to overcome distance and publish in Britain suggests that this was, in fact, one of the better choices.

I would argue that the distances involved in New Zealand's participation in the colonial writing world were much less of a hindrance than is commonly assumed, and it was not necessary to be physically located in Britain to overcome them. In the era before airmail services people were accustomed to waiting months for replies to letters; they rejoiced when, with the introduction of steamships, the expected time for sending and receiving mail markedly decreased. By the 1900s the voyage from New Zealand to Britain took only about a third as long as in the early 1870s.[35] From the 1870s, when the trans-Pacific route (via New York) began to be used, the time for mail journeys became shorter, and it was '31½ days between Auckland and London' at the turn of the century.[36] This fairly sudden shrinking of international space made the heart of the colonial writing world seem much closer.

Just as correspondence within New Zealand could be extended to include Australian writers, there existed lines of communication between New Zealand and Britain that maintained the two countries' interdependent relationship. These 'dynamic' links were the result of colonial exploration and continuing colonial connections and mobility.[37] The Jesuit priest C.C. Martindale met Eileen Duggan while visiting New Zealand and as a result asked Walter de la Mare to write an introduction for Duggan's *Poems* (1937). Because of this the two writers struck up a correspondence between London and Wellington which lasted for the next 18 years. De la Mare felt, through these letters (as well as his correspondence with Katherine Mansfield and Ian Donnelly), that 'New Zealand gets nearer and nearer', although his hope of meeting Duggan was never fulfilled.[38]

Mobile or not, New Zealanders were experts at negotiating the networks of the colonial writing world. Authors could overcome the drawbacks of distance with the use of certain techniques. The employment of a literary agent – a practice that became increasingly common from the late nineteenth century – made long-distance negotiations simpler. J.B. Pinker, one of the better-known agents in London, represented William Satchell. Pinker facilitated the publication of *The Land of the Lost* in 1902,[39] and it was followed by *Toll of the Bush* in 1905 as No. 500 in Macmillan's Colonial Library. Pinker also became Edith Lyttleton's agent while she was still in New Zealand. Her international success prompted him to approach her and ask if he could represent her.

Following the success of *Sons o' Men* and *A Spur to Smite*, Pinker 'solicited her business for a number of years ... before persuading her to dispense with her Melbourne agent, H.H. Champion, in 1908'. (Lyttleton left New Zealand for the first time in 1909.)[40]

There were some difficulties that were particular to transnational authors, and Edith Lyttleton eventually decided her agents were more hindrance than help. Her American agent, Francis Arthur Jones, arranged a contract for her book *Pageant*, but she was very unhappy with it as it bound her to accept the same terms for her next book.[41] This, and the conflict that followed, caused her to write to Jones:

> *It may interest you to know that you have reduced me to such a state of nerves and exhaustion that I have had to give up writing altogether. I feel that I never want to write another book. My agents always make me bad contracts and then make me fight for what I can get ... if anything.*[42]

Her multiple contracts meant she lost a lot of her profits to different taxes. For every £100 she earned in Australia, she ended up with £16 after paying Australian and American tax, two publishers' commissions and one agent's fee – and she still had to pay New Zealand tax.[43] Lyttleton was unusually successful, which compounded these issues, but agents proved useful in most cases, especially if the author had not been published before.

In the end, it was often influential people in the literary establishment – particularly those with transnational connections, like Pat Lawlor – who helped establish publishing relationships for New Zealand writers overseas. Jane Mander wrote to Monte Holcroft in 1934 suggesting he send his manuscript to Endeavour Publishing (an arm of the *Bulletin*, based in Sydney), which was responsible for over 2000 copies of Edith Lyttleton's *Pageant* being sold in New Zealand. Pat Lawlor was Endeavour's New Zealand agent, and Mander advised using him as a go-between, saying 'though he pub-crawls at intervals he is a live wire on the selling side'.[44] Alan Mulgan and John Schroder had existing literary contacts that could be utilised. Duggan wrote to Nettie Palmer in 1936 informing her that 'at the request of Mr Kavanagh and Mr Mulgan Mr von Haast is taking the M.S. of my rhymes to London'.[45] Duggan's *Poems* was published shortly after by Allen & Unwin.

Many writers utilised overseas contacts to simplify negotiations with publishers.[46] Ursula Bethell was well connected, since her grandfather had been

Shelley's housemaster at Eton.[47] She had also boarded with Arthur Mayhew's family while at school in Oxford, and many of her poems were addressed to Arthur's sister Ruth, who became her lifelong friend. Arthur Mayhew had an imperial career as an educator and in educational administration – he worked in India, taught classics at Eton and served in the Colonial Office in London.[48] He was also, conveniently, the long-time friend of Frank Sidgwick of the publishing firm Sidgwick & Jackson. Bethell sent Mayhew a selection of her poems; he liked them and showed them to Sidgwick. 'With little fuss,' says Holcroft, *From a Garden in the Antipodes* was published.[49]

Others used the services of friends who were already in England. Geoffrey de Montalk acted as a go-between for A.R.D. Fairburn before Fairburn himself went to London, and succeeded in getting *He Shall Not Rise* published by Columbia Press in 1930.[50] While Dan Davin was away serving in World War II, he managed to keep up his rates of publication in England because his wife, Winnie, was able to continue negotiating with publishers on his behalf. She found a publisher for his first book, *Cliffs of Fall*, while he was away, and wrote to him in 1944: 'On Monday morning the Cheque from Nancy Pearn for advance on *Cliffs of Fall* arrived – £75 less commission = £67-10s net. I banked it on Tuesday, but I've felt frightfully pleased all the week. It's very concrete, isn't it, darling?'[51]

In some cases London publishers were so keen to publish colonial manuscripts that they solicited submissions. This still involved some kind of go-between, such as a local publisher or a friend in England to deal with contracts. Thomas Fisher Unwin wrote to Australian firm Angus & Robertson in 1897, saying: '[F]rom time to time when authors speak to you with regard to the publication of their work, and you yourself do not care to take up the venture, or to publish for them locally, then, if you think well, I shall be happy for your clients to forward the MS. to me for consideration.'[52] Unwin claimed to have 'published more Foreign and Colonial books than most publishing houses', but still seemed keen to do more. This mindset was continued by his nephew, Stanley Unwin.

It was more difficult for new writers, especially poets, to secure publication – but not impossible. After the publication of *From a Garden in the Antipodes*, in a letter to Frank Sidgwick Bethell quoted a piece she had read by Edward Thompson, which said: '[T]here is at the present moment no publisher who would at his own expense publish a new poet (if there is, let him speak, that we may all look at a brave man)'. She went on to ask: '[H]ave you spoken? Or should it be my pleasant daring to write to ... Edward Thompson & reveal you?'[53] Publishing Bethell's work was an unusual risk for Sigwick to take: he mentioned many times the probable lack of profit and his intention to make sure that 'the author is aware poetry as a rule is not remunerative'.[54] But, in reply to Bethell's letter, he protested:

> there is 'at the present moment' ... 'a firm of publishers' [his own] that has always been ready to 'publish a new poet at their own expense' – and has done so before the striking MS. from New Zealand reached them.[55]

The impressive list of published authors in both New Zealand and Britain testifies to the truth of Sidgwick's claim.

Without connections, some authors simply sent their manuscripts off to British publishers and waited hopefully for a reply, relying on luck in their inter-hemisphere negotiations. This could have some success. Monte Holcroft adopted a vigorous 'hit-and-miss' technique, sending stories and articles to one publication after another, a process that is well documented in his notebooks in the Alexander Turnbull Library. One notebook records, for example, that in January 1925 he received three pounds and three shillings from *Punch* for 'Over the Wall'. In 1925 he sent the story 'Treasure Trove' to the *Bulletin*, *Punch*, the *Herald* and the *Sunday Times* before finally getting it accepted by *John O' London's Weekly* in February 1926. Other times Holcroft had quick success, as when 'The Lesser Lights' was accepted immediately by *Punch* in April 1925. The income that he derived from short stories and essays sent to periodicals in 1925 amounted to £160 10s. 5d.[56] – which was not bad considering the median yearly income in 1926 was £235.[57]

Frank Sargeson also adopted a scattergun approach to courting publishers in London. He says in his autobiography *More Than Enough* that upon receiving a rejection for the manuscript he had sent to Jonathan Cape he 'recovered immediately ... by posting it away to another London publishing house. For several years this posting back immediately to London was a regular routine.'[58] Luke Trainor describes the practice of sending work 'without specific invitation' to British publishers. A study of Macmillan readers' reports resulting from these submissions from 'the late 1880s to the early years of the 20th century' included 260 Australian and New Zealand examples. Ninety-two per cent of these submissions were rejected, but Trainor says that this 'rejection rate is not excessive' and that 'Antipodean manuscripts were quite up to the average'. A quarter of the 260 submissions were from New Zealanders, which means that New Zealand was slightly over-represented based on relative population sizes.[59]

While writers' complaints occasionally indicted both the New Zealand and the London literary scene for a lack of support and encouragement, their absence of success was sometimes the result of their own lack of initiative or effort. R.A.K. Mason's complaint is often cited as a prime example of New Zealand's failure to foster its writers. He wrote despairingly: 'The Virgils [...] starve in our English streets, / But oh, Maecenas, hard you are to find!' Maecenas, as Rachel Barrowman writes, was the patron of Horace and Virgil, and literary patrons were harder to find than Mason would have liked.[60] He wrote this on the back of a rejection letter for a temporary teaching job. Yet Mason was approached repeatedly by British bookman Harold Monro, who was very keen to publish his work and generally promote him within the English literary scene (Mason had initially, enterprisingly, sent Monro 50 copies of *The Beggar*). Mason neglected to reply to his letters and thus failed to take advantage of a willing patron. This was not because of some sort of loyalty to local publishing (at this stage there was very little to be loyal to, except Whitcombe & Tombs).[61]

Authors dissatisfied with the opportunities available to them in New Zealand sometimes complained that British publishers were not interested in New Zealand material. This further fuelled rumours that it was disadvantageous to be a New Zealand writer. Upon hearing that *Pageant* had not been selected as the Book Society's 'Book of the Month', Edith Lyttleton remarked, 'I'm afraid there must be some truth in the assertion that England is not interested in Australia or New Zealand.'[62] Nelle Scanlan was so convinced by the assertion that she set her early books in London.[63] Jane Mander wrote in the *Sun* in 1925: 'Many of our writers are successful, as far as magazine work goes. But when you talk of colonial "literature" to a London critic he asks you exactly what it is.'[64] Alan Mulgan noted in an article for PEN that the British public was 'not much interested in New Zealand' and that they did not 'seem to care for' novels about the country.[65]

However, these complaints were not borne out in reality, as Nelle Scanlan discovered, for New Zealand material was actually a very marketable commodity. Rather than being forced to deny her national origins to achieve publication, Scanlan's most successful novels were a tetralogy about the Pencarrow family, set in Wellington, the Wairarapa and Marlborough. She was initially under the impression that British readers would not be interested in New Zealand themes, believing that '[s]omething romantic and dramatic can happen in Piccadilly Circus but not on Lambton Quay'.[66] It was only at her publisher Robert Hale's suggestion that she chose the New Zealand setting, with very pleasing results that proved her initial misgivings to be unfounded.[67] Indeed, most works written by New Zealanders and published in Britain had New Zealand content, as the following table demonstrates.

Table 4.3: Content of books by New Zealand authors, 1890–1945

Place of publication	All or mostly NZ content	Some NZ content	No NZ content	Content unknown
New Zealand	171	50	80	43
United Kingdom	150	19	99	44
Australia	11	5	21	9
United States	5	0	7	1
Other	1	0	0	1
Total	**338**	**74**	**207**	**98**

Fifty-six per cent of the books with known content published by New Zealand authors in Britain in this period had all or mostly New Zealand content (63 per cent, if those with some New Zealand content are added).[68] Books that are judged to have no New Zealand content include many for which the setting is unspecific. These are usually books of poetry. Sixty-three per cent of the books published by New Zealanders in Britain had at least some overtly New Zealand content, putting paid to the idea that New Zealand content did not get published. Fifty-seven per cent of books published in New Zealand between 1890 and 1945 had all or mostly New Zealand content, a figure that is strikingly similar to that for books published in Britain, indicating that the place of publication made little difference to the content.[69]

When these figures are provided just for novels published in this period, the importance of New Zealand content becomes even more obvious.

Table 4.4: Content of novels by New Zealand authors, 1890–1945

Place of publication	All or mostly NZ content	Some NZ content	No NZ content	Content unknown
New Zealand	36	1	6	3
United Kingdom	119	4	73	23
Australia	6	0	11	3
United States	4	0	7	0
Other	0	0	0	0
Total	**165**	**5**	**97**	**29**

Sixty-one per cent of the novels by New Zealand writers published in the United Kingdom whose content is known had all or mostly New Zealand content. The percentage for novels published in New Zealand was even higher, at 84 per cent.

All of the novelists mentioned so far in this study, with the exception of Monte Holcroft and Dulcie Deamer, created work in a New Zealand setting, or with colonial characters in an English setting. This was not dependent on genre. Ngaio Marsh, for example, was extremely successful as a crime writer in the English tradition, but liberally used New Zealand settings and characters throughout her novels, taking advantage of the unique perspective to which she had access. Three of her pre-1945 novels, *Vintage Murder* (1937), *Colour Scheme* (1943) and *Died in the Wool* (1944), were set in New Zealand, and she had her protagonist Inspector Alleyn posted there during the war on counter-espionage duty. British readers were deeply interested in the colonies and were often surprisingly well informed about obscure parts of New Zealand. An article in the *Press* on Samuel Butler noted that a Cambridge academic was astonished to find:

> to what an extent English people looked upon Butler as a New Zealander, and how interested they were in his New Zealand experiences. Men of letters who did not know that there is such a city as Auckland or Wellington, know all about a sheep run called Mesopotamia, and a river called the Rangitata.[70]

While New Zealand content was popular, particularly in novels, it appears that some of the writers themselves were not aware of this, at least initially.

Nor were all New Zealand authors necessarily aware of the large numbers of New Zealand books published in Britain. Jane Mander gave a talk in 1932, and was reported in the *Auckland Star* as saying:

the numbers of New Zealand authors who had been published in London was very small. She mentioned [Isabel] Maud Peacock[e], Nelle Scanlan, Hector Bolitho, Edith Howes and a few others, not more than ten. Yet hundreds of novels were sent to the publishers with the hope that they might be accepted.[71]

In fact, between 1890 and 1932, 50 New Zealand authors had succeeded in getting a total of 130 novels published in the United Kingdom (this is excluding the 120 novels of Fergus Hume). This total would obviously be higher if pre-1890 novels were included. Mander was right, however, about the 'hundreds of novels' sent to publishers in the hope of acceptance.[72]

In reality it was useful to be a New Zealand writer when grappling with the British market, because New Zealand writers were able to take advantage of the British appetite for the 'colonial exotic', which was staple fare within the colonial writing world. The exoticisation of elements of colonial life and experience began as soon as Europeans started to explore far-flung parts of the world and brought back tales of curious lands and strange peoples. This cult of the exotic was tied up with the tropes of European romanticism and modified in the nineteenth century, influenced by the likes of Jean-Jacques Rousseau and proponents of the Gaelic revival.[73] Metropolitan audiences were not necessarily concerned about autochthonous colonial literary development, but their curiosity about exotic climes created an opportunity that colonial writers could exploit.[74] New Zealand was no exception, and Patrick Evans has noted that the introduction of tourism in the 1880s meant that 'the Antipodes became a stage in a world circuit of marvels to be gazed at by touring Europeans'.[75]

British readers were particularly fascinated with tales of indigenous peoples, something that New Zealand could provide in abundance. Tales of pre-contact Māori appealed to British idealists who had embraced the romantic concept of the 'noble savage', defined as 'an idealized concept of uncivilized man, who symbolizes the innate goodness of one not exposed to the corrupting influences of civilization'.[76] Descriptions of Māori life and culture fulfilled this need, in the eyes of British readers. There was a demand for exotic tales, both from newspapers and from overseas publishing houses. These were not realistic descriptions of contemporary Māori, but rather appropriated and romanticised stories from pre-contact times, popular both from an ethnographic point of view and because of simple curiosity. Stafford and Williams describe the allure of indigenous themes in 'Maoriland' literature, read by New Zealanders and 'a British readership agog for adventures of empire'.[77] This romantic treatment of Māori reflected the fact that by the 1890s they were thought to be a dying race and no longer a 'threat'.[78] The modern reality of Māori life was not deemed an appropriate or necessary subject to write about. Māori writers in English numbered very few at this time, but no doubt would have attracted great interest in Britain.[79] Stafford and Williams note the value placed on Alfred Domett's epic and unwieldy poem *Ranolf and Amohia* because of its indigenous themes, despite its being as far removed from colonial life 'as fact is from fiction'.[80] For the same reason, Alfred A. Grace's *Tales of a Dying Race* sold well in Britain, having 'taken a firm hold upon the British book-buyers'.[81]

Another type of writing that fascinated English readers dealt with the adventures of pioneers: tales of Britons in far-flung places overcoming the elements. One such book was George Chamier's *Philosopher Dick: Adventures and contemplations of a New Zealand shepherd*, thought to be autobiographical, which focuses on a young gentleman immigrant. Chamier himself immigrated to New Zealand in 1860 and spent about two years as a cadet on a North Canterbury sheep station.[82] He spent only a decade in New Zealand before he left for Tasmania, and he was in Adelaide by the time *Philosopher Dick* was published in 1891. Many books were written dealing with the tribulations of life on the frontier; William Satchell's tale of the Northland gumfields, *The Land of the Lost*, is an example.[83] Edith Lyttleton's *Promenade* is an at times fascinating account of the early days of settlement in Kororāreka (Russell) before and after the signing of the Treaty of Waitangi. Adventurous narratives had a political role, as they developed and perpetuated colonial attitudes towards the rest of the world.[84] Robert Dixon refers to the role of colonial adventure stories in reasserting colonial dominance in the later decades of the nineteenth century as the British Empire showed symptoms of decline: according to Dixon, 'tales of regenerative violence on the colonial frontier' became important to address anxieties about this, which perhaps explains their continuing popularity.[85]

Pioneering life also made an excellent backdrop for another very popular genre: the colonial romance. There are many examples of this among the list of New Zealand publications, all eagerly buying into the romantic tropes of the time. These stories often featured an unconventional heroine and a reticent but capable hero, revealing much about stock tropes of the colonial character, and were obviously designed to strike a chord with readers throughout the colonial writing world. Walter Smyth's *Jean of the Tussock Country* was published by Mills & Boon in 1928. In this story, an English 'new chum'[86] has to prove himself to the surly locals and at the same time falls in love with the boss's daughter, an 'outdoorsy' type with 'unruly copper coloured hair that refused to remain concealed under her broad-brimmed felt hat' and a face 'tanned a delicate shade of brown, which harmonised perfectly with the deeper hint of her humorous eyes'.[87] Isabel Maud Peacocke's *The Guardian* also features a tomboyish heroine who falls in love with an uncommunicative but dependable farm manager. Another example is Alice Kenny's *The Rebel*.[88] Mary Scott's first few novels were historical romances set in the far north. Indigenous appropriation and miscegenation were often themes of this type of story: Arthur H. Adams' *Tussock Land* features the love interest Aroha, who is part-Māori and the apotheosis of the new New Zealand nation, to which Adams' protagonist King Southern finds he must return from a sojourn in Australia.

Guidebooks and travelogues were frequently produced to promote New Zealand as a tourist destination, and literature that dealt with the country's exotic scenery and nature was also marketable overseas. The interest in New Zealand writing sometimes had more to do with interest in antipodean lifestyles and scenery than in literature, and there are several examples of poor quality writing that seem to have been published only by virtue of their entertainment value as 'colonial exotic'. F. Hellier's novel *Colonials in Khaki*, which was published in London in 1916, reads like a tourist guide cut and pasted into a stilted conversation. It follows the round-the-world trip of two New Zealand girls, one of whom exclaims at one point that Kipling's lines about New Zealand are 'a perfect description of the whole of New Zealand, which with its romantic scenery might well be numbered amongst the Pacific Gems'.[89] This is followed by conversation stoppers like: 'Every inch of New Zealand is worth seeing, from the snow-clad Alps to the thermal regions of Rotorua. Why, the mountain, lake and river scenery is magnificent!'[90]

Character development is non-existent and the intrusion of human emotions or relationships is a shock. The fact that the book achieved publication is testimony to the appeal of New Zealand themes.

The settlement of New Zealand had been seen as a social experiment, stemming from Edward Gibbon Wakefield's attempts at systematic colonisation. Innovations where New Zealand led the way were of great interest to people debating political and social issues in their own countries, and experiments such as the introduction of women's suffrage were watched eagerly from Britain to see how they would turn out. British suffragists were interested in hearing of New Zealand's success to fuel their own campaigns, as Raewyn Dalziel argues.[91] By 1908 there was a majority in the British House of Commons for women's suffrage but, to the chagrin of suffragists, progress was held up by political factors including the opposition of Prime Minister Herbert Asquith. As New Zealand and Australia had already implemented reform, there was a lot of interest in literature from these countries that touched on the relations of men and women. Edith Searle Grossmann's *In Revolt* was published in London and Sydney in 1893, the same year that women gained the right to vote in New Zealand. It tells the story of the turbulent existence of Hermione, who tries to escapes from a brutal husband. The sequel, *Hermione: A knight of the Holy Ghost*, was published in London in 1907. In this, the protagonist Hermione aims to 'repudiate all together the subjection of women to men'.[92] She is eventually forced to go back to her husband, resulting in her suicide. Writers who questioned the role of women and the immorality of extra-marital relationships, such as Jane Mander and Jean Devanny, were often less well received in New Zealand than overseas. British publishers and readers were more accepting of their work than the New Zealand public were, and it was British publishers who put out other feminist novels by Louisa Baker, Constance Clyde and Susie Mactier.

The inclusion of New Zealand elements in their work gave New Zealand writers an edge that appealed to publishers and the reading public. Reviews of New Zealand books in the *Times Literary Supplement* between 1890 and 1945 have a recurring theme: although the reviewer did not think much of the book, a redeeming feature was the unique colonial or native element. A review of Rosemary Rees' *Home Is Where the Heart Is* from 1935 stated: 'The setting of this novel in the New Zealand sheeplands gives a fresh charm to an otherwise undistinguished romantic narrative.'[93] Similarly, a reviewer of

Sophie Osmond's *Ponga Bay* found it redeemed by its New Zealand content: 'The narrative is weakly constructed, but the author obviously knows her New Zealand well, and the main interest of the book lies in its drawings of native life and character.'[94] The obvious 'colonialism' in Arthur H. Adams' *Tussock Land* was described as 'the source of freshness and interest in his book' in an otherwise unenthusiastic review.[95] Rees' *Heather of the South* is described as 'ordinary, almost humdrum', but 'the author's work is of interest in exhibiting the essential contrasts between New Zealand and Great Britain, and in displaying from an intimate knowledge the life of that country'.[96]

Appearing in a collection of works grouped under an 'Australasian' or 'New Zealand' umbrella could also be helpful. The reviewer of the *Kowhai Gold* anthology in the *Times Literary Supplement* supported the claim in the book's introduction that '[t]he future no longer seems full of emptiness, and the foundations of a New Zealand literature are being laid'. He went on to say that 'New Zealand is probably at the present time richer in literary originality than any other Dominion' and that at least 12 of the book's contributors were 'poets of distinction who can write on occasion verse that is delicately memorable and who, even in their less inspired moments, are fresh and individual'.[97] Had these poets been English writers struggling on their own in London, they might not have attracted such favourable notice. Some allowances might have been made for the colonial status of the authors, and the perception of 'freshness' might have stemmed partly from the poems' colonial setting. R.A.K. Mason tried to tap into this novelty factor when he wrote to Robert Graves:

> *If you do publish, I think you can rely on a fair number of extraordinary sales owing to the fact that I am a New Zealander. For one thing, it is so remarkable that anyone here should do anything decent. Again, there are a fair number of collectors here who will buy it just to add to their collection of New Zealand books, even if they do not appreciate it.*[98]

New Zealand motifs were popular, but there were also certain tricks of the trade that could be useful. Some themes were more likely to succeed than others and the work had to conform to English standards of presentation. As Mander advised Holcroft: 'If books are to be published in London they must be as English as possible in phrase unless their merit rests upon their strangeness … there should be as few as possible mannerisms or local touches in any book, wherever written, that has to do with universal character.'[99] She also advised him to approach the publishers Hodder & Stoughton, as 'they are more friendly to stuff set overseas than many other firms'.[100] A few writers ran into difficulties because their writing was too firmly based on New Zealand idioms. Frank Anthony's 'Me and Gus' stories had to be rewritten, 'toning down much of their lively original vernacular flavour', when they were presented to English publishers.[101]

In the later twentieth century, local critics and literary historians generally dismissed material published in Britain by New Zealand authors: it was seen as largely low in quality or, at any rate, not 'authentic' New Zealand literature. This means that much writing by New Zealanders has been completely ignored, including a number of gems that emerge when a more inclusive approach is employed. Interesting social commentary abounds, for example in Prudence Cadey's temperance novel *Broken Pattern*. This book shatters the expected portrait of New Zealand as a settler paradise: it describes 'higgledy piggledy little houses with their corrugated iron roofs; or the dusty, littered streets',[102] and the grand scenery as 'so different from what we expected. It's so bare and bleak and desolate. It frightens me.'[103] It also confronts social issues such as alcohol abuse, which Cadey depicts as a 'great big black ogre' hanging over the country.[104] The colonial writing world gave New Zealand authors the freedom to say these things about their society, whereas local publishers were reluctant to touch them.

Much writing, like *Broken Pattern*, has been ignored or forgotten, creating the mindset that hardly anything of a literary bent was happening, and writers were obliged to leave. Writers could access a multitude of overseas opportunities without leaving New Zealand's shores, but this fact is not often acknowledged. Despite the emphasis that has always been placed on expatriatism among New Zealand writers, a significant number found they could stay in New Zealand. Colonial mobility helped to maintain colonial links for all members of colonial society, whether they themselves went to other places or not. For writers, the existence of the colonial writing world removed the necessity of going overseas. In fact, of 118 traceable writers who published books between 1890 and 1945, only 55 (47 per cent) left New Zealand for a year or more – in other words, 63 (53 per cent) were able to function successfully as writers entirely in New Zealand.[105]

CHAPTER FIVE

Failure or exile? Reactions to 'overseas' writing and writers

I n 1945 the novelist Dan Davin completed *Cliffs of Fall*, a novel set in Otago featuring a young man stifled by the 'narrow interests' and 'restraints' of the small Irish Catholic community in which he grew up.[1] Joan Stevens, in her 1966 survey, characterises this as 'no new type in New Zealand fiction, even in 1945; "Get out, young man" … "the godwits fly" … these are old compulsions. "I want to get out of this country and over the sea," says Mark.'[2] *The Godwits Fly* is the title of Robin Hyde's fourth novel, and like *Cliffs of Fall* it has much more to say about growing up in New Zealand than simply the impulse to leave it (despite the title). Nonetheless, many of those interpreting these novels have seen them as proof of the inevitable and all-consuming desire of young writers to escape New Zealand. In *Cliffs of Fall* the action takes a darker turn than usual, as James Bertram describes:

> *Endlessly, in New Zealand writing of this time, the dilemma of the young man driven to 'leave for overseas' has been canvassed; only Davin was bold enough to embody 'New Zealand' in the figure of a loved but inconvenient woman, and to cut the Gordian knot with murder (and infanticide).*[3]

The book addresses the impulse to escape from a small town: Mark is pleased to return to university in Dunedin and throws himself enthusiastically into the debates of the time, despite noting that they were out of date compared to what was going on in Europe. Yet the critical response has focused on the few passages that suggest discontent with New Zealand, perhaps because Davin himself went overseas to live (as did Hyde, briefly and disastrously). This anxiety about New Zealand's literary history always returns to the idea that the most talented writers have been forced to leave, a theme supposedly reflected 'endlessly' in their writing.

Davin was not the first or last writer from an ex-colonial outpost to describe feelings of artistic and social constraint, but he and other early-twentieth-century New Zealand writers have been drawn into the prevailing narrative of expatriate 'exile' or failure. For sociologist Andrew Gurr, 'writers in exile' are those born in the 'small, immobile, close-knit communities which sociologists call *Gemeinschaft*' – communities where 'art tends to be conservative, traditional, conformist'. He writes: '[James] Joyce, Katherine Mansfield, [V.S.] Naipaul and Ngugi [wa Thiong'o] all grew up in colonial or post-colonial provinces which gave them little option but to detach themselves and adopt the life of the exile.'[4] This detachment refers to a second type of exile peculiar to expatriates, which was the state in which writers supposedly found themselves having left their constrictive communities for the 'seductive freedom' of the *Gesellschaft* – 'large, impersonal and individualistic societies' – which include cultural metropolises such as London.[5] In this scenario, writers were regrettably obliged to give up ties to their native country in order to have any chance of success – thus going from one kind of 'exile' to another. New Zealand writers' condemnation to exile, either at home or abroad, is a common theme in the country's literary history, and the process of trying to be a writer has been frequently associated with struggle and/or existential suffering.

Just under half of the New Zealand writers who published books between 1890 and 1945 did not leave the country at all during this period.[6] Despite this, attention has frequently focused on the writers who did leave, often without consideration of the length or permanence of their absence, but presenting it largely in a negative light, conjuring images of 'brain drain' and loss. Eric McCormick commented on the ship journey from England described in William Satchell's *The Elixir of Life*:

> Had the voyage been made in the opposite direction, the list would almost certainly have included one writer or more, for from the time of B.L. Farjeon and Fergus Hume there had been a steady export of New Zealand talent which reached its greatest dimensions in the years after 1918.[7]

By acknowledging only the writers leaving, McCormick gives the impression of a permanent, one-way flow of writers from the colonial periphery to the centre. This kind of confirmation bias has stood in for any real interrogation of the phenomenon. It ignores, for a start, the number of writers who came the other way, like Satchell himself, and others such as Ursula Bethell and Blanche Baughan. Beginning with William Pember Reeves, McCormick wrote of the lure of foreign lands: in 1896 Reeves 'had left for England, thus choosing his "way" which was, generally speaking, to be the way for the next thirty years both in art and in letters'.[8] In McCormick's account, Reeves was joined by Alan Mulgan and Katherine Mansfield. According to James Smithies, McCormick's implication was that 'the trip "Home" was taken by any writer who could afford it in order to avoid the loss of cultured society on the periphery of empire'.[9] This model of New Zealand literature suffering from an inevitable loss of talent to overseas has come to be widely accepted, but its glaring inaccuracies mean it needs to be challenged. To do so, we must first determine the origins of this idea.

The roots of these anxieties about New Zealand cultural society lie in a complex collection of attitudes to publishing and writing overseas. A 'cultural cringe' (inspired by jealousy, frustration and self-defensiveness stemming from being part of a small, recently formed, self-conscious nation) fuelled the idea that 'New Zealandness' was antithetical to writing. As a reaction against this, defiant and proscriptive nationalism contributed to a general negativity towards overseas endeavours, which became increasingly entrenched from the mid-1930s onwards. This led to an overemphasis on the division between New Zealand and 'overseas', leaving just two perceived alternatives for writers: failure or relinquishment of New Zealandness. Failure would result from remaining in New Zealand, but also from going overseas and not giving up one's New Zealandness to an adequate degree ('New Zealandness' here means ties to New Zealand and any cultural signifiers unique to people from New Zealand). Success overseas came at the cost of New Zealandness, and thus those writers were likely lost to New Zealand writing, as well as (somewhat paradoxically) being condemned to life as rootless 'exiles' because of the impossibilities of rejecting one's origins. So many commentators have focused on this aspect of writers' lives that, for many, Katherine Mansfield's dual traumas of languishing in New Zealand and suffering overseas represent the only two options available to New Zealand writers, at least until the late 1930s. Some of the traction behind the myth may stem from contradictory and resentful attitudes to New Zealand's perceived cultural reliance on overseas.

A belief that has existed almost as long as European settlement in New Zealand is that it is necessary for New Zealanders to prove themselves by being recognised overseas before their talents are acknowledged and appreciated in New Zealand. Jane Mander wrote to Monte Holcroft in 1931 that she was homesick and considering returning to New Zealand, adding '[b]ut I do need the publicity of a book or two to start me off as a writer out there, and so I am hoping to get yet another book that I have started finished before I come'.[10] Australians also thought that their work needed to be published overseas in order to be respected at home. Henry Lawson noted that Australian readers were only interested if books were published in Britain,[11] while Christina Stead recalled showing a collection of her short stories to Angus & Robertson only to find they rejected it, 'saying that she would have to be published in London first, before they would take her work'.[12] These assumptions may or may not have been correct, but it should not be automatically assumed that the writers considered this to be a problem, or were primarily focused on their reception at home. Nelle Scanlan was relatively well known in New Zealand but her major readership was undoubtedly located overseas. When called upon to give New Zealand-specific figures for sales of *Pencarrow* she had no idea of the numbers, as her statements from Robert Hale covered the whole field.[13]

Some writers and many later commentators, though, disliked the idea of needing overseas approval, and these negative attitudes have been exacerbated by the erroneous conflation of the need to *publish* overseas with the need to *go* overseas. In his 1940 assessment, Eric McCormick wrote that 'the voyage "Home" had become an established institution' because, for writers, 'there were cogent economic reasons' to travel to Britain.[14] This belief has permeated into more recent times: Louisa Baker, according to Kirstine Moffat, was 'the first New Zealand woman to succeed in making a career out of writing novels, publishing seventeen books between 1894 and 1910'. Moffat goes on to say:

> [T]his success was only possible when Baker left New Zealand to pursue her literary career in England, a departure that later authors, such as Jane Mander and Katherine Mansfield, were to follow ... Baker's predicament was typical of the dilemma facing creative artists in colonial New Zealand ... the few publishing companies based in New Zealand were reluctant to publish works by unknown local authors. Baker had no option but to pursue her literary dream overseas.[15]

Thus Moffat, like many others, equates publishing overseas with literary expatriatism.

But of course, getting recognised overseas did not require expatriation. Moffat and McCormick exhibit ignorance of (or, in McCormick's case, perhaps a disinclination to acknowledge) the more common approach made possible by the existence of the colonial writing world: many writers had books published in Britain while they remained in New Zealand. While writers were often obliged to seek a publisher overseas, this was not the same as being forced to go there themselves. As Heather Murray observes, New Zealand women writers 'were successful in having their books published by British publishers – in 1932 alone eleven women had novels published in London – so there was little need to migrate for that purpose'.[16] As the previous chapters have demonstrated, the limited local writing infrastructure did not automatically force writers to leave the country, as through the colonial writing world they had access to overseas publishing infrastructure, while being supported by local initiatives at lower levels.

Besides, success overseas did *not* guarantee success at home, and attitudes to those who had achieved overseas acclaim were contradictory. It was quite common for writers to be highly successful overseas and virtually unknown in New Zealand. This was true both of those who wrote from outside the country, such as Rosemary Rees, and those who never left, such as Isabel Maud Peacocke. Whether New Zealanders were interested in a writer's work may or may not have been the writer's primary concern, and in any case mattered little in monetary terms as the local market was insignificant compared to the British one. As Aorewa McLeod notes, the 'small and conservative New Zealand readership was not the major audience for novels written by New Zealanders or about New Zealand'.[17] This was partly because, as Terry Sturm points out, some New Zealand writers were less widely read in New Zealand than overseas 'primarily because of poor distribution arrangements by their British publishers'.[18] Authors who encountered this problem included Peacocke and Edith Lyttleton. Indeed, in Peacocke's case, '[m]any novels sold out in England before reaching New Zealand'.[19] While Guy Scholefield, journalist and later parliamentary librarian, greatly doubted whether 'the New Zealand public has any keen desire to read books about this country',[20] poor local sales were more likely the result of British publishers' neglect of the New Zealand market.

Writing which was successful in London could have a different reception at home. There are a number of examples of writers being successful and highly praised overseas but disliked or strongly criticised in New Zealand. Margaret Escott's *Show Down*, for example, was praised in London but 'some New Zealand critics found it problematic because of its departure from recognised themes and techniques'.[21] Hector Bolitho compiled a book of his reviews to highlight the discrepancy between the English and New Zealand responses, as Peacocke (writing under the name Isabel Cluett) reported: '[E]ven now these stubborn New Zealanders, despite the flattering extracts from English reviews with which his books are hall-marked, so to speak, maintain their critical and half-scornful attitude towards their native son and his work.'[22] Winifred Tennant wrote to Pat Lawlor in 1936, 'Did you ever see Hector Bolitho's pamphlet with English comment and New Zealand criticisms on his books? They were printed in black and green inks, and the English opinions made much pleasanter reading than the New Zealand gibes at a successful countryman.'[23] In 'The Heckling of Hector', Lawlor wrote that 'Hector was hurt very deeply over the unkind and unjust criticisms hurled at him by the press of his own country, but, in the security of the fame he has won abroad, he can smile.'[24]

The harsh scrutiny afforded to local authors might have resulted from a New Zealand version of what A.A. Phillips described in 1950 as the 'cultural cringe'[25] – the inferiority complex that Australian intellectuals felt when comparing their compatriots' work with that of their British and European counterparts. This attitude might have meant that New Zealand writers had to work much harder to be accepted in New Zealand than non-New Zealanders did, especially if their writing was about New Zealand. New Zealanders were unaccustomed to the use of their immediate surroundings as subject matter for highbrow art. A reviewer of the play *Rose Lane* in the Dunedin *Evening Star* in 1936 commented that the audience laughed when a character mentioned going to find a job in Invercargill. He said: 'The mere mention of Invercargill shatters, for a moment, all the illusion of drama.'[26] Alan Mulgan suggested that New Zealanders were not interested in reading about local themes, such as gumdigging in Auckland: 'Romance was something that came from the African spaces or the Hudson Bay Territory, not from the other side of one's own hills.'[27] Whether or not this was true of New Zealand audiences and affected the sales and reputation of New Zealand works locally, as demonstrated in Chapter Four, overseas audiences were much more enthusiastic.

Critical and/or realistic descriptions of their own society inspired self-defensive and hostile reactions in some readers and critics. Readers who were also subjects did not necessarily appreciate the portrayal of their own communities in a light they did not endorse. If controversial themes were addressed, the result could be extreme criticism or even censorship, as was likely to happen in any small community. Jane Mander's *The Story of a New Zealand River* is a reasonably frank portrait of Northland society and of the illogicality of trapping people in unhappy marriages. New Zealand critics responded to the book by labelling Mander as sex-obsessed, a criticism that was 'hurled at her from all sides', while in America and England only one reviewer drew this conclusion.[28] In New Zealand literary legend, the book was placed on the 'discretionary shelf' at the Whāngārei Public Library.[29] Dan Davin's *Cliffs of Fall* 'won for Davin a modest but solid reputation in Britain and the USA. In New Zealand its reception was more mixed.'[30] British critics described the novel as 'a bold attempt at an immensely difficult subject'. In New Zealand, predictably, 'it was read as a startling and uncomfortable revelation of scandalous goings-on in a respectable Presbyterian city'.[31] Government censors in New Zealand banned Jean Devanny's *The Butcher Shop*, officially because its frank portrayal of life on a sheep farm had the potential to do harm to immigration. The book also, however, showed the consequences of repression: the previously virtuous farmer's wife ends up slitting her lover's throat.[32] James Courage expected his depiction of Christchurch in *The Fifth Child* to create a scandal, '[e]specially after a number of not-quite-impartial N.Z. critics have had slaps at it in their weekly rags'.[33] These bad reviews never actually eventuated, probably because he disguised Christchurch well in his books.

If unwilling to accept candid description of their own society, critics were unlikely to say so outright – usually, rather, they expressed this by being overly critical of the accuracy of the portrayals. Cluett's explanation for the unpopularity of Bolitho's books in New Zealand was that his writings were jarring to the native ear because of 'a host of … small, but significant, inaccuracies which, to any reader with a knowledge of New Zealand, are irritating and distasteful, giving an altogether false impression of the country'.[34] This is all the more pointed given her apparent disapproval, a few paragraphs earlier in the same article, of the New Zealand critics' 'half-scornful' attitude to his work. In the case of Jean Devanny, Cluett again was the reviewer. She wrote of Devanny: '"Bushman Burke" may be said to be a riotous "saga of sex"', and 'though her stories all have a New Zealand background, and her descriptive scenes ring true enough, the dramas she unfolds have very small relation to New Zealand life, its conditions and traditions'.[35] It is possible that it was the themes Devanny addressed and their consequent association with New Zealand communities that reviewers found jarring, as well as sensitivities about the representation of societies.

Actually going overseas could increase the levels of hostility towards writers from their fellow countrymen and women. Some believed the authenticity of the writing suffered if the writer was distanced from the subject matter (although the opposite opinion, that distance was helpful, was also prevalent – see Chapter Six). Bill Pearson decided while in England that he needed immediate experience of New Zealand in order to write about it. He said of John Guthrie, who had moved to London, that 'if he had stayed home he might have become a very entertaining novelist or journalist. Since he writes now as if continually clearing his way through a fog, one wonders if the sophistications and pressures of London have left his mind … punch-drunk …'.[36] The bulk of Hector Bolitho's fiction was published while he was overseas, and he was accused of being out of touch with New Zealand because his writing included imagery of 'bright and lingering twilights; of oysters growing on mango trees; of rubber trees growing wild'.[37]

There was perhaps an element of parochial jealousy in the attitude of some to the 'big shots' who went overseas. This not only indicates that overseas success did not necessarily enhance local renown, but also illuminates the attitude of New Zealanders to those classed as expatriates. In 1940 the Dunedin journalist David W.M. Burn suggested a 'Centennial survey on expatriates doing well overseas'. According to manuscript sources quoted by Chris Hilliard, the editorial committee 'rejected the suggestion for fear that it would "excite jealousies" and "degenerate into a catalogue of undistinguished names"'.[38] The perceived trend of the best and brightest leaving the country was interpreted as a criticism or rejection of New Zealand and inspired scepticism about overseas writers' status as New Zealand writers and their authority to speak about New Zealand subjects.

Increasingly from the 1930s, combined with the rise of cultural nationalism promoting New Zealand literature beholden to no one, these contradictory attitudes to writers who pursued overseas publication or went overseas took a more consistently negative turn. Proponents of nationalism were resentful of New Zealand's cultural reliance on Britain and blamed this for the lack of 'authentic' local culture. In their estimation, all that had been achieved so far were cringeworthy attempts to adapt imported culture to the local environment (rather than something new that belonged uniquely to New Zealand). McCormick mentioned the 'dangerous' effects of a literature based on English models, when New Zealand-born writers visited 'in their literary excursions solely a region of scenes, images, and ideas not merely foreign to them but, in some respects, contrary to the facts of their experience', exacerbated by the reliance on overseas publishing and overseas literature.[39] As a cultural nationalist, Allen Curnow believed that this state of affairs was untenable, and for him it was the crux of the country's culture problems. Curnow wrote in his introduction to *A Book of New Zealand Verse 1923–1945*: 'Already, by the [1890s], it had become natural for the more active-minded New Zealander to regard literature, poetry most of all, as a thing disembodied from any living and tangible surrounding.'[40] This state of affairs did not allow, he thought, for the creation of something unique and vital to New Zealand.

Proponents of cultural nationalism blamed the dominance of imported culture for driving creative spirits into exile and believed the British literary canon to be problematically irrelevant to New Zealand life. In their view, the disconnect between literary subject matter and reality was to blame for the prevalence of expatriatism among New Zealand writers, as they assumed that reading imported literature inspired an exodus to its geographical setting. For Allen Curnow, this cultural reliance meant that '[f]ine talents had to leave this unreal community, which had lost its footing in history and could find none on its own ground; they sought some reality, some point from which thought could depart or imagination take flight'.[41] The idea of living in two worlds at once was a cause for concern, although in reality it was a natural consequence of the colonial condition.

Publishing and going overseas were associated with the need to rely on overseas publishing and pander to overseas preferences, and thus resented. Australian nationalists in the first few decades of the twentieth century bemoaned the damage done to Australian writing by the forced deference to the tastes of British audiences. The British publishers' idea of what the British public would be interested in had the potential, in the minds of the nationalists, to undermine the authenticity of the writing. Nationalist loyalties dictated a preference for Australian publishers, as when the novelist Joseph Furphy declared in 1897: 'Heaven forbid I should think of treating with an English publisher.'[42] Henry Lawson's sardonic 'A Song of Southern Writers' from 1892 calls on Australians to:

> Write a story of the South, make it true and make it clear,
> Put your soul in every sentence, have the volume published here,
> And 'twill only be accepted by our critics in the mist,
> As a 'worthy imitation' of a Northern novelist.
> For the volume needs the mighty Paternoster Row machine,
> With a patronising notice in an English magazine.[43]

Lawson's negativity about the inconvenient need to appease English critics and the effect of having to answer to foreign standards reflected the feelings of the other Australian nationalists, such as Vance Palmer, the 'self-conscious heir to *Bulletin* nationalism',[44] and his wife, Nettie. Their opinions, and those of a few others, have been made to stand for the general consensus. As a result, says John Barnes, '[i]n the absence of detailed publishing histories of the relationship between Australian writers and English publishers, the model of Australian creativity and originality unappreciated by London publishers has been generally accepted'.[45] Later literary historians, from an age in which nationalism was more prevalent, searched for distinctively Australian material to include in their literary histories, and the talent of Lawson, A.B. Paterson and a few others demanded their inclusion. Those historians also accepted the nationalists' fulminations against British publishers.

As John Barnes concludes, however, at the 'very least' this 'needs to be questioned', as attitudes were varied and contradictory.[46] The nationalist viewpoint was just one of many. Literary nationalists, although often singled out for attention by later historians, were a small minority of the Australian literary community and were therefore unlikely to be representative of the wider literary community's attitudes towards publication in Britain. The majority of writers might well have been quite happy with the situation, as publishing in Britain was a natural and accepted result of membership of the colonial writing world. While some were interested in the balladry, vernacular and values that would come to define early 'authentic' Australian writing, other well-known writers, like the poet Christopher Brennan, continued to write in traditional styles. This was true even of those who wrote for the supposedly nationalist *Bulletin*, which, '[a]lthough it did pride itself on its bush balladry ... published considerably *more* genteel verse by Australians – Victor Daley, Roderic Quinn and a host of others – than it did "rabid" bush ballads'.[47] Moreover, many of the *Bulletin*'s leading figures (and nationalists) were in fact themselves British immigrants for whom nationalism and doubts about links to the British Crown were logical extensions of the republicanism that flourished amongst working-class radicals in Britain in the 1870s.[48] As mentioned earlier, several key literary editors of the *Bulletin*, such as Arthur H. Adams and Douglas Stewart, were born and raised in New Zealand and led trans-Tasman lives, continuing the trend of outside influences.

New Zealanders, and Australians, did not necessarily view British cultural influence negatively, as they might not have seen it as 'overseas' culture. Nationalism for many, John Barnes says, still 'defined itself in the context of imperialism',[49] meaning that the division between local and overseas was not as strongly felt. There was nothing particularly unusual or troubling about the bulk of literature emanating from elsewhere. Literature is virtually always read 'disembodied' from its surroundings. The majority of nineteenth-century people reading Wordsworth, for example, were not in the Lake District at the time. They were more likely to be in a built-up, noisy, polluted city. The rural scenes of New Zealand were more easily relatable to English pastoral imagery than was London. It is not a requirement of literature to be about the place the reader is in, and sometimes escapism requires the opposite. Citizens of the colonial world were likely to be accustomed to such feelings of disembodiment, rather than compelled to leave or culturally traumatised because of them. Overseas cultural influence did not cause great mental conflict for the people it affected, beyond a general curiosity to see the places of which much of the available literature spoke and acceptance of their place in a shared colonial identity. Curnow's concerns were shared by few writers outside of his own group of cultural nationalists.

Equally unconvincing is the idea that New Zealand writing relied on the adaptation of foreign poetic techniques and language to describe a land never before encountered by the cultural owners of these techniques. Surely 'unstoried waters' could be 'storied' without that much trouble?[50] (Of course they were not unstoried – to claim so was to ignore centuries of Māori tradition.) Language, like culture, is not necessarily fixed to a location. The more florid English clichés involving gently rolling hills and pleasant meadows might have been unusable, but there is no obvious reason why other English words could not be used to describe the new scenery. No one ever suggested that New Zealanders had to invent an entirely new language to live and communicate in New Zealand, yet it has been argued that they needed to do this to describe it.[51] When Curnow, Denis Glover and friends began their attempts at fashioning a new way of writing New Zealand literature they merely simplified the language they used, removing the more hackneyed expressions of poetry. This might have been a different way of proceeding, but the impulse was not new. New Zealand writers had been attempting this for a long time. The use of clichés was a sign of a poor writer, not a reason to flee overseas.

There is one less lofty explanation for the attitudes of the cultural nationalists of the late 1930s and why they saw fit to identify publishing location as a crucial marker of 'national' writing. Their own importance on the local scene had a lot to do with the development of local publishing infrastructure from the 1930s onwards. They asserted that local publishing was intrinsically superior, which not only advanced the cause of cultural nationalism but served the interests of writers, like Glover, who were associated with the local presses (particularly the Caxton Press). Australian nationalists had vested interests as well: Paul Eggert suspects George Robertson of Angus & Robertson in Australia of 'playing the nationalist card'.[52] Allen Curnow's assessment of New Zealand literary development required local publishing initiatives to be in place before the country's writers could 'look to their own creative resources'.[53] By emphasising the dearth of other publishing options and the damage done to nationalist concerns by overseas publishing, the *Phoenix* group made their own contribution seem particularly vital. They promoted the notion that the situation of the New Zealand writer was intolerable until cultural nationalism – and the associated growth of local publishing and an inward-looking literary culture – came to the rescue. In fact, the complaints about overseas publishing often come from publishers (or people closely associated with publishers) rather than authors. For example, in 1946 A.W. Reed complained that 'the dice are loaded against the New Zealander in his own country'.[54] These negative aspects might even have been artificially emphasised by those with vested interests.

To back up their assertions, nationalist publishers used examples of the sorry fate of writers of local-flavoured literature at the hands of overseas publishers and the market. Frank Anthony was one of these examples. His moderate success as a writer in New Zealand inspired him to try and 'make a go of it' in England. His style was a 'racy, masculine vernacular idiom',[55] which aligned with Allen Curnow's vision of autochthonous New Zealand writing. Despite toning down the local content, however, Anthony failed to make his work palatable to English publishers. He did not break into the English market and died early and obscure, in a boarding house near Bournemouth in 1927. Terry Sturm follows the cultural nationalists in blaming the reliance on foreign publication for Anthony's failure. Anthony had tried to alter his writing style and produced the novel *The Cruise of the Phyllis, Captured by Maori Cannibals*, prompting Sturm to write: 'As an attempt to satisfy an English audience's romantic image of the South Seas as an arena of savagery and exotic adventure, it provides a sadly ironic illustration of the pressures which an English market imposed on expatriate writers.'[56] Anthony's work was discovered in the 1930s by the *Phoenix* group, who made sure to assert that this would not happen under their jurisdiction.

Stories like this promoted the idea that the two options for New Zealand writers had been failure (either at home or abroad), or success overseas at the expense of their New Zealandness, before the *Phoenix* group came along to fix the problem. This led to the 'catch-22' situation where it was seemingly impossible to both be successful and remain a New Zealand writer, since being overseas affected one's authority to write about New Zealand. Literary nationalism had a central problem with accepting foreign publication of local writing, and an even greater problem in accepting such writing if the author was actually living overseas. The idea that New Zealand writers could be just as successful in England and with British audiences jarred with the sentiments of the cultural nationalists, who believed that New Zealand writing should relate to New Zealanders alone. McCormick wrote:

> *A few of New Zealand's literary émigrés were to learn in the conditions of exile a new understanding of their country. But the greater number quickly discarded all traces of their colonial origin, merged themselves in the English literary world, and devoted their talents to the cultivation of some current literary fashion or to the glorification of those circles of English life which they had come to regard as enshrining the social absolute ... [and] neither their country's literature nor the world's has been greatly enriched by their self-imposed exile.*[57]

Thus, in McCormick's estimation, aside from 'two notable exceptions', writers were obliged to abandon their hopes of being New Zealand writers and settle for being mediocre British ones, or return home.

The belief that New Zealand overseas writers were forced to live as exiles and distance themselves from their native roots ties in with a worldwide fascination with the supposed rootlessness of literary expatriates. Even Katherine Mansfield, the most successful of the expatriate New Zealand writers and also one of the few who overtly resisted her colonial origins, did not manage to merge seamlessly with the European literary world – she is, presumably, one of McCormick's exceptions. Yet, at the same time, Mansfield embodies expectations of overseas writers. She unsettled herself frequently, moving to different places because of her ill health and an inability to write effectively if she remained in one place for too long. According to Lydia Wevers, this manifested metonymically in Mansfield's work with a 'recurrent motif of transport'.[58] Angela Smith sees this edginess appearing surreptitiously in Mansfield's fiction in the form of an ever-present sense of liminality, manifested in the recurrent images of edges and shorelines and the 'spaces in-between' throughout her work.[59] Vincent O'Sullivan describes 'Mansfield's sense of exile' as 'not so much the feeling that there is a country she will not return to, as a state of normality which she can no longer reach'.[60] She remained unsettled to the detriment of her health and personal relationships. She tried to reject her colonial ties but found this to be impossible: she complained of being an outsider after having escaped New Zealand for Europe, and never felt 'at home'. She wrote about her awkward position among the London literati:

> I am the little colonial walking in the London garden patch – allowed to look, perhaps, but not to linger. If I lie on the grass they positively shout at me: 'Look at her, lying on our grass, pretending she lives here, pretending this is her garden, and that tall back of the house, with the windows open and the coloured curtains lifting, is her house. She is a stranger – an alien. She is nothing but a little girl sitting on the Tinakori hills and dreaming: "I went to London and married an Englishman and we lived in a tall grave house, with red geraniums and white daisies in the garden at the back". Im-pudence!'[61]

Mansfield's example has often been seized upon as the blueprint for the fate of New Zealand writers abroad: they were doomed to live on the margins of society forever, purely because they were presumptuous enough to be both artists and New Zealanders.

The correlation of the lives of writers with dislocation and exile can at least partly be blamed on the influence of modernism. The literary modernist movement reached its height in Europe in the 1920s and 1930s, and the movement is often associated with expatriate writers and 'exiles'. Scholars have frequently connected the ethos of modernism to themes of dislocation, reactions to loss of tradition and certainty, and the artist's struggle against a world largely populated by philistines. Discussing George Steiner's book *Extraterritorial* (1972), in 1978 Malcolm Bradbury repeated Steiner's observation that a 'large part of modernist literature has been written by the writer "unhoused"'.[62] Over 40 years later Peter Kalliney reiterates that '[t]ravel and translation are right at the core of modernism's aesthetics of motion and dissonance'.[63] The new guard who became New Zealand's literary arbiters saw modernism as the height of highbrow culture, so it is not surprising that writing was equated with the need for some kind of adversity arising from dislocation: exile at home or overseas both fitted the bill.

Indeed, many writers involved with European modernism had come from somewhere else, in some cases even against their will. Many of the leading lights of the literary establishment were originally from outside England. Ezra Pound, Henry James and T.S. Eliot were all emigrants from America in the late nineteenth or early twentieth century. Some studies of 'writers in exile' have remained loyal to the original dictionary definition requiring forced expulsion from one's homeland, as in the case of *Transcending Exile: Conrad, Nabokov, I.B. Singer* by Asher Z. Milbauer. In this case, the writers being discussed were political exiles.[64] Joseph Conrad, born in Berdyczów (now Berdychiv, Ukraine) as Józef Teodor Konrad Korzeniowski, was exiled with his family by the Imperial Russians, and after some years at sea ended up in England, beginning his literary career in 1894. Vladimir Nabokov was an exile from Russia in the time of the revolution, and Isaac Bashevis Singer was a Jewish refugee from Poland.

Some people go so far as to suggest that exile is necessary for writing. Andrew Gurr says: 'In varying degrees the normal role for a modern writer is to be an exile. He is the lone traveller in the countries of the mind, always threatened by hostile natives'.[65] The author of *Three Writers in Exile: Pound, Eliot and Joyce*, Doris Eder, says: 'Exile was an essential condition of [James] Joyce's art. He needed distance in space as well as time in order to write about Dublin and to create the uncreated conscience of his race'.[66] James Bertram shares this view, saying of Jane Mander and Katherine Mansfield that 'some writers succeeded (usually through some years of study or residence abroad) in distancing themselves from the country of their birth, and so gaining a truer perspective on its manners and customs'.[67] The emphasis here is still on creating the best conditions for a 'true' representation of the country, which is highly subjective and not dependent on a simple choice between distance and proximity, as discussed in Chapter Six.

In fact, the very edginess that Mansfield thought made it difficult to be a writer in England was her passport to inclusion in the most rarefied of literary circles, as a sense of exile was virtually a prerequisite. Literary quality aside, Mansfield embodied the romantic ideal of a tortured artist. In order to claim to be on the cutting edge of literary fashions one needed proper credentials: fulfilling expectations of truly innovative contributors to literature required overcoming some kind of hardship. Fleeing a hostile environment and spending some time impoverished in a garret somewhere was a good start, as was struggling to survive outside of the mainstream, and, ideally and most importantly, occupying the role of an exile.

If the idea of a writer was automatically equated with the idea of exile, without meaning to belittle anyone's struggles or personal circumstances, it is not too difficult to imagine that some people played up to this trope. There were those who chose to reject colonial ties and emphasise the cultural deprivation they had overcome. The idea of the literary exile was a part of European modernism to the extent that it might have been seen as a desirable situation. Patrick Buckridge describes the Australian writer Godfrey Blunden as unusual because he was genuinely exiled: he was unable to return home for a number of reasons, including being a bigamist.[68] The usual persona of an exile, however, involved conscious 'self-fashioning', and living out the life of a tortured artist, which was a fashionable pursuit in Europe. Malcolm Bradbury claims that Ernest Hemingway left Paris 'in part because many Americans read his book *The Sun Also Rises* (1926) and promptly decided to become expatriate writers in Paris, whether they wrote or not, so swamping the "serious" writers'.[69]

It is a distinct possibility, then, that writers or people with ambition to be writers would have invented or exaggerated difficulties to emphasise their 'exile-ness' and therefore bolster their modernist credentials. Some New Zealand writers expressed dissatisfaction at the cultural life of the colony

– A.R.D. Fairburn described Auckland as 'an intellectual rat-hole', and a 'spiritual cesspool'.[70] While this might have been a fair assessment, playing up to this idea also increased his clout as a tortured intellectual fleeing oppression. Frank Morton believed that Jane Mander's complaints and her tendency to 'snap at the queer little harmless, cramping things in the New Zealand country that exasperated her as a young girl' arose from attempts to 'épater les bourgeois' (shock the middle classes) rather than genuine adversity, although his assessment is highly patronising and dismissive of women writers in general.[71] Katherine Mansfield enjoyed every material and educational advantage available to her in New Zealand but preferred to emphasise the deprivations of colonial life. Widely accepted without question, these attitudes further reinforced ideas about New Zealand as a cultural desert.

As well as the prestige gained from escaping real or imagined oppression at home, living overseas allowed for a whole new set of hypothetical or deliberate hardships. Early-twentieth-century New Zealanders commonly had a network of colonial connections to call upon, especially in the United Kingdom. Sometimes these connections were deliberately spurned in favour of an independent, bohemian lifestyle. According to James McNeish, of the group of New Zealanders who feature in his book on New Zealand Rhodes scholars in the 1930s, '[m]ost of them had New Zealand relatives they could stay with or sponge off in England. None did, except [Jack] Bennett who couldn't afford to go anywhere … and [John] Mulgan, who had to borrow from an uncle in London to survive'.[72] A friend wrote to Frances Hodgkins in 1919 that she 'did not wish to reside in the "lovely house" of an aunt in London, since that meant that she would also "give up every freedom and give up every chance of seeing the world"'.[73]

A more extreme manifestation of this desire for independence came with those writers who deliberately pursued a bohemian lifestyle. The Hokitika-born poet Alison Grant arrived in London in the late 1920s and immediately sought a more simple life, 'ritually burning all her London letters of introduction, sleeping rough in Trafalgar Square and selling matches on Waterloo Station'.[74] Katherine Mansfield flatly refused to compromise her art for pecuniary gain. Though she received £100 a year from her parents,[75] this was not a lot of money; £2 a week would not have gone far. Mansfield at first lived a purposefully bohemian and impoverished life. Upon getting to England she decided to live by Oscar Wilde's doctrine of 'the artist's duty of experience.'[76] She wanted to marry a man 'without prejudices' who would support her as an artist. She found a music teacher who complied, 'married him, found him absurd, and left him after a few days. A period of extreme loneliness and depression followed.'[77] She was in poor health, 'she had no real home, and sought vainly for a possible refuge'. She was also carrying a child, not her husband's.[78] Her deliberate attempts at rejecting a comfortable existence for an edgy, bohemian one, in the end, perhaps compounded her ill health and led to her early death.

Discomposure arising from living in several places during one's lifetime was one of many aspects affecting writers' outlooks and could inspire literary responses. Unease, which might naturally result from being far from one's home and family, sometimes manifested in the fiction of New Zealanders. Dan Davin wrote in 1956 about how 'by crossing the sea you had abolished your right to a past, to a background'.[79] Louisa Baker gave herself the pseudonym 'Alien', which, according to Kirstine Moffat, 'speaks of both her sense of dislocation from her New Zealand home and her sense of isolation as a professional and artistic woman in a patriarchal environment'. She felt 'like a permanent exile'.[80] Edith Lyttleton travelled frequently and wrote her fiction from a number of different national perspectives, causing Terry Sturm to say that she never felt at home anywhere.[81] The kind of permanent dislocation and longing for home articulated in A.R.D. Fairburn's poem 'To an expatriate' was thought to be the standard fate of New Zealand writers who went overseas:

> *The embers of your old desire*
> *remembered still will glow, and fade,*
> *and glow again and rise in fire*
> *to plague you like a debt unpaid,*
> *to haunt you like a love betrayed.*[82]

Themes of not belonging overseas while being unable to return home occur reasonably frequently in New Zealand writing and in writing about New Zealand writing.

It is the way that these expressions have been interpreted and problematised that is the issue – turning mobility and overseas connections into something that had a destructive effect on the development of New Zealand culture rather than extending its possibilities. Negative or uncomfortable responses attract more attention, but these were not the only responses from New

Zealand writers, and disaffection might have had many different origins. Dominating the historiography of New Zealand literature is an assumption that there was something wrong with New Zealand that drove its brightest literary talents to leave the country. The cringe factor also extended beyond New Zealand's shores, contributing to the belief that association with New Zealand was a barrier to success overseas. Conclusions resulted that life overseas was traumatic, and more often than not led nowhere, unless a writer was willing to give up on being a 'New Zealand writer'. These ideas came from a number of sources relating to New Zealanders' self-defensive attitudes, their need to defend their own patch against perceived criticisms, the association of literary merit with suffering and dislocation and, in some cases, the unrealistic expectations writers had of their own talents as artists. When they found they did not achieve publication as freely and easily as they perhaps thought they ought to, they assumed it was due to being in New Zealand, and insisted that writers must leave to achieve success. Similarly, though, poor reception overseas was attributed to the inadequate removal of colonial shackles. Absorbing these perspectives gave people the unsubstantiated idea that failure was the result of being too closely associated with New Zealand, a point further explored in Chapter Seven.

CHAPTER SIX

New Zealand writers and the modern world

I n 1932 literary critic and writer Winnie Gonley wrote, 'Jane Mander has written four novels of New Zealand life, but, receiving little encouragement in this colony, she has gone to America.'[1] Although one reason for this might have been Mander's desire to escape the 'soul-searing silence', another contributing factor was the aspiration to study at the new School of Journalism at Columbia University, in New York. Leaving in 1912, she took one novel manuscript with her and on her way to America visited London, where the book was turned down by four publishers. She continued to write novels and stories, and by 1918 had had a novel accepted by John Lane. Mander moved to London before her fourth novel, *Allen Adair*, was published. She remained connected with the New Zealand literary world and eventually returned.

Her life story is more complicated than a simple trajectory of an artist fleeing an oppressive society (as in Gurr's *Gemeinschaft*). As I will argue in this chapter, she and other writers are better described as 'rootful' rather than rootless, whether they travelled the world or remained in New Zealand, as they maintained many connections to different places. Similarly, there is no standard pattern for the lives of mobile New Zealand writers in the early twentieth century, and certainly not one that equates to an exodus of writers fleeing literary oppression in New Zealand only to be faced with exile and/or failure overseas.

Stuart Murray compares Jane Mander's experiences to Mansfield's, saying that 'Mander's life appears at times to [be] a shadow version of Mansfield's earlier engagement with London literary culture, but without the heady Bloomsbury connections.'[2] Katherine Mansfield, despite being patently exceptional, is the archetypal model of an early-twentieth-century New Zealand writer against which other writers are measured. James Bertram wrote in 1971 that 'Katherine Mansfield and D'Arcy Cresswell are both exact representations of the expatriate New Zealand writer – uneasy wanderers between two worlds, living in a love–hate relationship with their own country.'[3] Eric McCormick used a comparison between the first and last publications of Katherine Mansfield and those of Blanche Baughan and Alice Webb to demonstrate the lack of advancement in the work of the latter two writers, proving (in his eyes) that New Zealand lacked 'all but the minimum conditions necessary for the creation of literature.'[4]

The career trajectory of one individual cannot be said to represent those of an entire literary generation, however, especially someone as unique and complicated as Katherine Mansfield. She was an exception not, as McCormick claimed, because she enriched her country's literature while overseas, but because, if the prevailing narrative about her is to be believed, she so stridently tried to reject her ties to colonial New Zealand.[5] Her contribution to literature describing New Zealand life came almost in spite of her efforts to have nothing more to do with the place. Mansfield desperately wanted to leave New Zealand, yet when she did she was haunted by memories of her birthplace, felt she did not fit in to English society because of being a colonial, and wrote about New Zealand in her most famous stories.[6]

Even this account, Ian A. Gordon argues, may be exaggerated: he claims that the portrait of Mansfield as 'distraught sufferer' drawn by Ruth Mantz in her influential biography, 'on which all subsequent versions have been based', comes from a flawed interpretation of the primary material relating to Mansfield, and the editorial choices made by John Middleton Murry about posthumous publication of her letters and journals.[7] An unmediated reading of the material reveals someone eager and interested in her surroundings, intent on recording as much as possible for future use.[8] Most writers (although they may have expressed dissatisfaction with New Zealand) were not intent on leaving permanently and cutting off all ties, and they often had little in common with Mantz's version of Mansfield. And it seems that even Mansfield might not fit easily into the category she supposedly exemplified. Because of the huge variation in the experiences of overseas writers, expatriation does not have as much explanatory power as it has been credited with when it comes to the success or failure of writers, but its importance has been taken for granted.

New Zealanders existed in a world of possibilities, where mobility and overseas connections (both for those who travelled and those who did not) were relatively normal. Leaving the country did not automatically create an exile. Instead, New Zealanders were citizens of the modern world. The colonial world was the product of the mass disruptions resulting from the advent of modernity, which exploded traditional European society structures and scattered people across the globe from the seventeenth century onwards. By the turn of the twentieth century colonial expansion and technological advancement had made the world more mobile and interconnected than ever before. These developments resulted in a kind of 'world connectedness' or multiplicity of connections, which was a particularly crucial lifeline for those who had made it as far as New Zealand. What is interpreted as exile is simply the growing mobility and distance from tradition that became increasingly common in the modern era. Living in the colonial writing world allowed the acquisition of a transnational perspective that could in fact be an advantage.

Having multiple affiliations and attachments resulted not in rootlessness or a permanent state of exile, but something more like 'rootfulness'. Many writers reported feeling an intense homesickness when they travelled overseas, implying the opposite of rootlessness; instead, they retained a strong connection to their native land. This was a common experience if they had been anticipating a pastoral paradise and instead encountered London. According to Vincent O'Sullivan's biography, the English winters depressed John Mulgan and made him long for the year-round warmth of the top of the North Island.[9] Though Mulgan was not fooled by nostalgic portrayals of what England would be like, he exhibited a common antipodean reaction to the reality: disappointment mingled with homesickness. A.R.D. Fairburn reported after his visit to Kew that he had encountered a 'tea-tree bush which nearly made me cry'.[10] Dora Wilcox also found London depressing and described the effect it had on her writing:

> *And when I look on London's teeming streets,*
> *On grim grey houses, and on leaden skies,*
> *When speech seems but the babble of a crowd,*
> *And music fails me, and my lamp of life*
> *Burns low, and Art, my mistress, turns from me,*
> *Then do I pass beyond the Gate of Dreams*
> *Into my kingdom, walking unconstrained*
> *By ways familiar under Southern skies.*[11]

In order to write, she implied, she had to imagine herself back in New Zealand. Such feelings reflected the reality of life in the modern world, where uninterrupted ties to a single place were much less common, and it was quite possible to have strong connections to one or more of these places.

A model that juxtaposes colonial backwaters with a distant metropolis does not make sense in the context of the twentieth-century colonial world. Colonial society in New Zealand formed well into the modern era, and there is a great deal of doubt about whether New Zealand qualified as a *Gemeinschaft* at all. Rather than being organised into 'small, immobile, close-knit' village-like groups, society in early New Zealand was, according to Miles Fairburn, highly mobile and fragmented. Because of the pioneering nature of society and the itinerant nature of jobs, 'community structures were few and weak and the forces of social isolation were many and powerful'.[12] Rather than being 'close-knit', Fairburn argues, the people were 'atomised', meaning socially isolated from one another. The nature of work in the early colony meant that itinerancy was common, as workers moved around to temporary jobs wherever they were available. New Zealand communities, therefore, were not 'immobile' either.

Towards the end of the nineteenth century, when New Zealanders lived increasingly in towns and small cities, they were still not living in a *Gemeinschaft*. The timing of colonial expansion when it reached New Zealand meant that it was part of advances brought about by the industrial revolution. The institutions of modernity reached New Zealand simultaneously with the creation of these communities. Thus, people were organised into social groups, but these were not organic, primitive communities. Rather, they were 'instantly modern', and sometimes deliberately planned to be so. New Zealand cities were examples of 'planted communities', planned overseas and transplanted whole to the colonies.[13] Moreover, with New Zealanders' high rates of literacy, their wealth and their links with Britain as the world's first industrial nation and the centre of the empire, they were able to gain access to much that was up to date. A stark dichotomy between 'the untamed bush' and 'civilised England', although sometimes portrayed in literature such as Edith Grossmann's *Heart of the Bush*, simply was not the reality for the majority of New Zealanders, who mostly lived in cities or towns and had access to the modern world.[14]

It was not unusual to have various influences and perspectives within the

context of multiple backgrounds facilitated by colonial world mobility. Douglas
Stewart, for example, had an Australian father, but was born in Eltham, New
Zealand. He spent his life moving between Australia and New Zealand, which
gave him a broader perspective when writing about either country. Such
complexity is often presented as a problem, or something out of the ordinary:
his biographer, Nancy Keesing, describes him not as an 'Outsider' but 'a man
from another country looking at natural features'.[15] Brigid Magner's study of
trans-Tasman literary expatriates continues to problematise expatriatism.
She focuses on the 'various impostures' and 'elaborate subterfuges' that four
writers were forced to perform to counter the effects of living between two
literary traditions.[16]

On the contrary, colonial world connections and mobility were a common
reality for New Zealand writers. Of the 118 traceable writers in my dataset,
40 per cent had come to New Zealand as migrants; 22 per cent were adults
when they arrived. Between 1890 and 1945, 47 per cent of these writers left
New Zealand to live somewhere else for more than a year. Only 23 per cent
were born in New Zealand and died there without leaving for more than
a holiday.[17] The life story of any Pākehā New Zealander was likely to be
connected with some sort of cross-border travel, either to New Zealand or
from it. This migration had nothing to do with a lack of support for writers.
Miles Fairburn has posited that the only really exceptional thing about
New Zealand in the first half of the twentieth century was that it was the
'most globalized society in the world', meaning that New Zealanders were
uniquely indebted to outside influences.[18] It is a possibility that, because New
Zealand was a young country whose settlers arrived mostly after 1860, early-
twentieth-century New Zealanders were the most migratory people in the
British world. When migration is compared in four British settler colonies
in 1920 (by means of calculating total departures and arrivals as a percentage
of total population), New Zealand had a greater number of both departures
and arrivals per capita than the other nations.[19] Fairburn argues that New
Zealand's physical isolation, among other things, caused it to be settled later
than anywhere else. Thus New Zealand is a uniquely young country and as
a result must have had an unusually high number of migrants or children of
migrants, making the population particularly modern and transnational.

Early-twentieth-century New Zealand was a land where, aside from the
indigenous population, everyone had arrived within the last 80 years. Even

if New Zealand-born, they dreamed of visiting the places they read about and that their parents had told them about. In *The Passionate Puritan*, Jane Mander wrote:

> *No Englishman is capable of feeling for London that concentrated reverence and yearning that comes to the dreaming colonist on a New Zealand hilltop or an Australian plain. To most of them London has the painful lure of the unattainable – the mournfulness of saying year after year 'Perhaps I can manage it next', and of fearing the while that it won't be managed. But the illusion is hugged and fed and never allowed to die. There is always the prospect that something may happen – and one may really get there at last.*[20]

This heightened awareness of what was over the sea has also had a profound effect on New Zealand's literature and on the country's literary criticism and conception of its own literary history. It has given rise to the fruitful, transnational perspective brought about by New Zealand's participation in the colonial writing world. If national identity is 'the product of a constant interplay – of personal mobility and negotiation, of familiarity and distance, of nostalgia and disavowal,'[21] as Stuart Murray claims, the colonial writing world model allows for the expression of these qualities. In J.G.A. Pocock's view, history itself is never quite at home, but is 'transplanted by voyagings and generated by settlements and contacts.'[22] The model acknowledges this, where the portrayal of literature as a national project has denied it and turned transnationalism and dual identity into something negative.

Determining authority to write about a place based on either distance or proximity is not a zero-sum game, and how well literature portrays a national culture is not the only measure of literary worth. Beyond this, what Pocock calls the 'antipodean perspective' could be an advantage, as living in more than one place allows for different perspectives and perhaps a more nuanced view of the world in general. Salman Rushdie writes of his initial concern that living in London and writing about India meant that he would never be able to capture the reality of his homeland, that his 'physical alienation from India almost inevitably means that we will not be capable of reclaiming precisely the thing that was lost; that we will, in short, create fictions, not actual cities or villages, but invisible ones, imaginary homelands, Indias of the mind'. Once he had experienced writing overseas, however, he saw that the added perspective was actually an advantage, and 'the broken mirror may actually be as valuable as the one which is supposedly unflawed'. Thus, 'it was precisely the partial nature of these memories, their fragmentation, that made them so evocative for me'. Being away from one's native land like this may, says Rushdie, 'enable [the writer] to speak properly and concretely on a subject of universal significance and appeal'.[23] The goal might be to more faithfully represent one's place of origin, or to pursue insight on a universal level, or something else entirely, but these first two options are not mutually exclusive (although they are often presented as such).

The antipodean perspective was not limited to those people who had moved countries at some point, as colonial mobility had broader-reaching effects. All Pākehā New Zealanders at this time were closely related to migrants if not migrants themselves. Thus the poets Jessie Mackay, Eileen Duggan and Alice A. Kenny, who were born in New Zealand and never left (or, in the case of Mackay, only left later in life for a brief visit to the United Kingdom), still possessed this broader perspective. It manifested itself in their writing, which was infused with a preoccupation with the issues of the old world, passed down to them from their immigrant parents. Jessie Mackay was intensely interested in the cause of Scottish and Irish home rule, and this appeared in poems like 'Scotland unfree' in her 1935 collection *Vigil*.[24] Eileen Duggan had a strong emotional attachment to Ireland, and had grown up on tales of oppression by the English (both her parents were from County Kerry). A review of her poetry in the *Irish Homestead* declared: 'We might almost suppose she was living in Ireland.'[25]

Modernism is often taken to be a reaction to the turmoil caused by modernity, and its expressions inspired by the disruption to traditional communities and modes of thought caused by the Enlightenment, exploration and European colonialism. George Steiner wrote that modernist literature largely came from 'unhoused' writers, but as a result of modern upheaval, everyone living in the post-Enlightenment world was 'unhoused' in some way or another. Physical expatriation was not necessary to experience this kind of dislocation from tradition, especially for those who found themselves in New Zealand (a recent product of these ruptures).

Along similar lines, J.G.A. Pocock writes that the state of being a New Zealander is one of never feeling at home. This is not necessarily a negative outcome in his eyes: he sees the work of Allen Curnow as celebrating the creative energies that this encourages, while presenting 'an imagination which could never be fully at home where it was, could never fully return to where it might have come from, and had travelled too far to fly off and live anywhere else.[26] Cultural nationalism is simply another expression of the need to replace traditional ties with those of a newly created 'imagined community'.[27] Aligning with English modernist ideals, Curnow and associates constructed themselves in opposition to people with international ties in order to increase their own local importance, creating this myth of the binary division between those with national and those with international interests (while in reality everyone had international interests to some degree, and the cultural nationalists' new ethos was also imported). Modernism could be both an essential description of place and the essential expression of displacement. While critical studies tend to focus on one or the other,[28] it was, in fact, both of these, and neither, because in the early twentieth century people lived in a mobile world with a multiplicity of attachments. Modernism expressed the 'unhoused' nature of life in the modern world just as well from 'the so-called outposts of empire' as in 'cosmopolitan ... urban streets, cafes, and salons'.[29] As Mao and Walkowitz describe, current transnational modernist scholarship goes beyond this dichotomy and 'emphasizes a variety of affiliations within and across national spaces', which could perhaps be seen as 'many houses'.[30] Also beyond this dichotomy lie the majority of New Zealand writers who visited or lived in Europe in the early twentieth century.

The prevalent idea that most writers were forced to become expatriates, condemned to live as 'uneasy wanderers between two worlds', does not make much sense in the context of mobility. In this context, the 'expatriate' label is not very useful for determining the concerns, outlook or contributions of writers. While the pattern is seldom questioned, there is little consensus over the actual reasons behind the supposed mass exodus afflicting New Zealand, and certainly no attempts to quantify the phenomenon or compare those who stayed and those who left. The reality is fragmented and varied; writers left for a multitude of reasons, some of which were to do with the strictures of society and smallness of intellectual life, and some of which were not. They undertook a variety of activities while overseas and made different numbers of trips of different durations and levels of permanence.

The urge to travel and see the world was as common as in the present day, and some writers spent time abroad purely for this reason. Because Alan Mulgan's visit to England was, he said, the inevitable result of a youth spent absorbing English literature, which led him to 'fix [his] thoughts ever on England', McCormick alleged that Mulgan shared this widely reported compulsion to leave the country.[31] The truth is that he had long wished to see the places immortalised in literature, and this desire was satisfied by a relatively short visit. Mulgan did not wish to go and live in England; his vision was historical and nostalgic, and he had no desire to engage with the modern realities of the country, managing to find 'something fitting and beautiful' even in the streaks of dirt on the public buildings.[32] Ten of the 118 writers in my dataset, including Mulgan, journeyed overseas largely for sightseeing purposes, and their trips lasted for a year or less.[33] One other of these was Jessie Mackay, who visited Ireland and England and was a delegate to the Gael Race Conference in Paris in 1921. Anne Glenny Wilson travelled to Britain in 1897 and was able to view the work of William Morris. Isabel Maud Peacocke spent a year in Europe in her early twenties. All of these authors remained in New Zealand except for these brief forays overseas.

Fifty of the 118 writers were not born in New Zealand, and 25 of that 50 left New Zealand at some point between 1890 and 1945. To call these writers 'expatriates' immediately raises questions, as it is not clear what they would have classed as their homeland anyway. The colonial world often created people who were difficult to classify. Rudyard Kipling is most usually referred to as an English writer, but he was born in Bombay and spent the first 25 years of his life living alternately in England and India, until in 1892 he and his wife embarked on a round-the-world trip. They unexpectedly spent four years living in Vermont and travelled extensively; Kipling was the author of several travel accounts as well as famous 'empire-based' poems and short stories. Kipling and others like him were British imperialists (and certainly his expressed views reflect that), and had what could be called a 'pan-British' identity. His audience thus included colonists of British origin in Australia, New Zealand and the rest of the empire. But identifying the 'home' that he would return to, with his audience famously scattered throughout the empire, is not straightforward, and his life story is outside of the paradigms of simple migration, travel or expatriation.

Writers born outside of New Zealand, such as Edith Lyttleton, cannot be uncomplicatedly counted as New Zealand expatriates, as their allegiances were multiple. In more general use, 'expatriate' means a person who lives or works overseas for a time, but even this is not without ambiguity or descriptive inadequacy. The term works on the assumption that everyone has a single *patria*, or homeland. But how is one's *patria* determined? The most obvious factor is birthplace, but this is inconsistently applied to authors when determining if they are sufficiently 'of' New Zealand to be included in the national canon. The poet Will Lawson was numbered among New Zealand expatriate writers in Australia in 1962 by Pat Lawlor.[34] Lawson was born in the United Kingdom, emigrated to New Zealand at the age of four and when eight moved with his family to Brisbane, where he lived until the age of 16. He then 'alternated between Sydney and New Zealand', and to claim that his foremost allegiance was to New Zealand is quite an assumption.[35] Kirstine Moffat frames the novelist Louisa Baker as an unfortunate expatriate, forced to go overseas by the lack of support she received in New Zealand.[36] But she was already 'overseas' in New Zealand, having been born in England.

For those not New Zealand-born, it was common to make trips back to their homelands, to visit relatives or (like W.H. Guthrie-Smith) to get married. John Macmillan Brown (historian and writer of utopian fantasy novels), himself an immigrant from Scotland, visited England in 1884, where he was offered the prestigious position of the new chair in English literature at Merton College, Oxford. He declined, preferring to return to New Zealand. Comments about New Zealand's high rate of expatriatism often do not differentiate between those who intended to live permanently overseas, those who intended to be away for a time, and those people who left New Zealand with the intention of travelling then returning. Nor is there acknowledgement of the fact that the people concerned might have come from somewhere else in the first place.

For middle-class New Zealanders at this time it was not unusual to visit England, and this was not an indictment of the failings of New Zealand. James Courage, for example, was reportedly tortured by tension between home and abroad. Yet he came from a family that was part of the colonial gentry in Canterbury, 'was used to having relations come and go from England and was brought up, like many of his generation, to think of England as "Home".'[37] His family members were mostly Oxford-educated, so being sent to Oxford for his further education would not have seemed out of the ordinary. Courage remained in England after this, but did not necessarily leave New Zealand with the intention to stay away permanently. In *Settler Society in the Australian Colonies*, Angela Woollacott asserts that most residents of the Australian colonies (at least of the land-owning class) had personal connections that extended throughout the empire because of the fluid nature of colonial appointments. Thus it was not unusual for families in British colonies to be able to call on contacts in England and beyond.[38]

A nationalist approach to history has, in the past, led to misinterpretation of the natural patterns of global migration and movement. In contrast, the model of the colonial writing world by necessity embraces a transnational approach and accommodates these patterns easily. It can accommodate personal motives with no relevance to incipient nationalism or expatriatism, and it can acknowledge the impact of international events. As Denis McLean says in a review of James McNeish's *Dance of the Peacocks*, 'New Zealand is not a place apart, from which we view the global traumas at a comfortable distance. The whole country passed through the fires of the fights against fascism and communism.'[39] Despite being very far away from the powerhouses of Europe, through its ever-active colonial links New Zealand was affected by global transitions and involved in world events.

World wars affected New Zealanders both at home and through their direct involvement. Over 240,000 New Zealanders travelled to Europe because they were serving with the armed forces in World War I and World War II. This was the primary reason some writers went overseas, not because they were frustrated with New Zealand and its lack of literary nourishment. In World War I John A. Lee served in the New Zealand Expeditionary Force from 1916. He appears to have otherwise had no intention of leaving New Zealand. The call to arms was a common reason for going to Europe, for women also. Dora Wilcox was living in Belgium but travelled to England during World War I for 'war work', serving with the Voluntary Aid Detachment.[40]

Still more writers made the journey during World War II, including Denis Glover. Glover initially expressed pacifist views, but upon noticing all his friends objecting to the war he changed his mind ('looped the loop' in the words of his friend John Drew), saying: '[s]omebody's got to go.'[41] While on leave in London he met with Charles Brasch, and John Lehmann introduced him to literary types like Cecil Day Lewis and Stephen Spender. He returned 'reluctantly' to New Zealand.[42] Eric McCormick himself served with the 5th Reinforcements as a medical orderly, before being appointed assistant to the army archivist in Egypt. The politics of war had effects as well. Basil Dowling, for example, was imprisoned for expressing his pacifist views, and his expatriation came soon after his release.

New Zealanders were also not immune to the lure of such prestigious academic institutions as the universities of Oxford, Cambridge and London, as well as those America could offer. A number of writers initially left New Zealand with the sole motive of studying in one of these places, such as Jane Mander's trip to the Columbia School of Journalism. Again, this did not equate to a rejection of their country of origin, for within the colonial world it was common for young men and women to be sent overseas (to England in particular) to further their education. England had long-established and prestigious institutions that could assist a subsequent career back in New Zealand. Dan Davin attended Balliol College, Oxford, on a Rhodes Scholarship and read 'Greats'.[43] John Mulgan also made the journey to England to attend Oxford (Merton), though he had just missed out on a Rhodes; he was offered a job at the Clarendon Press before he had even received notice of his 'first' in English. James Courage received a second-class BA from St John's, Oxford, in 1927, the year that Charles Brasch started at the same college. J.C. Beaglehole, a historian who also wrote poetry, travelled to the University of London on the strength of a postgraduate scholarship; D'Arcy Cresswell initially went to London to study at the Architectural Association.

Study overseas was often a familial expectation rather than a choice made by the writers themselves. According to James McNeish, Charles Brasch was initially reluctant to leave New Zealand: 'Brasch who had been shipped off to Oxford as a schoolboy had at first been miserable in England. He had grown to love it …'[44] Bill Pearson had no particular desire to leave the country and won a scholarship only because Canterbury University College had put his name forward to go to England, unbeknown to him. Pearson himself felt '"tremendously ambivalent" to such a move'.[45] Departure from New Zealand was clearly not always the result of frustration at the lack of local opportunities.

Many writers were also journalists, members of a profession that enabled movement throughout the English-speaking world to follow stories and gain experience. Because larger countries offered more opportunities as well as the excitement of foreign shores, several writers left New Zealand to pursue their journalistic careers. Most went to Australia, as there was no need to go as far as London to get work on newspapers (as already discussed in Chapter Three). Their careers usually included stints in several parts of the colonial or wider world, rather than a long-term stay in any one place. When Nelle Scanlan first travelled to the United States to attend the Limitation of Arms conference in Washington, DC, she went as a journalist, and was the only woman reporter present.[46] In her capacity as a journalist she travelled the world; her successful career as a novelist was just a lucrative sideline. Eric Baume, author of 13 books, including the 'melodramatic romance novel' *Half-Caste*, left New Zealand for Australia in 1923 to advance his career as a journalist, reporting on the war in London and then returning to Australia.[47] Hector Bolitho, famed 'expatriate', was first and foremost a journalist and then a royal biographer.

It was quite possible to find journalism work in New Zealand, but unlike creative writing, which could be undertaken anywhere, reporting on news stories often required proximity. Roderick Cave includes journalism with bookselling and publishing as an occupation whose proponents invariably moved countries at some point – and this could just as easily be to New Zealand as from it: '[F]or a great part of the 19th century and beyond, practically every compositor or pressman or journalist or bookseller who worked in New Zealand came from outside.'[48]

For those of a more avant-garde literary persuasion, the small population of New Zealand (about 1.15 million at the end of 1918[49]) made it difficult to find a proximate group of people interested in providing an alternative to mainstream lifestyles and culture. Like-minded people were not numerous enough to form the self-sustaining subcultures found in larger cities elsewhere. A.A. Phillips wrote in 1950 of Australia:

> *I do not know if our cultural crust is proportionately any thinner than that of other Anglo-Saxon communities; but to the intellectual it seems thinner because, in a small community, there is not enough of it to provide for the individual a protective insulation.*[50]

The 'cultural crust' in large Australian cities might have been thinner than in London, but by the late nineteenth century it undeniably existed. In New Zealand, however, the situation was more critical, and those wishing to experiment with innovative ideas were unlikely to find a large group of sympathetic people ready to discuss them in close proximity. Ruth Park, writing about New Zealand in 1942, said: 'Some parts of Auckland were not intellectual deserts, but I didn't know of them.'[51] To some extent this problem was addressed by correspondence with other people throughout Australasia and the rest of the colonial world, but undeniably there was a greater concentration of intellectual company in larger cities like London, Sydney and Melbourne, where fringe cultures could develop that allowed people to escape the status quo. In London, people were numerous enough and anonymous enough for out-of-the-ordinary opinions to escape criticism, most of the time. Similarly in Sydney there was a bohemian subculture that Dulcie Deamer embraced then conquered when she left New Zealand: she was dubbed its 'queen' in 1925.[52] Described by Caroline Daley as an 'expatriate nudist',[53] Deamer mixed with 'starving artists, poor musicians, writers scratching for a living, bit actors, and people with all sorts of strange jobs'.[54] Sydney's Bohemia had clubs, societies and networks, but nothing like this existed in New Zealand at the time.

Mainstream culture in New Zealand was, by most accounts, rigid and conformist. Public requirements of respectable behaviour possibly resulted from a backlash against frontier unruliness. The suffrage movement gained strong and early support from some politicians because they hoped that women's votes would temper the wild nature of early settler society. Although the advancement of women was progressive, then, the successful nineteenth-century suffrage campaign was in one sense a conservative victory. The ideology behind the winning of the vote in 1893 did more to reinforce traditional gender roles than to expand the options available to women, according to Raewyn Dalziel.[55] The victory of the suffrage movement with its strong links to the temperance and social-purity movements reflected New Zealand's puritanical 'monoculture'.[56] Lawrence Jones blames Victorian 'lower-middle-class evangelical morality', which was brought over by British settlers in the second half of the nineteenth century, and a lack of diversity among immigrants to New Zealand.[57] Transgressions of this social code were avoided because of concern about what other people would think.[58] These social codes were present in other societies as well, but smaller communities left little room for alternatives in New Zealand society, with mainstream attitudes reflecting a 'sharp fear of and disapproval' of alternative lifestyles.[59]

A number of New Zealand writers expressed a desire to escape this inflexible society, to the extent that the plight of the beleaguered artist oppressed by puritans became a literary trope. An example of this appears in Jane Mander's semi-autobiographical *The Story of a New Zealand River*, where the character of Asia likely reflects Mander's own preoccupations. Asia wants to embrace modern ideas but is trapped in a society indifferent to such notions and dominated by Victorian puritanism. Mander criticised New Zealand's ubiquitous puritan culture, as well as its preoccupation with material gain and stifling conformity. In her later novel, *The Passionate Puritan* (1922), the residents of a Northland timber-milling settlement live in a line of houses all decorated identically with the 'accepted white bed quilt and white lace curtains', with no deviations from this model tolerated.[60] Mander was not alone in her dissatisfaction – A.R.D. Fairburn's assessment of Auckland as a 'spiritual cesspool' was expanded on by his friend and literary mentor, Geoffrey de Montalk, who wrote as he travelled to Britain: 'It's a good feeling, leaving cursed New Zealand four hundred miles further behind every day! Try it!'[61]

These expressions of spiritual dissatisfaction often came coupled with more mundane reasons for wanting to leave the country, and were not *only* the result of intellectual impoverishment. Like many young people, A.R.D. Fairburn coveted a more exciting, glamorous life in a foreign land. He was also struggling to find employment, and he wrote to Montalk in 1927: 'I couldn't get a job as a collector of night-soil in Freeman's Bay if I offered to do it for threepence a week. I have several times lately seriously contemplated stowing away on a boat to England. I'd probably starve when I got there though.'[62] As well as this, he was miserable about an ill-fated recent dalliance with a woman. He described his depressed state to R.A.K. Mason in 1930, saying, 'I *must* leave New Zealand,'[63] and revealed that he was 'contemplating simultaneously a desperate marriage to a girl who could only have been a disaster for him, and escape to Europe or America'.[64] Geoffrey de Montalk received a court order in 1927 instructing him to return to his wife and small child, whom he was charged with abandoning. Not long after, however, he 'filed for divorce and left for Auckland in order to make arrangements to flee the country's "suffocating philistinism"'.[65] His book *Wild Oats* was favourably reviewed by Ian Donnelly, but then ran into trouble with the country's dominant puritanism when it was 'rejected by the literary editor of one of the big dailies [Alan Mulgan], [who refused] a review because the author was in the process of dissolving his marriage'.[66] De Montalk might have interpreted this as an oppression of artistic temperament, but his other reasons for rejecting New Zealand were more practical and less impressive.

Other writers left for family reasons or because of difficult relationships. Aorewa McLeod suggests that some writers chose to leave New Zealand in order to escape from duties that prevented them from writing. In the case of Jane Mander, McLeod's primary example, the motive was to get away from frustrating domestic tasks and parental control. Mander's writing might have been hindered while in New Zealand because of having to housekeep for her father, and this might have added to her reasons for leaving the country (although she had already written her first novel when she left).[67] Edith Searle Grossmann decided to travel extensively after the breakdown of her marriage. Her husband, Joseph Grossmann, had become embroiled in scandal and fraud allegations at Auckland University. She also wanted to seek treatment for her son, Arthur, who suffered from a mental disability, the details of which are not clear.[68] Grossmann's unhappy home-life was the catalyst for her departure, though she did express a dislike of the colony's ways. Louisa Baker was also unhappily married, and moved first to Dunedin and then overseas because of this.[69]

For some, this dissatisfaction went deeper. For those whose natural inclinations fell outside the mainstream moral code, life in New Zealand could be difficult. Roles for men and women were clearly defined, and women were faced with the options of being a wife and mother, or choosing the life of a quiet spinster. Robin Hyde found she naturally fell outside of these categories and led a troubled life as a result, failing, according to her son and biographer Derek Challis, 'to find a niche in which to secure and sustain her nature and talents'.[70] She was a single mother, her child born out of wedlock, and she had to work for various newspapers to earn money, which 'absorbed the energy and time that might have gone into more meaningful work'.[71] She wrote: 'I seem to dry up and become hard and metallic whenever I make a reasonable effort at working for a living. Tropic island and banana trees for one, please.'[72] Her first child died, and she regretted bitterly that society's 'narrow conventions and lack of sensitivity decreed that she should deny his ever having lived'.[73] Hyde found life very difficult in New Zealand, and this was probably the reason she left, though her brief life overseas was no easier.

There is evidence that marriage made it difficult for women to be writers, and that because of this women writers were less likely to marry. Information on marital status is available for 94 of the writers in my traceable dataset, 37 women and 57 men. Of the men, 49 out of 57 (86 per cent) were married at some point, compared to only 54 per cent of the women. Members of either group may have been in same-sex relationships but this is not well documented. Five of the men are known to have been homosexual (including D'Arcy Cresswell, who was also married); only four of the others remained unmarried. According to the 1936 census, 70 per cent of adult males were married, and 76 per cent of adult females.[74] These figures include divorced and widowed people (everyone except the 'never married'). When writers are compared to the national averages, the rate of marriage is considerably less for women and more for men, leading to the conclusion that marriage and writing were less easily combined for women than for men because wives were expected to engage in the more-than-full-time job of supporting their husbands' careers, keeping house and raising children. Altogether, 298 books were published by 116 women between 1890 and 1945 as compared with 417 books by 204 men.[75] Many of the more well-known women writers of this time remained unmarried, by choice or necessity, including Ursula Bethell, Edith Lyttleton, Jane Mander, Ngaio Marsh, Rosemary Rees, Robin Hyde, Eileen Duggan, Blanche Baughan, Nelle Scanlan and Jessie Mackay.

Particularly problematic at this time in New Zealand was the public's attitude to male homosexuality, which was explicitly illegal. For gay men like Frank Sargeson, growing up in a small, conservative city like Hamilton was challenging. Though homosexuality was also illegal in England, a significant proportion of the leading figures of the writing world were gay, and many found it relatively easy to move in circles that took homosexuality for granted. This was not the case in New Zealand. D'Arcy Cresswell left the country soon after he was involved in an entrapment and blackmail scandal with Whanganui mayor Charles Mackay which resulted in his being shot by Mackay.[76] Hector Bolitho, James Courage and Charles Brasch might also have been inspired to leave the country in the hope of greater sexual freedom overseas. Although there is some uncertainty about Geoffrey de Montalk's sexuality, he was unimpressed with the closed-mindedness of New Zealand society, where he was expected to be a dutiful husband. He wanted to go to Europe, where he thought he would be able to embrace his more unconventional tendencies.[77]

The 'strictures of society' did inspire some people to go overseas, but this is often wrongly confused with literary reasons for leaving. The two are entirely separate issues, as the social constraints did not necessarily prevent people from writing. The narrowness of mainstream society was not, as such, hostile either to literary creativity or the life of the mind. It is commonly assumed that puritanism stifled creativity. In fact, it could *inspire* creativity, and the results could be published overseas thanks to the colonial writing world. Nor was this restricted to people reacting against puritanism, as Kirstine Moffat lists some 28 authors who published books before 1940 that showed puritanism in a 'predominately positive light'.[78] Plenty of other writers were inspired to write in reaction against puritanism, including Jane Mander, Hector Bolitho and Frank Sargeson (Moffat lists 12 particularly significant authors).

The freedom to write was a luxury only afforded to those of a certain class, and men and women might have been prevented from achieving publication because of the competing demands of feeding and housing themselves and their families. Mary Scott and her husband ran a back-country sheep farm, and it was only when her eldest daughter was able to take over her household duties that Mary found the time to write.[79] Writers need time and financial support to practise their craft, and working-class people would have been short on both, as well as potentially lacking access to the education levels and cultural capital required. This is not something that would have forced aspiring writers overseas, however. While Catherine Bishop has shown that the world of imperial mobility was not limited to elites and wealthy individuals,[80] and members of all levels of society had and maintained colonial contacts, a certain amount of spare time and money was necessary to actually visit friends and family abroad. Impoverished New Zealanders would not necessarily be able to afford to try their luck elsewhere, and were probably aware that less well-off people had an even smaller chance of advancing beyond serial drudgery in other parts of the world.

The more common, mundane reasons many had for going overseas are often ignored entirely in favour of blaming New Zealand's cultural and social limitations. Yet in the majority of cases writers did not go overseas just for literary reasons. Of my dataset of 118 traceable writers, 55 left the country at some point between 1890 and 1945 for two years or more. David McClelland and H.B. Marriott-Watson provided no obvious clues as to why they left New Zealand. For the remaining 53, only 24 per cent were mainly occupied with creative writing while overseas.[81] Leaving New Zealand solely because one could not be a writer in New Zealand was certainly not the norm, though a few people thought it would boost their chances. Frank Anthony decided to try his luck in London on the strength of his moderate literary success in

New Zealand. Monte Holcroft went for similar reasons, though he had had little success previously. Even if a desire to further their writing career was a motive for travel, writers often engaged in several activities during the course of their time overseas. Other forms of work, when counted together, were more common (such as journalism or other work). For shorter journeys to the United Kingdom (a year or less), travel was the main occupation. There is no obvious overall pattern, with writers going abroad for a variety of reasons and spending their time in a variety of ways. It is clear, too, that expatriation was seldom permanent, as many people went on short trips.

The colonial world provided opportunities and pitfalls that were not necessarily foreseeable from the outset. It was not uncommon for people to live and work within the British colonies without knowing what their ultimate destination would be. The model of deliberate withdrawal resulting in exile does not account for people who left the country without the intention of staying away for a long time, or whose plans changed. Quite a few New Zealand writers ended up doing something different from what they had originally intended, particularly when war intervened. D'Arcy Cresswell went to London to study architecture, but World War I broke out soon after he arrived and he ended up serving as a private with the Middlesex regiment. W.H. Guthrie-Smith was also in Britain on one of his 'periodic visits' during World War I and found himself 'managing the gardens of a London hospital.'[82] Randal Burdon went to England in 1914 'hoping to study law', but these plans were interrupted by World War I.[83] Later, John Mulgan and Dan Davin both went to study at Oxford and then worked at Clarendon and Oxford University presses respectively, but spent some years serving in World War II. None of these forays overseas necessarily constitute deliberate and permanent withdrawal.

The majority of New Zealand writers who were in London were not trying to earn a living as writers, often because they were overseas for other reasons, and often because they had other sources of financial support. Some were supported by their parents, like Charles Brasch, who was free to travel about in Europe as he chose. Others were there to study and later found employment, such as James Courage, who worked in a bookshop. Creative writing was just a sideline for many. Most, like Ngaio Marsh, were involved in more than one line of work. When Marsh arrived in London in 1928 she stayed with the Rhodes family, whom she knew from New Zealand, where they had owned Meadowbank Sheep Station in Marlborough. With Nellie Rhodes she established an interior decoration shop called Touch & Go, in Knightsbridge, and wrote a detective novel that was published by Geoffrey Bles in 1932. Rosemary Rees was overseas primarily because she was on a prolonged theatrical tour. Edith Lyttleton left for England having already published several books, and her main reason for going was to accompany her family.

McCormick's examples of 'literary émigrés' are not convincing proof of the importance of expatriate exiles to New Zealand literature in the early twentieth century, nor of their prevalence. The three key examples chosen by McCormick (William Pember Reeves, Alan Mulgan and Katherine Mansfield) could not have been more different in terms of their individual career trajectories, preoccupations and motivations. Reeves was primarily a politician and left New Zealand because he had been appointed as agent-general for New Zealand in the United Kingdom. His departure had little to do with literary exile. Mulgan, a self-confessed Anglophile, travelled to England in 1926 on a cultural sightseeing mission. His visit was in no sense a literary exile and it was his only foray out of the country. Both before and after his trip, he was heavily involved with the business of creating New Zealand literature and was always an effective intermediary in the colonial writing world. Mansfield, on the other hand, had an antagonistic relationship with colonial culture. She was not involved in any New Zealand literary projects (or, at least, none that were apparent at the time) and sailed for England intent on leaving everything related to her home country far behind, in particular her parents.[84] The three writers lumped together by McCormick are similar only in that they happened to have been born in the same country.

Jane Mander's story is much more closely related to that of other members of the colonial writing world, like Nelle Scanlan, who remained part of the New Zealand literary scene while overseas. These two writers were not atypical. Many people enrich their lives with a period overseas, but this is not exile. Often the idea of 'necessary expatriatism' has been confused with the enhanced perspective that spending a few years living in a different place can provide. What Mansfield and Mander did have in common was their place in the modern world as 'rootful' New Zealand writers, unable to depend on the certainty of tradition. For Mansfield, focusing on whether she represented New Zealand, or European modernism, is 'limited and parochial', according to Vincent O'Sullivan: what is more of interest is her 'modern, extremely clear, extremely tested twentieth-century voice'.[85]

Going overseas was often not a permanent move, even for those going for longer periods, as they usually returned to New Zealand. Out of the 65 who left New Zealand between 1890 and 1945, 41 returned at some point; 32 died overseas and 33 returned and lived for the rest of their lives in New Zealand.[86] Of the authors who spent the rest of their lives in the United Kingdom, four died young, so it is impossible to determine whether they would have stayed away permanently. Robin Hyde was certainly very unhappy in London, and John Schroder was trying to make arrangements to bring her home when she died. John Mulgan had also expressed the intention of returning to New Zealand, but died young by his own hand, suffering from depression after the war.

Most of the writers who ended up spending the rest of their lives overseas returned to New Zealand at some point, either for a visit or an extended stay, rather than staying away permanently. It was rare for a writer to leave and never come back. In fact, the writers who intended to leave permanently and those who ended up staying overseas are in the small minority. Going from New Zealand to the United Kingdom was not out of the ordinary: as the protagonist's grandmother in James Courage's *The Call Home* says: '[W]e have none of us lost the link with England'.[87] In some ways the transition was easier then than it is now, because New Zealanders had free entry to Britain. Between 1948 and 1973 the words 'British subject and New Zealand citizen' appeared on every New Zealand passport, and before 1948 just 'British citizen'. From 1974 the wording read 'New Zealand citizen'. It was only in 1962 that the British government decided to restrict entry for members of the Commonwealth, fearing mass immigration from its former colonies in Asia and Africa.[88] The majority of writers who did go overseas spent at least some time in London, and this is the focus of Chapters Seven and Eight.

CHAPTER SEVEN

'The whole thing's been a farce': New Zealand writers in London and overseas

Newly arrived in London in 1929, hopeful novelist Monte Holcroft had come from New Zealand to 'try for a foothold' among the literary greats. It was not to be a simple undertaking, however. One can only imagine how disheartening it was for him to hear from Jane Mander, soon after stepping off the boat, that he ought to go immediately back to New Zealand while he still had the money to buy himself a ticket.[1] Life in literary London was not easy, and Holcroft soon learned that being there would not necessarily increase his chances of becoming a best-selling author. He found the cold of the London winter 'demoralising':

> *after the peace of Lourdes and the excitements of Paris the big city seemed damp, cold and indifferent. I had found it easier to write in Lourdes and looked now for a place in the country which would give me similar quietness and perhaps a touch of human warmth.*[2]

This interlude did not last long; fearing that he would be 'overtaken at last by grinding poverty', Holcroft returned home to Christchurch after receiving a ticket from a concerned family friend. He was in part reluctant to leave, but also attracted by the idea of returning to the 'haven' 'in *my* own country and among my own people, in a city not far from mountains, with everywhere a feeling of space and freedom'.[3] If writers left New Zealand expecting their luck to change suddenly then they were inevitably disappointed.

Rather than coming to the realisation that being in London was not a guarantee of success, as they could already do most things from home, Holcroft and other New Zealand writers tended to blame their frustrated suppositions on the fact that they were New Zealanders. Partly to justify their own decisions to go to Britain, they sometimes assumed that success required becoming an 'exile' and rescinding all ties to New Zealand. This was in part because of expectations resulting from the trope of the writer as 'exile' that strengthened with the growth of the modernist movement (and 'deliberate' exiles are discussed more fully in Chapter Five). The mistaken belief that they were disadvantaged in New Zealand gave some writers unrealistic expectations of success in Britain. Meg Tasker describes a similar misplaced belief among Australian writers: that London, as the 'centre of literary culture', was 'the best place in which to exercise their talents and ambitions'.[4] Initial enthusiasm more often than not turned to disillusionment as they discovered that the London literary scene and London life in general were more challenging and less glamorous than they expected. Instead of acknowledging their unrealistic expectations or even their own failure to produce quality work, they tended to blame the attitude of the British to 'outsiders'. Some even came to the conclusion that the only two options were remaining as 'outsiders' and failing, or losing their individuality and resigning themselves to overseas exile.

When writers did leave New Zealand, they most often went to London. To some New Zealand literary imaginations, London in the early twentieth century represented a wealth of opportunities that were not available at home. They described in vivid detail the shortcomings of the land they were leaving behind, then projected contrasting virtues onto England. Geoffrey de Montalk told A.R.D. Fairburn in 1927 that 'poets are as badly treated in this land of white savages and All Blacks as they are feted and laurelled and crowned in Merrie England'.[5] The pages of Hector Bolitho's autobiography are filled with his hopes of escaping New Zealand. He complained of not having any like-minded friends with whom he could discuss his advanced literary tastes.[6] He first went to Sydney, and expected even more from England.

New Zealand writers sometimes had expectations that simply being in London would be a ticket to literary stardom. Whatever their motivations for going there, some arrived in the metropolis hopeful of fulfilling their literary aspirations and expecting to find a more sympathetic environment for their writerly lifestyles. De Montalk wrote in 1927, 'I am going to London, with not more than £30 in my pocket, to try and conquer the world of letters, or die in the attempt.'[7] Monte Holcroft too, initially spurred on by the myth of London's magical abilities to bring literary and intellectual fulfilment, described himself as a 'literary pilgrim, ready to worship at the older shrines, but with a screed or two of my own to sell by the way'.[8] A.R.D. Fairburn was thrilled to be in

London at first as well. He described his early exhilaration as 'the exuberance of the colonial's "discovery" of London'.[9] Soon after his arrival, Hector Bolitho had tea with a New Zealand friend whose voice 'already had an English chill', and was excited to learn that the friend had 'spoken to G.K. Chesterton on the telephone and had seen D.H. Lawrence eating a boiled egg at the Trocadero'.[10] The literary world seemed within easy reach.

London in the early twentieth century did have a cornucopia of literary opportunities on offer, for those who knew how to take advantage of them. This was the result of a vast increase in demand for literary works during the nineteenth century through the creation of a 'mass reading public'. The spread of literacy and rising incomes created a large audience of potential readers, and literature was no longer confined to the privileged elite. New technology (such as gas lighting and better public transport) meant that people had more time to read.[11] At the same time that popular demand was increasing, improved methods of printing and distribution were reducing the price of books, making them more readily available. A host of new publications sprouted up, including 121 literary magazines that appeared between 1837 and 1913.[12] A number of new publishing houses were founded in the latter decades of the nineteenth century by people like Gerald Duckworth, Robert Hale, Matthew Hodder and Thomas Stoughton, and Arthur H. Stockwell.

However, although there was a significant increase in opportunities for publishing in London, there was also a rise in the number of writers trying to take advantage of this. Inexperienced writers struggled to deal with the dense maze of publishers and agents and with competition from more established authors. So, the apparently vast prospects for writers were tempered by the reality of complexity and competition, and hopeful arrivals from New Zealand found that they were very small fish in a very large pond. When Nelle Scanlan described the difficulties she faced in London, she said that 'all the literary talent of the world seemed pooled in this great city'.[13] The reality for most in this fiercely competitive environment was that publication was a struggle and it was difficult to derive any sort of useful income from writing. Most writers remained what Edith Lyttleton described in the 1930s as 'makeweights' – 'lowly, ill-paid authors whose stories (four of five per issue) were used as "fillers"' – as opposed to 'established' authors, who were 'much better paid, [and] whose name would appear on the cover of the magazine'.[14] Even Lyttleton struggled with this despite being already a successful author, having had two novels published by Andrew Melrose of London (before she left New Zealand) and a number of stories in prestigious international magazines.

The romantic grandeur of the England that people in New Zealand grew up hearing about was rarely comparable to the reality they encountered. While initial impressions could be of a bustling city of delights, the realities of London soon hit those people brought up on their parents' rose-hued nostalgia. J.C. Beaglehole, upon arriving in London at the age of 25, remarked:

> The journey from Tilbury to St. Pancras was pretty dirty on the whole, though at first there were a few fields & haystacks & churches that looked like the England of romance. But then we came to interminable lines of houses all built in the same way in big blocks or separately, which were uglier still. So a station or so farther on I nearly got out & came back home; but I decided I would see what St. Pancras was like anyhow. It was all smoke & uproar but having got so far I decided I would give London a go.[15]

Geoffrey de Montalk described this same journey from Tilbury, the port on the Thames where the steamships arrived, to St Pancras in the heart of London. He too was horrified by the sight of 'all those miserable little houses between Tilbury and St Pancras, grey and all that'.[16] London was usually a lot dirtier, bigger and more confusing than its pilgrims had imagined when envisaging their romantic introduction to a city filled with charming experiences and literary greats. The writers could only console themselves by turning their disappointment to literary inspiration. Dan Davin's *The Sullen Bell* depicts a group of New Zealanders in London as 'ghosts, the people who having got Home after a lifetime's dream longed to be back at home and dreaming again'.[17] The reality could rarely live up to the legend.

Writers and artists who had entertained notions of quick success rapidly became disenchanted. Douglas Glass, a New Zealand photographer living in London, wrote to R.A.K. Mason in 1929 that 'life over here is a hell of a strain and a man is lucky if he ever gets any writing done. That is real creative work. I find it very depressing and may return to New Zealand after another year of it.'[18] He went on to say: '[M]ost people who come here & write home to N.Z. or return after six months are too bloody selfish or stupid to tell the truth.'[19] Being outside of London was even worse. A.R.D. Fairburn wrote to Mason from the Wiltshire countryside in 1931: 'I wish to the devil you could come over here. Except when I go to London I am just as much intellectually isolated as you are. More so, perhaps.'[20] Frank Sargeson embarked on an ambitious reading programme in the British Library, but soon became overwhelmed by the task and the 'intolerable weight of so much civilisation'.[21] Arthur H. Adams went to London in 1902 to 'make his name', but his initial fascination soon gave way to unhappiness. In 'Introduction: The Web' in his volume of poems *London Streets*, 'the overall impression is of London as a web of "Great Greyness" which has "shrivelled and long sucked dry" Adams' "alien heart"'.[22]

The political atmosphere of pre-war London would have been a shock to new arrivals from the other side of the world. Visitors in the 1930s found Europe heavy with a sense of impending doom, especially in the lead-up to World War II. Fairburn's initial enthusiasm wore off and was replaced by despondency. He said that Europe felt like a 'mortuary' and that the atmosphere in London was one of 'utter and hopeless decadence'.[23] In 1931 he wrote to Mason: 'I have the feeling of being in a crumbling world.'[24] In 1932 he continued: 'Perhaps you don't see, out there in N.Z., away from Europe as you are, just what is happening. What is indisputably, unmistakeably, inevitably happening. We are ending.'[25] Charles Brasch believed that James Courage was only able to write effectively after World War II, once 'the terrible constriction and oppressiveness of the 1930s, heavy with the growing threat of war, had been resolved. The relief, the release, were enormous.'[26] James Bertram's time at Oxford as a Rhodes Scholar altered his perceptions, according to James McNeish: 'By 1935 Bertram's view of England was shifting from the Wordsworthian picture he had imbibed at Waitaki, of a green and sunlit land, to one of a society that had so many things wrong with it that it was becoming rudderless internationally.'[27]

The reasons that so many people had left London in the first place to go and live in the colonies had not gone away. Overcrowding and bad living conditions were common, and ways around them were only available to those with enough money. The lack of unpolluted air and sun, the crowding and the anxiety experienced living in a large European city in the early twentieth century caused many health problems.[28] Arnold Wall, an emigrant to New Zealand from England, was surprised to be homesick for such an unlovely place, expressing astonishment that his 'tough Colonial heart should turn / To London; to the sour, revengeful town, / Whose smoke, whose smells and vapours all her own, / Drove me, a willing exile, from her arms.'[29] David Lynn, a New Zealander who went to London, described it in realistic terms in his novella *Love and Hunger*: 'The East End of London: what a conglomeration of twisted humanity! Millions burrowed in their fetid warrens like rabbits: born, lived and died there.'[30] In comparison to this, New Zealand probably did not seem like such a terrible alternative.

The epicentre of the literary universe was not necessarily a good environment for writing. Writers were just as likely to complain about life in London as New Zealand. Jane Mander had thought that she needed to leave New Zealand to find the intellectual stimulus she required, but ended up saying that 'nobody who wants to create should ever live in "the swim" of a big city'.[31] She wrote to Holcroft in 1932: 'In many ways I envy your hermit existence in N.Z. You may be suffering over it now, but it's out of just such isolation that really great books come … Then authors come to London, get ruined by adulation and bold advertising and proceed to write inferior books.'[32] Boredom could encourage writing: Madeline Duret appears in A.G. Stephens' collection of autobiographical notes of Australasian authors. She found the slower pace of life in New Zealand more conducive to writing: having moved to Dunedin from India via Wellington she reported that she 'found it deadly dull, took to writing, received no rebuffs, delightful editors'.[33] Eileen Duggan, who never left New Zealand, decided that the advantages of being in London were not worth the loss of credibility, saying 'if the colonial way is slower, at least it is purer', and: 'It is good for us to be here away from the marketplace', as she 'would sicken of a praise begotten of propinquity'.[34]

The freedoms that New Zealanders hoped for were not guaranteed in the larger cities either. England in many ways was just as conservative as New Zealand, but there was a large enough population to allow self-sustaining fringe and bohemian subcultures. The highly public trial and subsequent imprisonment of Oscar Wilde (leading to his later exile in France) made it very obvious that homosexuality was officially as ill-tolerated in England as in New Zealand, although gay people were common enough among the literati for A.R.D. Fairburn to complain of anti-heterosexual discrimination.[35] Nonetheless, despite the existence of pockets of tolerance, homosexuality or 'alternative lifestyles' were still subject to social and legal discrimination, and Geoffrey de Montalk's predictions about the freedoms that London was going to afford were checked somewhat on his arrival. In 1928 he wrote: 'I have been in the papers here during the last few days, together with Douglas, as we went into a West End restaurant in silk shirts and blue trousers, but no coats. We were refused service.' The newspapers contributed headlines like '"Poet in Silk Shirt" and all that sort of rubbish.'[36] He was referring to Douglas Glass, who was arrested soon after Montalk arrived for stealing from his place of employment, a menswear shop.[37] By 1930 Glass had fled to Paris. De Montalk was eventually imprisoned for attempting to publish a bawdy poem he had written for Fairburn, and was adopted as a cause célèbre by the leading literary figures of the day.

Many of the complaints of New Zealand writers and their subsequent disappointment with London were probably the result of the myths they had grown up with that promised intellectual and cultural fulfilment in England or Europe. However, if they were not successful from New Zealand there was no reason to suppose they would be in England; London was not an automatic ticket to success. *London Called Them* (a novel by Isabel Maud Peacocke about young New Zealanders in London) features the hopeful artist Dick Travers, dispirited by his lack of success. '"The whole thing's been a farce," he laughed rather bitterly – "me coming here to set the Thames on fire when I couldn't even make the Waitemata smoke."'[38] Dan Davin also mocked this idea, satirically portraying those whose imaginary England was unlike the real London: 'Who would have believed that feet could become this sore in Oxford Street as in Karangahape Road ... that if you were without love in your own country you were without love everywhere?'[39]

It was true that being outside literary circles made life difficult: unknown writers usually had at least one of two obstacles to overcome. Firstly, they were often not known by English publishers. Unless they were fortunate enough to have influential contacts, new writers had to be very lucky to get their work published. Secondly, 'outsiders' found it difficult to make inroads into literary circles, for being successful in London was often a matter of one's contacts and level of involvement in cliques. Arthur H. Adams encountered this in London and wrote about it in the *Bulletin* on his return:

> *The London editor doesn't know you, doesn't want to know you, has never heard of you or your work. And he does know your London rival. He was at Oxford with his father, or a bishop has mentioned his name, or they both come from the same county, or he's a friend of somebody in the Stock Exchange.*[40]

In the novel *London Called Them*, the young New Zealand writer Ngaere complains of not being given a chance by publishers because 'we're not smart little Oxford or Cambridge undergrads, with smart little nasty minds ... they despise us overseas writers as literary barbarians just because we weren't born in the Strand or Little-Muddle-in-the-Mud and haven't been to their mouldy universities.'[41] Peacocke's assessment of the situation is very similar to one of Jane Mander's descriptions. Mander said in a letter:

> *Nobody knows better than I that the way of the writer is long and hard, the overseas one at any rate. We have more than ever now to contend with in the horde of clever young Oxford and Cambridge graduates who are all writing books of one kind or another ... We outsiders have to be so much better than they to get any notice at all.*[42]

She was paraphrased in the *Auckland Star* as saying: 'Too much favour is shown by publishers to the young men just down from Oxford and Cambridge, like Beverley Nicholls, irrespective of the quality of what they have written.'[43] Peacocke was heavily involved in literary circles in New Zealand, particularly in Auckland, where Jane Mander was based from 1932, so would have spoken to authors with first-hand experience of life in London. Thus she was aware that being unknown and outside literary circles was a handicap, although this could be overcome by influential connections, provided one was lucky enough to have them.

London had a multitude of cliques and clubs, and just knowing which one to approach was difficult. In a talk given to the Lyceum Club in 1933 Jane Mander explained:

> *The artist set of New York is a huge fluid affair in which everybody knows everybody, for the Americans have a peculiar form of inferiority complex which leads them to get a severe pain if they don't meet everybody, whereas in London there are some twenty odd circles and sets which don't mix in anything like the same general scene.*[44]

The complicated workings of the literary social scene would have been a mystery to those newly arrived. The credentials required for membership in these societies often ruled out writers who were not already successful, creating a paradox that was difficult to overcome. London's Lyceum Club, for example, was designed to help women writers, but gaining membership required already having had a book published, having university qualifications, or being the wife or daughter of a 'distinguished' man.[45] Writers were invited to join PEN once they had already had some success.[46]

The Lyceum Club was especially important for women because many of the prestigious clubs in London dedicated to the arts and literature were restricted to men (such as The Athenaeum and the Savage Club). The bohemian circles of Sydney, also, were not necessarily accessible to everyone. Members of Sydney society formed clubs such as The Casuals and the Dawn and Dusk Club, but these organisations 'excluded women either deliberately or by meeting in places like bars, that were hard for women to enter'.[47] Women were included only if they used their sexuality, according to Drusilla Modjeska. Sydney-based Nettie Palmer conducted her literary business almost entirely through letters. Just being in these places did not guarantee access to artistic circles.

Even if in London, writers could still be disadvantaged because they lacked essential knowledge about the publishing industry. A writer inexperienced at dealing with British publishers would not necessarily know how to write the kind of work that London publishers were likely to be interested in. Jane Mander described the 'awful rubbish' that could be found in English magazines, but made the point that 'there are experts in rubbish as in everything else', and in order to produce writing that would be accepted a writer needed 'knowledge of the market and the public that no colonial writer can acquire at once'.[48] Some publishers were more likely to be sympathetic to new writers or writing with a colonial setting than others, and it helped to know who they were. Edith Lyttleton's American publisher, Curtice M. Hitchcock (of The Century publishing company), sold the rights of Lyttleton's popular book *Pageant* to Allen & Unwin because of their 'unusually good Colonial connections' and because he expected there would be 'a good colonial return' on the book.[49]

In an industry where contacts were so helpful, another possible stumbling block for the unconnected writer was the process of securing a review. The literary review was a phenomenon that developed during the nineteenth century, and since its arrival on the scene, the power of reviewers to make or break a writer had increased. Some people took this idea to extremes, and 1819 a bad review of Keats in the *Quarterly Review* was 'widely supposed' to have been the cause of his death.[50] Reviewing relied heavily on the whims of the reviewers, and could be a very fickle affair. For example, those in the industry knew it to be unwise to publish a book in the spring: in naming their 'book of the year' at the end of the year, reviewers rarely managed to remember further back than autumn.[51] According to the British novelist Marie Corelli, reviewing was always done by favour.[52] In *London Called Them*,

Ngaere deplores her chances of gaining recognition, saying: 'What chance have I got, or others like me? No influence – no pull anywhere. I don't know any best-seller novelist who'll pull the strings for me, if I do the same for him when his next piece of tripe appears.'[53] In some people's opinion, even a bad review was better than being ignored, as what really counted was being talked about by the 'metropolitan elite' and being the 'gossip of the clubs and dinner tables.'[54] Again, being well-known in society was invaluable for writers, and thus reviewing – or the lack of it – was yet another way in which the impenetrability of London's literary networks hindered new writers.

Professional endorsement was important, and competitions and prizes could 'make' a new writer. Both the United Kingdom and United States publishing industries selected a 'Book of the Month', which could boost sales immediately. Andrew Nash writes: 'In 1928 a Book of the Month [US] selection meant an advance of $500, a minimum order of 35,000 copies and the added benefit of publicity.'[55] The Book Society in the United Kingdom was so powerful it could even control how novels were written. 'In 1932,' writes Nash, 'the Book Society informed Chattos that they would select David Garnett's *Pocahontas* as their monthly choice for January 1933 provided that alterations were made to the opening chapter.'[56] This referred to some troubling scenes of violence, which Garnett obediently removed.

When writers did manage to get their manuscripts accepted, inexperience could again work against them as they tried to negotiate a favourable contract. Unknown writers were in less of a position to bargain, and even successful authors were not guaranteed a healthy profit. Up till the 1890s it was usual for publishers to pay authors a lump sum of £50 to £100 for the whole copyright.[57] In the new century it became more common for authors to negotiate royalty agreements and the process became even more convoluted and open to manipulation.[58] For women this was for some time complicated further by their being unable to sign contracts on their own behalf. New Zealand writer Clara Cheeseman's 1886 contract contained the clause 'In the event of the Author being a Married Lady, this Agreement should be countersigned by her Husband.'[59] As she was unmarried at the time, her brother responded to the contract. New writers risked making a loss if they did not possess the knowledge to prevent this. However, achieving publication was more important than how much a writer made on a first book.

The London literary scene was in some respects a rather impenetrable 'old-boys' club', which made life difficult for emerging authors. An example is the case of New Zealand author Rosemary Rees, who, despite having very convincing evidence, lost a case of plagiarism to Walter and Frederick Melville, who were well-known figures in the dramatic arts. Rees claimed that she had sold her play 'The Beggar Maid' to Walter Melville, who later sold it back to her for the same price, but kept a copy. Several months later he produced 'The Beggar Girl's Wedding', which had almost exactly the same plot. The two plays are summarised in the archives of the Society of Authors in the British Library and are basically identical, barring names and some wording. Surprisingly, however, Rees lost the case, and according to the Court of Appeal judgement, this was because '[i]t is clear that there has not been any deliberate or intentioned copying'.[60] The Melville brothers owned several theatres in London, including the Lyceum Theatre over which they reigned for 30 years.[61] It seems that Rees's word and evidence were not enough to convince the court to rule against members of the literary establishment.

The reality of 'making good' in London was hard. As Felicity Barnes says, 'For many writers, life was harder, and their work was less, in quality or quantity, than they would have liked it to be. The attractions of the metropolis were not necessarily equivalent to its rewards.'[62] Even the most successful of overseas artists had an initial struggle. When Frances Hodgkins left New Zealand to pursue a painting career, she never intended to stay in Europe for more than a year. In the end, she remained there for the rest of her life and became the first New Zealander to have a painting hung 'on the Line' at the Royal Academy of Arts in 1903. It took a great deal of perseverance, however, to get that far. Initially she had many set-backs, such as her failure to infiltrate artistic society in Cornwall. Work she sent to the New English Art Club was, in her words, 'REFUSED, REJECTED – spurned – flouted and returned'.[63] Hodgkins came from an advantageous background: her father was an art teacher and heavily involved in artistic circles. Like Katherine Mansfield, she had every opportunity but still found it difficult to break through in London. Being successful in London was simply very hard work.

In fact, London life was hard for everyone, not just newcomers from the colonies. Unconnected English people, whether moving to London from rural areas, a different city or merely a less fashionable part of the city itself (thus making them not part of the 'right' circles) could also face problems breaking into the literary scene in London. England's deeply entrenched class system created considerable barriers for many people. The British writer Arnold Bennett, for example, came from Burslem, now part of Stoke-on-Trent in Staffordshire, and had to work very hard to gain his later enviable position (he was recently described as 'the JK Rowling of his day'[64]). His social background – he came from a family of provincial shopkeepers – had taught him to see authors, especially metropolitan ones, as 'beings apart and peculiar'.[65] Katherine Mansfield and John Middleton Murry were very much part of the English literary scene by 1917, associating with 'members and friends of the Bloomsbury group: T.S. Eliot, Aldous Huxley, Lytton Strachey, Dorothy Brett, Siegfried Sassoon, the Woolfs, S.S. Koteliansky and Bertrand Russell'. Even then, however, 'Murry, perhaps because of his lower-middle-class background, was often seen as an outsider, as was Mansfield, the colonial'.[66] According to Peter Macdonald, social origin was important: 'Very crudely, for the culturally and socially privileged', involvement in highbrow literary circles was 'like speaking a first language', while, for the more marginalised, it was 'like learning a second late in life'.[67]

Even those firmly within the literary establishment did not necessarily feel that their path was an easy one. Virginia Woolf, it would seem, was the ultimate insider. Her father, Sir Leslie Stephen, as the editor of the *Dictionary of National Biography*, 'had known most eminent authors and journal editors'.[68] She was the centre of what came to be known as the Bloomsbury Group. As a woman, however, she often felt marginalised. In *A Room of One's Own* she described the disenfranchisement she felt when denied access to knowledge because of her gender. Attempting to enter a famous 'Oxbridge' library to consult a Thackeray manuscript, she was intercepted by 'a deprecating, silvery, kindly gentleman, who regretted in a low voice as he waved [her] back that ladies are only admitted to the library if accompanied by a fellow of the college or furnished with a letter of introduction'.[69] Women were also frequently disadvantaged, as mentioned earlier, by being denied access to the meeting places where cultural information was shared, such as clubs. The Royal Colonial Institute, for example, initially admitted men only, though women could join in subordinate positions from 1909.[70]

The term 'exile' originally meant 'banishment to a foreign country', often as a kind of punishment.[71] It is commonly used much more broadly than this: according to the *Oxford English Dictionary*'s longer definition it can mean 'prolonged absence from one's native country or a place regarded as home, endured by force of circumstances or *voluntarily undergone* [my emphasis] for some purpose'.[72] The term gets even more diluted when applied to literary 'exiles', to refer to anyone writing from a marginalised perspective, rendering the term somewhat meaningless. David Bevan, writing on exile, says, 'Exile, viscerally, is difference, otherness':[73] as such, the term has been extended to mean 'all conceivable forms of alienation'.[74] Thus the writing industry of London was peopled heavily with 'exiles'. Virtually everyone was marginalised – if not foreign, they were of the wrong class or the wrong gender.

The perception remained that writers from overseas would find it harder to earn money. Despite the seeming abundance of opportunities, for a writer newly arrived from the other side of the world with no alternative source of income, making any kind of living was difficult. Many people found themselves living much more frugally than they had hoped. In a large city, with no family or friends to help in times of crisis, writers could end up being impoverished unless they had a healthy allowance from home. In a 1924 article on the struggle of the overseas artist in London, Jane Mander advised people not to come over unless they had financial support. She calculated that the minimum cost for a woman living alone in one room in London 'could not be less than four pounds a week in any decent neighbourhood'.[75] It was necessary for writers to avoid boarding houses as they needed peace and solitude to write. Thus, a minimum of £2 out of the £4 went on rent, and for the rest:

> you would get only the cheapest of clothes and the poorest of food in the most sordid of places unless you could cook for yourself. You could never take a taxi. You could occasionally enjoy a theatre from the pit. You could not get out of London for week ends. It would help if you could make your own clothes, do your own washing and cooking, and eliminate all thoughts of having anything beautiful around you, or of entertaining a friend, or of buying books.[76]

Mander was supported by her father while in England, and tried to supplement this with writing and journalism, but admitted in 1924 to being 'hundreds of pounds in debt'.[77]

Monte Holcroft's pilgrimage to London ended in disenchantment, and he mentioned the pitying attitude towards writers from the dominions: 'Another poor devil come to London to starve.'[78] D'Arcy Cresswell resorted to selling his poems door-to-door. He found this 'financially rewarding', as the silver half-crown he could get for a set of poems 'would buy a meal at the diner François (in Old Compton Street), which would last you two days'.[79] When Hector Bolitho met D.H. Lawrence, Lawrence advised him that in order to succeed he must be prepared to leave London and 'be content to live on three pounds a week'.[80] This, like Cresswell's plan of having a meal every two days, was not the glamorous lifestyle Bolitho had in mind. Later, despite his success, he was still pleading poverty, writing to Chatto & Windus: 'I am desperately poor, as ever, and am now swimming manfully ahead on an overdraft'.[81] He complained of his impoverished circumstances, saying his figure was 'not Greek enough' to go about without clothes.[82] Fairburn wrote to Mason from London:

> *If you hear of any bright young souls packing their trunks to come over this way, just be kind to them: grab them by the coat-tails and jerk them back off the gang plank. I heard that Marie and Maud Ballantyne were thinking of coming. Unless they've got a lot of money in their stockings they're damn fools.*[83]

Financial difficulties, however, affected everyone, not just colonials and immigrants. Arnold Bennett was encouraged to enter a *Tit Bits* (magazine) competition, and when he won he began freelancing for this and similar publications (the *Sun*, an evening paper; *Cassell's Family Magazine* and the *English Illustrated*). He made little more than £15 a year doing this and had to supplement his income by working as a clerk. He reported in 1900 that, after covering the costs of having the manuscript typed, his book (*A Man of the North*) had earned him 'the sum of one sovereign'. This was nothing to grumble about, however. '"Many a first book has cost its author a hundred pounds", he noted later. "I got a new hat out of mine."[84] D.H. Lawrence came from very humble beginnings and was forced to give up a scholarship to high school to work in a local factory at the age of 16 in 1901. Fatefully he contracted pneumonia, which forced him to quit his job, resume his education and begin writing. He supported himself through teaching until a gradual build-up of success allowed him to pursue full-time writing from 1911.[85] These well-respected writers were not automatically part of the literary scene and had to work against fairly difficult odds.

To be experimental meant even greater risk of impecuniosity. Even the most highly regarded members of the modernist movement faced impoverished circumstances. Those at the forefront of literary innovation were not the same writers who found themselves on the bestseller lists, at least not in their own time. The mainstream book-buying and book-borrowing public set parameters of profitability for the publishing companies, giving a heavy advantage to books with obvious popular appeal. Libraries that operated on a 'tuppenny' system depended on books being quickly read, and thus preferred to purchase shorter and more undemanding pieces.[86] Libraries were significant consumers of books – Boots Booklovers' Library bought 'over a million books a year' according to chief librarian F.R. Richardson.[87] Andrew Nash notes that leading literary figures, with the exception of E.M. Forster, all had 'uneasy relationships with the market' and had to find alternative channels of publication:

> [D.H.] Lawrence struggled to find a market after the banning of The Rainbow *(1915), and had to publish* Lady Chatterley's Lover *(1928) privately in Florence. [Virginia] Woolf found editorial freedom in a form of self-publication by the Hogarth Press; [T.F.] Powys's most famous novel,* Mr Weston's Good Wine *(1927) was first published in a limited edition; [James] Joyce's* Ulysses *(1922) was published by the specially-created Shakespeare and Company in Paris.*[88]

Continuing into the 1930s, more 'intellectual' books became more accessible through institutions like the Penguin Classics library, which deigned to publish them and sell them at an affordable price. Largely, however, writers wanting to create cutting-edge literature had to occupy a very privileged position or be extremely lucky. Lawrence, Woolf and Joyce all had their most famous books published independently or overseas because mainstream publishers were unwilling to take such risks.

If writers were really to establish themselves in the literary scene, they had to maintain a careful balance between financially profitable work and work that was intellectually interesting. The literati looked down on the lowbrow pursuit of commercial gain and held profit-motivated authors in low esteem. Genuinely highbrow writers had to be indifferent to public tastes and marketable fashions, or at least had to appear that way.[89] In reality almost everyone was a mixture of the 'purist' (interested only in writing for its own sake) and the 'profiteer' (writing to make money).[90] Joseph Conrad had to write saleable short stories to earn money without harming his intellectual integrity. Even when he had broken into the market he still had to find a patron to endorse his work. New Zealand writers faced this same conundrum.

Searching for available outlets for Dan Davin's writing, his wife Winnie (née Gonley) wrote to him:

> I've had a letter from Nancy Pearn which will annoy amuse & I hope please you. She has sold 'The Vigil' – but to 'Good Housekeeping' – but for six guineas. She realises that you will probably have mixed feelings about this, but as you know her policy is to build up as wide an audience for your future stuff as possible, & this high-class Women's mag. certainly has circulation. Also the fee is excellent, isn't it?[91]

Winnie was aware that *Good Housekeeping* was not Dan's ideal outlet for his work, but, practically speaking, all avenues had to be pursued. Other, less discriminating writers might have been quite satisfied with an arrangement like this, however.

Writers, wherever they were, often felt the need to protect their egos by blaming their environment (including their location) for their lack of success. When they were in New Zealand they blamed their distance from the springs of culture in places like London, but when in London they blamed British publishers, the snobbish attitude of the English and the 'closed' London literary scene. Hector Bolitho was successful, and though this was helped along by the reputation he gained by accompanying the Prince of Wales on a tour of Australia, as Robin Hyde said this 'would have meant nothing ... had he not been prepared to work as few New Zealand writers, largely though they talk, would ever dream of doing'.[92] Many writers thought that what was holding them back was the lack of opportunities available in New Zealand. What they did not admit or even realise was that, through the colonial writing world, they had access to almost all of these opportunities without leaving the country. This meant that unless they were exceptionally lucky or well connected, they were not necessarily advantaged by going to London. While the idea that they needed to leave New Zealand to be successful writers was a myth, so was the idea that in many cases replaced it – that it was the particular difficulties encountered by colonial writers overseas that prevented them from enjoying the success they envisaged. Some returned home disillusioned and attributed the success of others to their selling out in some way, perhaps by abandoning their principles or their former identity.

CHAPTER EIGHT

Setting the Thames on fire

A number of New Zealand writers managed to successfully immerse themselves in British or European literary circles while remaining connected to New Zealand writers and writing. Nelle Scanlan, for example, kept company with a long list of literary notables through her involvement with London society and the group PEN. At one point she was asked to tea by John Galsworthy, largely because he wanted to talk about his visit to New Zealand.[1] Jane Mander was also well connected and lived in Paris for a time while reading manuscripts for the owners of a small press who were 'friends with Gertrude Stein and Ernest Hemingway'. This was living 'la vie bohème', according to Alex Calder: 'the kind of existence now memorialised for tourists by the Shakespeare Bookshop or the Chelsea Hotel'.[2] At the same time, Mander continued to write articles for the Christchurch and Auckland *Sun* newspapers.[3] Both she and Scanlan eventually returned to New Zealand, continuing their involvement in bookish society there. Edith Searle Grossmann successfully established herself on her own in London after escaping a difficult marriage. As well as engaging in British literary circles, she embraced colonial networks both in London and those that connected her to the New Zealand literary scene. She continued to contribute to New Zealand publications such as the *New Zealand Illustrated Magazine* and the *Auckland Star*, and topics 'relating to New Zealand remained favourites'.[4] New Zealand writers did not have to choose between their New Zealand connections and engagement with overseas literary scenes: while they did not necessarily greatly improve their situation by making the journey, they were not especially disadvantaged as a result of being New Zealanders.

In the same way that writers were able to write in New Zealand and publish their work using colonial networks, so too could they write and remain connected to literary goings-on in New Zealand while overseas. Despite what the proponents of literary nationalism would have us believe, physical location is not all that important for literary production. Writing is less affected by location than other artistic pursuits, and thus 'expatriatism' has less impact on New Zealand writing than assumed. This is because of the portable nature of a writer's work, as Ngaio Marsh pointed out in her entry on 'Expatriates' in the 1966 *Encyclopaedia of New Zealand*. She wrote:

> *Writers are in a different class. A writer is the most solitary of craftsmen and the most self-contained. Whether, like James Courage, he works and publishes in England, or whether, like the best of our poets, he stays in New Zealand, his books appear and are read in both countries by people whom they are likely to please. Janet Frame lives in England and writes about New Zealand.*[5]

Jane Mander echoed these sentiments in her novel *The Strange Attraction*, set in New Zealand:

> *A book is a book, and a boat a boat, and a fire a fire all the world over. And then this business of being in the swim in London or Paris or New York is only another of the hypnotisms men succumb to to please themselves. It isn't as important to live in London as they think it is.*[6]

Concern about the physical location of authors came from the mid-twentieth-century adoption of nationalism as the driving force behind all cultural history worthy of notice. Although modern critics have left this behind, the legacy of this preoccupation is certain persistent assumptions about the negative experiences of literary 'expatriates' in Britain. This concern disappears when we use the 'colonial writing world' model.

Although it was common to hear complaints about the difficulties of writing in the frantic environment of London, it was just as common to hear complaints of isolation and quiet being barriers to working. Jane Mander had been one of the main proponents of this view, protesting about life in 'sense-stultifying' New Zealand,[7] but changed her mind after going to London. Monte Holcroft took an extended holiday in the New Zealand countryside in 1934 so he could concentrate on his writing. Before long, however, he was writing to Ursula Bethell saying that it was too peaceful and he was unable to work (preferring the more urban environs of Christchurch):

It really begins to seem that I shall have to let everything go until I return to Chch. There was a sort of [asceticism] in my life there that helped me to write. And while I was there, of course, I complained against the lack of food and rest and longed for the kind of life I am having now. Aren't we impossible creatures?[8]

Dan Davin complained of 'culturally barren' New Zealand, but while enduring his first northern-hemisphere winter he turned his criticisms on England, finding that the 'food was bad, the cities filthy, the people intolerable, the culture shallow'.[9] In general, writers were capable of complaining wherever they were. As A.R.D. Fairburn wrote to R.A.K. Mason in 1931: 'As far as I can make out, there seems to be a universal belief held by every mother's son that he would be perfectly happy if he was somewhere else but where he is now. The whole world's infected.'[10] This suggests it was something other than location that determined writers' success.

The location of the author did not greatly affect their productivity as measured by book publication. Table 8.1 shows the place of publication of books by New Zealand authors between 1890 and 1945, sorted by the location of the author immediately before publication. Books have been omitted where the author's location is not known, as have the 120 novels of Fergus Hume.[11] 505 books are included in the table.

Table 8.1: Books by location of author and place of publication

Place of publication	Location of author					
	NZ	UK	Aus	US	Europe	Total
NZ	214	1	1	0	0	**216**
UK	116	95	19	3	4	**237**
Aus	13	0	27	0	0	**40**
US	4	2	1	4	0	**11**
Europe	0	0	0	0	1	**1**
Total	**347**	**98**	**48**	**7**	**5**	**505**

Writers who had books published in the United Kingdom were likely to be located in New Zealand or the United Kingdom, with slightly more in New Zealand. 116 books were published in the United Kingdom while the author was in New Zealand (23 per cent of the total number of publications), as opposed to 95 (19 per cent) while the author was in the United Kingdom. Overall, the location of the author did not greatly affect the likelihood of getting a book published in the United Kingdom. While the largest proportion of books (214, or 42 per cent of the total) were those published in New Zealand by writers who remained in New Zealand, most of these were books of poetry. Table 8.2 shows the figures just for novels.

Table 8.2: Novels by location of author and place of publication

Place of publication	Location of author					
	NZ	UK	Aus	US	Europe	Total
NZ	26	0	0	0	0	**26**
UK	77	72	17	3	0	**169**
Aus	5	0	13	0	0	**18**
US	4	2	1	2	0	**9**
Europe	0	0	0	0	0	**0**
Total	**112**	**74**	**31**	**5**	**0**	**222**

The figure for books published in New Zealand while the author was in New Zealand has reduced dramatically: just 26 out of a total of 222 novels (12 per cent). However, the proportion of books published in the United Kingdom remains similar. This is not surprising, as novel publishing was not well advanced in New Zealand, while it was relatively easy to get a small run of a book of poetry published locally (often subsidised by the author). Moreover, the restricted market for poetry made it difficult for large overseas firms to take an interest in it. In the case of novels published in the United Kingdom, however, there is little difference between the figures for New Zealand-based authors and United Kingdom-based authors – 77 and 72 respectively. This indicates that the location of the author was not nearly as important as other factors, such as the place the book was published.

While New Zealanders did not necessarily gain an advantage by going to London, they were not disadvantaged either. Some were extremely productive while overseas, and had successful careers based mostly in London. They included Edith Lyttleton, Nelle Scanlan, Rosemary Rees and Ngaio Marsh. Jane Mander, despite being one of the most vocal in her complaints about the difficulties of being a colonial writer in London, wrote her second and third novels in New York, and the next three while in London. She wrote only her first novel while in New Zealand, taking the manuscript with her when she left. D'Arcy Cresswell produced many of his published poems while wandering in England. Many writers enjoyed relative success in London due to individual talent, luck and/or the employment of various coping mechanisms. What one writer considered 'success' may not have satisfied another's criteria. Generally speaking, however, success in the form of publication and recognition hinged on the ability to capitalise on opportunities or novelties they could exploit rather than proximity to literary infrastructure, and New Zealanders were just as likely to break through the barriers as anyone else.

The obstacles to literary production and publication were not insurmountable. The techniques employed by writers 'on the ground' in London were not all that different from those of the writers who remained in New Zealand or far away: they still revolved around a combination of talent, tenacity and good luck. Even writers based in London often found it necessary to use an agent. The expanding marketplace and rising number of professional authors led to the employment of experienced negotiators to act in the authors' interests. A.P. Watt was the first to work as a literary agent, with others like J.B. Pinker following in his footsteps. Pinker represented a number of literary notables, including Oscar Wilde, Joseph Conrad, H.G. Wells, Henry James and D.H. Lawrence, and was 'initially regarded by London's publishers with fear and suspicion'.[12] He also represented several New Zealand authors, such as Katherine Mansfield and Edith Lyttleton. Jane Mander advised Monte Holcroft to get an agent, as she had found this very useful. In a letter to him in 1933 she recommended her agent, Leonard Moore (who also represented George Orwell). Moore was able to advise her on which publishers to approach, an important consideration since there were 'certain publishers to whom it would be quite hopeless to send' New Zealand or colonial material.[13]

Edith Lyttleton's disillusion with agents and publishers' transnational dealings meant she dispensed with them altogether while in London. She wrote in 1933: 'When I came to live in London I found that I could do very much better for myself without an agent, and in three years I had contracts with all the magazines I could write for, and had raised my prices from 7 guineas a story to 7 or 8 guineas a thousand words.'[14] Lyttleton's complaints about her British agent, J.B. Pinker, were perhaps unfair: according to Terry Sturm, Pinker was 'assiduous in carrying out her wishes and promoting her interests'.[15] Lyttleton was immensely successful by this stage and very experienced in dealing with editors and publishers. In most cases it would seem an agent was helpful for those with less experience, whatever their background.

Even for London-based writers, letters were still a primary form of communication, although they could result from actual meetings, or facilitate them. These methods required a certain level of persistence. Though established writers complained of the swathes of letters they got from third-rate poets hoping to win their support, some hopeful writers used this method with success.[16] Hector Bolitho wrote to G.K. Chesterton: 'I met you once, at a garden party, so I feel that I may begin in this way.'[17] D'Arcy Cresswell approached T.E. Lawrence by letter, and was pleased to receive a reply: 'I was delighted to get back and find you had answered so promptly. Ede said you didn't even open your letters for weeks … if my first letter was somewhat pompous, it was because I feared you might snub me.'[18] Cresswell's generally assertive approach, which included selling his poems door to door, seemed to work well, for despite the disputed quality of his poetry he returned home with a reputation as a 'man of letters'.[19]

Unknown writers required tenacity when approaching publishers. Moving in literary circles for a while could help, but success was largely reliant on confidence and determination. Hector Bolitho had never written a novel before, but managed to secure publication on the strength of his non-fiction work. Accompanying his manuscript of *Solemn Boy*, which he sent to Chatto & Windus, was a letter, which said:

> *I have had two or three unimportant books published – the main one the history of the Princes [sic] antipodean tour. I accompanied him.*
> *In Australia, Africa & N.Z., I have a 'name' as a writer: my last book sold 4800 copies in N.Z. & Australia & my newspaper stories & articles are always featured. I mention this because I am confident of a good sale of a novel in these countries, in all of which I have edited newspapers &*

magazines. In England I write for 'The Times', Manchester 'Guardian',
'Country Life' etc.

> *If you consider the novel has any merit, I'd like the opportunity of talking*
> *over the possibility of publication with you as there are certain reasons why I*
> *am assured a successful sale: too complex to explain in a letter.*[20]

This approach reveals a self-assurance that most new writers would not have possessed, whether they were in London or not. It had the desired effect, and the book was published.

Experience could also allow writers to overcome the obstacles that the review process provided, but again, this was more down to confidence and contacts than proximity. It helped to know how the system worked – some writers or publishers prearranged reviews of their books in sympathetic publications, evidence of which is 'not difficult to gather', according to Philip Waller.[21] Hector Bolitho was an experienced campaigner, and when *Solemn Boy* was published by Chatto & Windus, he sent them very strict and detailed instructions on which publications to send review copies to:

> *I am sending you herewith 7 letters to personal friends on New Zealand*
> *newspapers, also a list of other papers to whom I think you should send*
> *review copies. A similar list for Australia will follow. I am enclosing also two*
> *typed copies of another article on my book which your press representative*
> *might be able to place outside London. I am already making arrangements*
> *for the article to appear in London. [She] might have a number of copies*
> *done and send it to Provincial papers.*[22]

Bolitho was very confident of making colonial sales and possessed a vast amount of knowledge about how to use the facilities of the colonial writing world to his advantage. He is justly described as the 'king of expatriate networking' by Felicity Barnes.[23]

For someone less well-connected and less experienced it was more difficult. Margaret Escott attempted to exert her influence when her book *Show Down* was published, but could only come up with one suggestion: 'I have a friend who seems to know a great many people in the writing world, & although my name alone would convey nothing to them, if she added a personal note, this might do a [bit of] good.'[24] Perhaps as a result, *Show Down* was not a success initially. Harold Raymond of Chatto & Windus replied to Escott's letter saying that the novel was selling very slowly. The book had sold 450 copies, and 100 of these went to an agent in Canada.[25] The letters reveal that Escott wrote another book which she submitted for publication to Chatto & Windus, called 'Face to Face'. The book was put through four separate readers, as Raymond obviously wanted to help, but despite saying that 'all of us very much admire portions of the book', he ended with, 'I am sorry to say that we do not feel we could get away with it'.[26] Soon after the publication of *Show Down* Escott returned to New Zealand via Australia and never published anything else, although *Show Down* did eventually enjoy modest success. In her case, being in London did not prove helpful.

Some female New Zealand writers deliberately concealed their gender to help their chances of publication and success, as women writers were taken less seriously than men and could be limited to certain genres. Edith Lyttleton was better known as G.B. Lancaster, and with this gender-ambiguous name many people were not aware that she was a woman. A 1904 review of *Sons o' Men* in the *Times Literary Supplement* referred to her as 'Mr. Lancaster'.[27] She used this pseudonym, however, mainly because her family deeply disapproved of her writerly profession. We cannot know how being known as a woman would have affected her sales: the rustic, pioneering world she wrote about might have been perceived as unbecoming subject-matter for a woman. In reviews of her early books, *A Spur to Smite* and *Sons o' Men*, about rough working life in New Zealand and Australia, words such as 'virile', 'forcible', 'strong' and 'masterful' recurred again and again.[28] She was more likely to be criticised for lack of 'authenticity' if known to be a woman, as in an *Evening Post* review which praised her descriptions of scenery but said: 'If she could only depict the "sons o' men" themselves as faithfully, she would scarce have a rival in contemporary fiction'.[29] Others expressed incredulity that a woman could have written such material.

For some, concealing their gender was a more deliberate ploy to achieve publication. Jessie Weston, who wrote the New Zealand novel *Ko Meri: A story of New Zealand life* in 1890, travelled to England to publish it and once there became an established journalist writing on politics and for military magazines under the name 'C. de Thierry'. Only her editor knew she was a woman.[30] It is less likely that she would have been received seriously as a writer on these topics if her gender had been known.

Again, proximity did not help with this technique – concealing gender would have been easier from a distance. Most of the examples described here of writers' techniques to achieve publication would have worked at least equally as well by letter if the writer were located elsewhere. A writer could still strike up a correspondence with a well-known author, or send off their manuscript, from overseas. There might have been some advantage to being 'known' if able to attend literary and social events, but being published and reviewed in important newspapers was probably more useful.

Writers did not face a particular disadvantage because of being New Zealanders if they were able to use some of these techniques or employ contacts. Some writers did well in London and were able to learn the art of writing for money. Jane Mander complained of the volumes of 'expert rubbish' that English writers produced, but also said that 'it is quite true that once you have learned the knack of writing the popular short story you can make a living out of it'. Describing these sort of stories as 'machine-made', she credited Edith Lyttleton with being an 'old hand' at this process.[31] In a 1905 *Bulletin* article, Arthur H. Adams wrote of his experience with such techniques: '[I]t took me exactly eighteen months to get down to the level where I could see things from the English point of view. It isn't necessary to write from that point of view; it is essential to find out what it is, and allow for it'.[32]

It was certainly possible for New Zealand writers to have warm receptions from the literary community, whether they renounced or declared their origins. John Brodie, who wrote under the pseudonym John Guthrie, had a largely positive experience in London. Rhonda Bartle writes:

> As for the rewards of writing, Brodie declared there was not much in the way of money, but 'a great deal in the feeling of attainment and a share in the life of literary London'. Among his notes ... are warm letters from such contemporary leading literary lights as Monica Dickens, Godfrey Winn, Somerset Maugham, Compton McKenzie, John Galsworthy and Siegfried Sassoon.[33]

Nelle Scanlan was also received amicably, and when she arrived in London she reported she already had 'a fair number of invitations'.[34] She was asked to a reception at the Duchess of Norfolk's house virtually as soon as she disembarked, and that same year was 'invited to a garden party at Buckingham Palace for the first time'.[35]

Some writers found their niche in England and stayed there. Hector Bolitho became a royal biographer and was invited by the Dean of Windsor to live in the cloisters of Windsor Castle. Robin Hyde was moved to write this poem about him:

When asked why he lived at the Deanery
Said Hector, 'I add to the scenery –
And the wily Yankee
If his luck's in, may see
Me peer like a faun through the greenery.'[36]

H.B. Marriott Watson moved to England in 1885 after being educated from the age of nine in New Zealand. He went on to write 43 'undistinguished but versatile novels',[37] but only one, *The Web of the Spider*, was about New Zealand.

Other writers also did well, but their stories are seldom well known. The reason for the longevity of the idea of the beleaguered 'expatriate' is that literary history is all too often based on colourful hearsay and complaints originating from frustrated authors, and not on empirical evidence. The story of David McClelland, who wrote under the name David Lynn, is a remarkable counter-example to this idea. John A. Lee, who reprinted McClelland's book in 1946, described him as '[t]he sensationally successful New Zealand writer, who landed in London penniless and ended by writing, publishing and selling his own novels, and as a result made a vast amount of money. He made £2,000 out of this book *Love and Hunger*, which is of rough, tough, raw-edged life.'[38] As Rowan Gibbs points out, however, there is very little other information available about McClelland, despite his publishing some 28 books in total. Like McClelland, many of the more prolific writers who went to the United Kingdom actually published more while they were there than at home in New Zealand.

The stories of writers who did well, like David McClelland, are generally ignored in favour of those who complained bitterly about the trials and tribulations of surviving in London. On occasion the successes of writers in England went unreported in New Zealand, as in the previously mentioned case of Isabel Maud Peacocke, whose writing was not well known in New Zealand due to poor distribution arrangements.[39] One of the main reasons that New Zealanders were not true 'exiles' was that they remained part of the colonial writing world. It was those who complained the most bitterly who also complained the loudest, and it seems their versions of events were the most often recorded. In fact the colonial writing world afforded them some advantages.

One possible advantageous by-product of relocating to London was that high productivity and acquiescence to the demands of the market were required in order to survive, as writers were less likely to have familial assistance to fall back on. This might explain why some writers were more productive in England – for some, their years there were exceptionally productive. This becomes clear if we look at the publication records of seven of the most prolific writers who spent considerable periods there. Louisa Baker, Edith Lyttleton, Jane Mander, Ngaio Marsh, Katherine Mansfield, Rosemary Rees and Nelle Scanlan collectively spent 131 years in the United Kingdom between 1890 and 1945 as adults. During this time they wrote (and had published) a total of 48 books. By contrast, during their combined 115 years in New Zealand they wrote just 22 books. That is a rate of 0.37 books per year in England, as opposed to 0.19 per year in New Zealand.

If literary productiveness can be quantified in terms of the number of books produced per year, writers who spent four or more years in the United Kingdom produced an average of 0.19 books per year. In New Zealand, however, writers produced 0.11 books per year.[40] These figures are only approximate, however, due to the transient lives of some of the featured writers.

These figures seem to indicate that London was better for writers in terms of productivity, though D'Arcy Cresswell, Denis Glover, Charles Brasch, Ngaio Marsh and Ursula Bethell were more productive in New Zealand. However, this increased productivity might be because some of these writers were going to England for a relatively short period in an attempt to succeed as writers, and would have expended the most effort during this time. Over their entire career, these years in a new place might represent the years of greatest determination. The time overseas is less likely to include the years of old age (although a few writers began their writing later on in life), or, for women, their time raising children. When the lengths of writers' trips are examined, writers who spent between two and five years in the United Kingdom had the highest rate of book production.[41] It was perhaps these shorter trips that generated the most enthusiasm for producing books. All this bears out the suggestion that a group of writers spent a few 'writing years' in the United Kingdom before returning to 'normal life'. Those who stayed in Britain long-term returned to 'normal life' there and their productivity declined, just as it did in the case of writers who returned to New Zealand. Short-term success could be explained by increased motivation rather than the benefits of being close to publishing houses.

Whatever the measures of success, the picture of unsuccessful colonial writers was in many cases incorrect, and this inaccuracy was compounded by the fact that the difficulties inherent in having to pursue publication in London were over-emphasised by those with a nationalist agenda. John Barnes cites the example of Henry Lawson, who made negative comments about Australian writers leaving for England before making the journey himself. Lawson's largely positive experiences in London were overshadowed by the 'received interpretation of [his] venture to the imperial centre' by later nationalists like Vance Palmer and A.A. Phillips, who turned it into a negative experience.[42] John Barnes also acknowledges that Lawson's poem lampooning the effects of British publishing on Australian writing, 'A Song of Southern Writers', was written several years before he went to England, after which his attitudes changed.[43]

Discrepancies could exist between writers' perceptions of their circumstances and experience, and incontrovertible biographical details. Holcroft was negative about his time in London, causing his biographer to write: 'A bleak period followed. The market for popular magazine fiction was declining and the competition for publication overwhelming; London was cold and aloof; and the reception of the romantic melodrama *Beyond the Breakers* and his second novel, *The Flameless Fire* (1929), was indifferent.'[44] However, Holcroft actually wrote two of his three published novels in this short three-year stint in England. Obviously he had grander expectations than mere publication.

New Zealanders did not *have* to go overseas to succeed, but they could succeed overseas without foregoing their ties to New Zealand. In fact, rather than being their downfall, New Zealanders' difference quite often proved to be an advantage, and maintaining their colonial writing world connections was often lucrative. This is completely at odds with the idea that distancing oneself from one's national origin was the only way to be successful. Being different, but not too different (they were not a 'visible', non-white, minority[45]) gave New Zealanders a point of distinction that they took advantage of. Their special status meant there were opportunities open only to them. Jane Mander said:

> One does not have to be a Londoner long to be able to pick out the outsiders.
> I do not mean the obvious foreigners, like the Hindoo law students ... I

mean rather the Empire visitors, who come branded with a different cast of face, freer movements, a less blasé air, and varied intonations. One can pick them anywhere.[46]

Being not quite foreign but not quite British meant New Zealanders and Australians had a unique position. If in some respects they were outsiders, this actually served them well, as they enjoyed more freedom than their British counterparts. Perhaps because of their scarcity in numbers, or else their relatively recent appearance on the English scene, New Zealanders had the advantage of occupying a unique position in English society, outside the standard class divisions. This was particularly true for women, as they found themselves outside the usual strict British codes of conduct, whose rules were not always applied to colonials in London. Colonial women, for example, had greater freedom to move around than their English counterparts, for an unmarried genteel English lady under 30 'could not go anywhere or be in a room even in her own house with an unrelated man unless accompanied by a married gentlewoman or a servant.'[47] Thus Virginia Woolf could be envious of Katherine Mansfield's freedom (though at the same time Mansfield was envious of Woolf's 'settled domesticity'). Certainly the distance from the constraints of familial disapproval could give them greater freedom (although some, such as Edith Lyttleton, brought these constraints with them).

While Felicity Barnes talks of New Zealanders' ability to overcome their somewhat ambiguous status as white colonials in London, replacing this with 'a form of metropolitan superiority,'[48] in fact it was their colonial status, and membership of the colonial writing world, that allowed them to function in a special way, with more freedom than the locals. New Zealanders and Australians were less accustomed to the more rigid class structure of Britain. The idea that New Zealand was a classless society was of course an exaggeration, but class barriers in New Zealand were more permeable and rendered less effective by egalitarian ideology. Rather than being intuitively constrained by their origins, then, New Zealanders were more likely to approach people and demand attention. Dan Davin's novel *The Sullen Bell* speaks of these 'confident colonials' who had come to conquer London, and who were 'sure that because they didn't have to stick to the rules they would get all the breaks'.[49] When D'Arcy Cresswell and Hector Bolitho wrote their daring and unsolicited letters to T.E. Lawrence and G.K. Chesterton, with whom they were not personally acquainted, they were exhibiting this tendency to ignore the conventions of English society.

Not being as strictly bound by convention gave New Zealanders more options, but sometimes their lack of knowledge or respect for convention could cause problems. An Australian reporter mentioned the little, unimportant things that Australians were not too precise about but were 'life and death' to a respectable Englander. He wrote: 'I remember one of us was sent to interview the Marquis of Salisbury at Hatfield. He went in a soft hat. Several personages were deeply pained.'[50] Australians and New Zealanders often shared a healthy disregard for such intricacies of custom.

New Zealanders, whether they liked it or not, belonged to a special club, and the prerequisite for membership was merely being associated with New Zealand. If stranded in London without contacts or support networks, New Zealanders were fortunate to have the option of grouping together with other visitors from the colonies. These antipodean networks included Australians, and this gave them the numbers required to function effectively, though New Zealanders were reportedly 'thick as peas' in London in 1902.[51] The networks provided colonials with support and advice from people facing the same obstacles as they did. Networks of London-based New Zealanders and Australians were so prevalent they were dubbed 'Anglo-Colonia'. Plumridge writes: 'Advice about "ways and means" was always shared among expatriates and intending expatriates ... there was a very high degree of this sort of informal sharing of information and networking among expatriates.'[52]

These networks began on the university campuses, in particular Edinburgh. In 1890 the Australasian Club there numbered 120, of whom 27 were New Zealanders. Fourteen years later, the New Zealanders were in the majority.[53] These were probably all men, though the first female undergraduates began at Edinburgh in 1892. Such networks were often utilised or even begun by New Zealand scholars overseas. J.C. Beaglehole went to London on a postgraduate scholarship, and for him '[f]ellow students – Australians, North Americans, a South African – provided intellectual stimulation, a diverse range of interests and lively company. He was less enthusiastic about the English, though there were exceptions.'[54] The group studying at Oxford found more companionship with working-class or grammar-school people than with those who had attended public schools, and grouped together with the other New Zealanders, although John Mulgan did seem to be reluctant to do this. They decided to resurrect 'the Hongi Club (an Auckland import – beer and talk, after sport)'.[55] These colonial networks would serve them well later in their careers.

The networks of Anglo-Colonia also functioned around clubs, notably the Lyceum, the Austral, and the Australian and New Zealand Luncheon Club. The Lyceum Club was founded by Constance Smedley as a meeting place for professional women and located in Piccadilly. It became 'one of the most prestigious and influential women's clubs of the early twentieth century'.[56] The Lyceum had a New Zealand Circle, of which Edith Searle Grossmann was a founding member. She also urged Australasian authors trying to make a name for themselves in Britain to join a club or the Society of Authors, arguing that the difficulties in finding a publisher were 'doubled for a colonial'.[57] Here Grossmann acted as 'New Zealand's literary spokeswoman', and at the club's Colonial Circle dinner she sometimes gave readings of the work of her New Zealand friends, including Jessie Mackay, Edith Lyttleton and Blanche Baughan. Through her involvement with the Lyceum she 'was most likely responsible for bringing these artists to public attention in London'.[58] The Lyceum Club actively tried to encourage colonial writers, at times holding literary competitions and inviting submissions of unpublished work from overseas.[59] The New Zealand Society was formed in 1927 as a dining club.[60]

While Anglo-Colonia provided the means for Australasians to meet each other and exchange information, publications like the *British-Australasian* enabled New Zealanders and Australians to publish their addresses. This weekly magazine also provided information about the comings and goings of antipodeans in the United Kingdom and Europe. For example, on 29 March 1906 it reported the arrival of the Beauchamps to collect their daughters,[61] one of whom was Katherine Mansfield. The 'Anglo New Zealand' section reported in 1906 that 'Miss B.E. Baughan, of Bank's Peninsula, is on a five or six months' visit to this country. Miss Baughan used to live here some years ago, but after two visits to the colony, she has decided to make her home in New Zealand.'[62] Another weekly newspaper, *New Zealand News UK*, was established in 1927.

New Zealand House was often a first port of call for New Zealanders in London, and many had their mail sent there. It was not uncommon to run into an acquaintance while visiting. Jane Mander commented that 'the Strand [home to the New Zealand and other colonial high commissions] is known in the summer as the Dominion Promenade'.[63] New Zealand House was designed as an institution to make New Zealanders at home in London, with 'facilities for travellers', 'reception and reading rooms, a library and poste restante service'. The House also functioned as a sort of bank for servicemen on leave. Denis Glover related that he was able to get a loan of five pounds there provided he filled in a form. He recounted that he was not allowed to write 'to carry on drinking until leave has expired' under 'Reasons for wanting this loan', and had to come up with something more suitable.[64] Where a New Zealand embassy was not available, a British one functioned in much the same way. Nelle Scanlan wrote: 'I always presented my credentials at the British Embassy wherever I went (New Zealand had few embassies in those days), and I found them most helpful.'[65]

The support and networks provided by Anglo-Colonia were invaluable, although New Zealand and Australian writers could find themselves in an 'involuntary ghetto'.[66] The colonial writing world thus solved the main problem overseas writers supposedly faced: being alienated from one's community. In many ways this gave them advantages over non-antipodean others who were in the United Kingdom but without ready-made networks, as the networks of Anglo-Colonia were so widespread and easily accessible.

Anglo-Colonia was particularly important because many new arrivals had unrealistic expectations of the reception they would get from the British. They assumed their status as displaced Britons would mean their automatic acceptance, because they had been raised on the idea that they had a special place in the regard of British people and a privileged place at the heart of the empire. A writer in the *Press* in 1927, for example, claimed that living in Christchurch prepared one for England, and enabled one to feel quite at home at 'Home'. New Zealand was the youngest of England's colonies, he said, 'and perhaps for those reasons alone a little dearer to the mother's heart'.[67] New Zealanders' immersion in British culture also led them to believe it would be a seamless transition if they did visit.

In actual fact, Britons were often indifferent to New Zealanders rather than welcoming them as 'one of their own', and were certainly unaware of the 'special' relationship that the latter believed they shared. Fairburn wrote bitterly to Mason in 1931:

> *It's so ridiculous when you come over to the Mother Country and find Mum smiling cynically at little Tommy's innocence. All those [things] we worship in N.Z. – patriotism, the Flag, Imperial ties (sorry – 'Bonds of Empire'), &*

so-on, are sneered at by a good many Englishmen, and taken lightly (oh, so lightly) by the rest. They realise their small importance.[68]

Felicity Barnes cites the example of World War I nurse Ella Cooke, who wrote heatedly:

As regards my opinion of English people it's quite altered now that I have lived amongst them. They seem to think the people in the colonies are not up to much and really don't know anything nevertheless at a time like this they ought to send all the men they can to defend England.[69]

According to Plumridge, the British were 'magnificently unaware' of the actual details of the colonies. They could even be downright prejudiced against colonials. She relates that the 'situation had somewhat improved since the 1870s, when any colonial was automatically blackballed from London clubs as a "cad", but there was still in the 1890s a mild contempt'.[70] Monte Holcroft felt that it was 'chastening to go abroad and discover how small a place these islands occupy in the seas that surround them and in the minds of continental people'.[71]

Americans were even less aware of New Zealanders' existence, but this actually worked in New Zealanders' favour – they enjoyed a special status because they were unusual enough to be interesting. Some found that this afforded them exclusive opportunities when in America. As a New Zealander in Washington, Nelle Scanlan was something of a novelty, was invited to speak at literary luncheons, and as a result became very well-connected. She went to the United States to participate in a conference as a journalist, and was initially involved in literary circles because of this. Scanlan was astonished at the ease with which social success found her, as when the British ambassador invited her to the embassy. She wrote to her family, 'It is all so wonderful, so unexpected, so undeserved – it bewilders me ... I haven't done a single thing to get this publicity – it has been absolutely thrust upon me – a sort of literary Cinderella business'.[72] She was also a clever manipulator: when speaking of a man who had an interest she did not reciprocate, she said: 'I don't think there is any chance of him doing much for me on the way to Washington – if I go, but he may be useful there. I haven't decided yet'.[73] Her success was probably at least partly the result of opportunistic use of the novelty value that New Zealanders enjoyed.

New Zealanders were also of interest to people overseas because of the social experiments the country had been involved in. Speaking of her time at Columbia University in New York, Jane Mander said:

> Before I had been very long at the university I was quite a pet, as I was the first New Zealand student to go there and somebody told the suffrage leader Mrs Carrie Chapman Catt about me. The full [thing] of the suffrage campaign for women was on there as it was in England, and Mrs Catt asked me to speak for her.[74]

As a result of their success in the US, Scanlan and Mander found they were easily included in London literary society when they continued on there. The connections that Scanlan made in the United States served her well across the Atlantic, as she was able to use her contacts. When she went to London, she got a book published and was invited to become a member of PEN in London as 'Herman Ould, the secretary, wrote to me and invited me to join'.[75]

New Zealanders' 'special' status deriving from their relative lack of numbers could allow advancement. So, while some found being labelled as 'colonial' caused difficulties, sometimes the opposite could be true. Forrestina Ross observed that the metropolis held 'many Aladdin's caves [for which] there is an open sesame in London in the password, "the Colonies"'.[76] Merely being a New Zealander could open doors like this. The reason Hector Bolitho was invited to tea with John Middleton Murry was only because, he said, he came from the same country as Murry's wife, Katherine Mansfield, who had died the previous January.[77] John Mulgan and Dan Davin got their advantageous jobs with Clarendon and Oxford University presses at least partly because they were from New Zealand. They were headhunted while still at Oxford by Kenneth Sisam, a New Zealander who presided over recruitment at the press and was keen on the idea of creating a posse of clever New Zealanders.[78] Dorothea Turner speculates that Jane Mander's successful application for admission to the new Columbia School of Journalism in New York was 'bolster[ed]' by her nationality because of what New Zealanders stood for as 'leaders in social legislation'.[79] Eric Baume wrote: 'I found in Europe that being a New Zealander and an Australian was a great help because they respected our individual point of view'.[80]

Though some New Zealand writers complained that they were disadvantaged as outsiders, in a lot of cases New Zealanders were the very insiders being complained about. Ngaere in Isabel Maud Peacocke's work echoes Jane Mander in claiming to be unable to compete with Oxbridge graduates, creating a picture of exile within the metropolis. Yet in some cases, the so-called exiled New Zealand writers were these very same Oxford graduates. James McNeish's group of 'exiles' consisted entirely of people who had attended Oxford, including Dan Davin and John Mulgan. James Courage and Charles Brasch also graduated from Oxford. Davin and Mulgan both had insider careers in the literary world (though Mulgan's was cut short by his early death). Davin in particular presided over a healthy network of New Zealand notables over whom he and his wife Winnie would hold court at the local Gardeners Arms in Oxford. Study somewhere like Oxford was likely to open up further opportunities. Davin, while there, 'crystallised his ambition to be a writer, beginning work on his first novel'.[81] Writers might not always have achieved everything they wanted while in England, but this was not the result of their being outsiders or exiles.

New Zealanders' novelty value extended to the selling power of their work, and they had access to an entire genre that was not available to non-colonials. As mentioned earlier, New Zealand material was a popular subset of a staple of the colonial writing world: the colonial exotic. The relocation of writers overseas did not stop them from writing about New Zealand, and doing so could actually enhance their chances of publication. Even in the case of poetry, which was notoriously difficult to sell to publishers, New Zealand content sometimes had a special appeal. For D'Arcy Cresswell, in England selling poems door-to-door, one '"sales technique" was to declare himself to be a "New Zealand poet"'.[82]

Almost all of the writers I have mentioned in this chapter created work in a New Zealand setting, or with colonial characters in an English setting. Rather than ceasing to be New Zealand writers when they left, many found that moving to England did not change the fact that they wanted to write about New Zealand, and they continued to do this, while functioning as part of the colonial writing world. Jane Mander said that 'there is no prejudice here, I find, against outsiders in the story world, and English magazines are becoming increasingly friendly to stories with an overseas setting'.[83] While Louisa Baker complained to a New Zealand magazine in 1903 that in Britain 'a story with an English setting is three times the value in London, commercially, of one with a colonial background',[84] she still persevered in this genre when in London, encouraged, it is said, by the example of the South African Olive Schreiner. Her decision was probably a wise one. When Jane Mander moved to London and had to write books in order to survive financially, she set them in New York and London and Paris. However, 'though technically accomplished',[85] they were not as successful as her New Zealand books and she returned home disillusioned. She remarked later that 'well-thought out stories of pioneer life from anywhere would receive a good hearing' from publishers in London.[86]

Table 8.3 shows the location of New Zealand authors on the publication of their books between 1890 and 1945 (excluding 213 where this information was not available, and the work of Fergus Hume), sorted by the content of the book.

Table 8.3: Author location and book content, 1890–1945

Author location	All or mostly NZ content	Some NZ content	No NZ content	Unknown	Total
Australia	14	2	26	6	**48**
Europe	1	0	0	4	**5**
New Zealand	184	42	82	39	**347**
United Kingdom	43	2	38	15	**98**
United States	5	0	1	1	**7**
Total	**247**	**46**	**147**	**65**	**505**

The majority of books with known content in the table contain New Zealand content. This is predictable for those written in New Zealand, but of the 83 books written in the United Kingdom whose content is known, 45 (54 per cent) have at least some New Zealand content. Clearly, being in another location did not stop New Zealand writers from writing about New Zealand. Nor did New Zealand content put off British publishers.

Writers did not have to forfeit their New Zealandness, and remained contributors to the New Zealand literary scene even when in London. Overseas writers often sent material to New Zealand publications and to New Zealand 'bookmen' for evaluation. The poems of overseas writers appeared in local newspapers. Geoffrey de Montalk, despite his expressed distaste for New

Zealand literary periodicals, sent poems to New Zealand, and when informed by A.R.D. Fairburn that 'Return to London' had been used by the *Sun* he wrote back that he was 'glad'.[87] Writers also wrote reports on their experiences overseas for New Zealand papers. Monte Holcroft wrote a series for the *Sun* called 'Who travels alone: The adventures of a low-brow novelist', which appeared in 1929. Ngaio Marsh contributed 'A new Canterbury pilgrim', a series of articles that appeared in the Christchurch *Press* and were syndicated to other newspapers. Louisa Baker, from 1903, 'maintained her New Zealand connection' by writing a weekly column called 'Alien's letter from England' for the *Otago Witness*. This was 'eagerly read'.[88]

Most New Zealand writers who went overseas still remained very much in contact with New Zealand through the same colonial writing world networks they utilised at home. Networks, by their very nature, do not just work one way, and information was transported to the metropolitan centre from the periphery as well as from the periphery to the centre. As Felicity Barnes says of Lawrence Jones's connection of expatriatism with 'silence or expatriation': 'Whilst struggle was certainly a factor for many writers, the association of expatriation with "silence" and "withdrawal" is not necessarily an accurate reflection of their experience.'[89]

Writers in New Zealand used letters to maintain contact with the wider world, and they also used them while overseas to maintain ties to the New Zealand literary scene. While in London, Jane Mander wrote to writers at home with advice and literary criticism. Those who benefited included Monte Holcroft. Hector Bolitho, so often used as an example of someone who fled the New Zealand literary scene, retained contacts with New Zealand. He returned several times, he communicated with Pat Lawlor by letter, he asked to be kept informed of literary developments, and he expressed interest in appearing in a New Zealand publication, saying in 1966, 'I still have a strange vanity about appearing in a New Zealand magazine.'[90] He was more concerned by his reviews in New Zealand than those from elsewhere (even though the ones in Britain were generally more positive). Writers going overseas were unlikely to sever all contact with their home, even after many years, and sometimes in spite of negative reactions to their work. As Eric Baume explained after a long time abroad, 'I have kept in touch with New Zealand for so many years because it is my home country and my father was born there just on a hundred years ago.'[91]

While overseas, writers and other artists often still identified strongly with New Zealand. Even Katherine Mansfield was said to wear a tiki and own several other Māori artefacts. Frances Hodgkins, too, was 'very much aware of herself as a New Zealander' and 'as a badge of nationality she wore a Maori *tiki*'.[92] Hodgkins relied on the New Zealand art community in London to come to her exhibitions, and she seemed overly concerned about the opinion of the New Zealand public.

The same publications that facilitated the internal workings of colonial networks in London also kept New Zealanders informed about what was going on at home. This further enhanced their participation in the colonial writing world. The *British-Australasian* (later the *British Australian and New Zealander*) was largely concerned with printing general news from home for New Zealanders and Australians living in London. It served as a voice for the antipodean literary community, and printed news about literary goings-on at home, as in the issue of 11 January 1906, which reported the death of the popular Australian poet Victor J. Daley.[93] The 25 January 1906 issue also reprinted, for the benefit of Australian and New Zealand readers, overseas extracts from some of the stories and poems printed in the Christmas numbers of the leading Australasian weeklies. This line-up included a poem called 'The man from Maoriland' by W.T. Goodge.[94]

Publications in New Zealand maintained the link with overseas New Zealanders by regularly reporting on what they had been up to, as when the *New Zealand News* in 1930 related that 'Count Geoffrey de Montalk, whose title is an ancient Polish one, recently paid a visit of two months to Lithuania'.[95] Newspapers, such as the Christchurch *Press* and the *Wanganui Chronicle*, often included a column entitled 'New Zealanders in London'. On 12 February 1929, for example, the *Press* included a description of a dinner party held by the High Commissioner for 'twenty-eight New Zealanders whose business in London is connected with journalism, literature, art or the theatre'. This particular party included Nelle Scanlan and William Pember Reeves, and Jane Mander and Hector Bolitho were among those who sent 'letters of regret for not being present'.[96] Australian readers also reportedly showed a great deal of interest in the 'doings of their contemporaries in the great metropolis'.[97] In this way writers remained very much involved with Australasian literary circles.

Many contributions of writers who lived overseas have not been properly acknowledged. The word 'expatriate' as applied to overseas writers perpetuates a location-based sense of nationalism, which is anachronistic if it is made the basis of judgements about New Zealand before the 1940s, leading to an array of gaps and misconstructions. Many people subscribed to this notion of nationalism without necessarily realising it, even those who were not overtly nationalist. Jane Mander said in 1932:

> In a way Robin Hyde ought to be an exceptional case, as she was not born in New Zealand, but in Australia.[98] Still, she was brought here as an infant and has identified herself with N.Z. life and journalism, is in the opinion of many our finest poetess, and has now written several books, of which Journalese and Check to Your King are local colour.[99]

While totalling the number of New Zealand novelists, Mander placed a slightly negative slant on Edith Lyttleton, who was 'a New Zealander only by adoption' and 'early left New Zealand for England and America'. The fact that Lyttleton's emigration to New Zealand at the age of six and eventual departure overseas should count for more than the 30 years she spent in New Zealand in between is telling. This pedantic attitude to national identity became widespread under the influence of cultural nationalism, and yet it was rarely consistent. Some required New Zealand birth as the measure of New Zealandness, some required New Zealand content in the writing produced, and some saw residence in New Zealand as the crucial factor.

New Zealand writers overseas at the time noticed this and complained about the attitude of nationalist literary critics to their work. Cultural-nationalist assumptions were absorbed into the mainstream way of thinking about New Zealand literature, and remained dominant even in the 1960s. Olaf Ruhen complained about them in relation to Joan Stevens' 1961 study, *The New Zealand Novel*:

> [I]f Joan Stevens (whoever she is) limits [the novels she includes] to work that has a New Zealand setting, I don't think she is entitled to her title. She has to overlook the Fergus Humes, for example; and Fergus Hume changed the face of the popular novel. Does she include New Zealand work written in London? … no matter how small a man's output [by Stevens' estimate], as long as he continues to live in New Zealand, he belongs; if he leaves, he doesn't.[100]

Robin Hyde, also, was underappreciated because of her internationalist outlook. Patrick Sandbrook argues that accounts of her lack of recognition have usually focused on attitudes to gender and personal circumstance. But the publication of her major work happened in the late 1930s after she had left the country and was 'away from the notice of some key commentators. The views of several influential critics were evidently formed on the basis of her early work and did not change', and Charles Brasch's 'assessment of her talent is therefore condescending and dismissive'.[101]

Many of the writers who were important contributors to the national canon *were* writing from overseas. Katherine Mansfield represents an ambiguity in the minds of New Zealand literary historians. She cannot be ignored as the most successful New Zealand writer of the period (in terms of critical acclaim anyway), yet she supposedly rejected her 'New Zealandness' (although not in her writing). The New Zealand literary canon encompasses many authors who wrote their novels while overseas, including James Courage, Dan Davin and Hector Bolitho, all of whom wrote about New Zealand. Many others also published their canonical works overseas. This criterion for exclusion is illogical and inconsistently applied, creating incongruities and problems of selection in much of New Zealand literary history to this day.

Membership of the colonial literary world allowed New Zealanders to participate in the London literary scene from New Zealand, but also to remain involved with New Zealand while in London. Far from being permanently dislocated from New Zealand, writers often remained physically in contact with New Zealand by visiting, or returning. This further strengthened and added to the links made by the colonial expansion in the first place, and is a physical representation of the way the colonial writing world worked. Writers overseas were not lost to the New Zealand literary scene, and many returned to make important contributions to local initiatives.

Concluding thoughts

From England in 1932 A.R.D. Fairburn wrote to R.A.K. Mason in a manner that contrasted sharply with earlier sentiments he had expressed about being desperate to leave New Zealand. He wrote:

> I'd like to go back to N.Z. and be a New Zealander. Not a wistful student of French Impressionism and Post Impressionism as some of our young artists would apparently wish to be. Not a follower of the Bolshevik Revolution – which is about as irrelevant to N.Z. as ham to a synagogue feast. Not a student of Anglo-Irish decadence – of Virginia Woolf, James Joyce & c. But just a New Zealander. I would like to live in the backblocks of N.Z. and try to realise in my mind the real culture of that country.[1]

Fairburn had previously demonstrated noticeably different feelings about being stuck in New Zealand. He could not wait to leave the 'intellectual rat-hole' and join the crowds of people trying to make their way in the United Kingdom. His time in England, it appears, had caused him to change his mind about his native country, and reversed his attitude to New Zealand and writing.

Fairburn's about-turn is not actually surprising. The realisation that London's literary opportunities were not exponentially better brought the New Zealand scene more sharply into focus for some writers. It became clear that there were advantages to being in New Zealand and that many of London's advantages had been available to them all along. The writers who went to England because, like Frank Sargeson, they expressed a feeling of being 'separated from the sources of culture that had meaning for [them]',[2] often realised on arrival that there was no distinct advantage to being physically in the same place as the objects of culture. Some found they disliked the pretentious ways of the London literati and preferred the more unassuming, straightforward colonial way. Fairburn came to realise that it was the 'simplest realities' that were important as opposed to the 'rather frenetic' climate of London.[3] Many writers came to the conclusion that London did not live up to expectations, for, like Sargeson, they 'had tried London and found it wanting.'[4]

Colonial networks and links meant that New Zealand remained in the forefront of the minds of writers overseas. Some writers actually had more contact with other New Zealand writers in England than they did in New Zealand. Indeed, James Courage became involved with these circles only when he went to England; it has been said of him that 'perhaps paradoxically, it was in London that he became immersed in the New Zealand literary scene, as a result of meeting many of the New Zealand writers visiting England at the time.'[5] It was at the Lyceum Club's New Zealand Circle that Edith Searle Grossmann made the acquaintance of other New Zealand authors, such as Kate Isitt, Edith Lyttleton and Dora Wilcox. She was on the council, and in this capacity attended the circle's inaugural dinner 'where she gave a lecture about the current status of New Zealand literature.'[6] Literary friendships were made overseas and literary business was conducted: the creation of the influential literary periodical *Landfall* was a result of Brasch and Glover meeting up in London. Glover recounted: 'It was in fact on Hampstead Heath one morning that we laid plans for the foundation of *Landfall* when and should the war end.'[7] Few would dispute that this was an important moment for New Zealand literature.

Writers who were already friends sought each other out. They continued to function as part of the New Zealand literary scene while in London, and even promoted writers from 'back home', as when Edith Grossmann promoted the poetry of Jessie Mackay and others at Lyceum Club dinners. Often it was being in England that brought New Zealand more clearly into the minds of those who had left. They became aware of being New Zealanders in ways they had not previously apprehended, and comparisons with the English highlighted the value of their colonial difference. Frank Sargeson was to remark, famously: 'Like so many of my fellow countrymen I had to visit Europe to discover that I was truly a New Zealander.'[8]

Some dealt with this discovery by writing about New Zealand, and many writers who never actually went back to New Zealand wrote about the land in which they had grown up. Even Katherine Mansfield eventually came to embrace her colonial past, at least in literature, writing her most successful stories about New Zealand. After the death of her brother she was overcome by nostalgia and found that she wanted to write of her 'own country' and make it 'leap into the eyes of the Old World'.[9]

Others returned home with a renewed zeal for New Zealand writing. Upon immersing himself in all the intellectual fare the British Library had to offer and finding it weighty and potentially irrelevant, Sargeson came to the realisation that he was 'determined to make his own literary effort in his own country',[10] though he had also run out of money. Monte Holcroft's experiences in England had a similar effect, and he remarked in *The Deepening Stream*: 'I had come back from England with a new feeling about my native country'.[11] Jane Mander wrote to Pat Lawlor the year before she left England for New Zealand, 'I have a hankering now to get back to my original environment in writing. Apparently no-one else will ever be able to do that gum country of the north which is in my blood and bones'.[12] John Mulgan, too, expressed a wish to engage with the literary implications of being in New Zealand, and wrote to his mother in 1934: 'We must all end up back in a few years' time, say 1940, prepared to do something'.[13]

Mulgan was not to return home due to his early death, but many of his compatriots did, and some did in fact 'do something'. Several writers and associates put their energy into creating a local publishing infrastructure, building on the earlier efforts of Denis Glover in the Students' Association's basement at Canterbury College. This was where the Caxton Club first began its printing ventures, and out of this the Caxton Press was born. Glover ended his time in the navy and gave up the excitements of London to 'return home to the responsibilities of a literary and publishing career, his true vocation'.[14] From the mid-1930s there was the deliberate creation of a national publishing industry that did not rely on external market forces. Before that, local publishing had really been a supplement for the publishing opportunities available in England and elsewhere.

Other initiatives coincided with Glover's effort, like the Unicorn Press, which was set up by Bob Lowry. With Ronald Holloway, Lowry printed D'Arcy Cresswell's *Lyttelton Harbour* and Sargeson's *Conversation With My Uncle*.[15] The group responsible for these initiatives was largely composed of cultural nationalists who later claimed that they had founded genuine New Zealand literature. While their claims are dubious, the purposeful construction of local publishing facilities certainly influenced the course of New Zealand literature and literary scholarship. The Caxton Press was willing to take risks because of a 'resolute commitment to the arts in New Zealand',[16] and because it was anxious to serve highbrow local literary aims.

As observed in Chapter Five, one way to deal with being 'unhoused' by the consequences of modernity and colonial upheaval was to focus heavily on creating a new tradition to replace the ones that had been lost. Fairburn might have not seen the relevance of Joyce and Woolf to New Zealand, but the first issue of *Phoenix* included a modernist manifesto that had more in common with the outputs of English modernists like D.H. Lawrence and John Middleton Murry than anything particularly local. Modernist literature by its very nature established itself as the pinnacle of literary achievement. This is not necessarily the fault of modernists themselves, but rather the critical legacy that has been calcifying around a corpus of classics ever since. Andrzej Gąsiorek takes issue with the idea that modernism is a retrospective critical construction, but finds some truth in this suggestion when applied to the production of modernism as a movement.[17] For Gąsiorek, the defining feature of the modernist movement was the impulse to 'defy conventions of literature and make something new',[18] which in this case meant striving to reject the literary conventions that represented colonial ties to Britain. In order to create something truly 'as immediate in experience as the island soil under [their] feet',[19] the editors of *Phoenix* had to assert that they were doing something entirely new and important, and dismiss what had come before. In reality, modernist writers shared certain attributes but had many, varied preoccupations, some of which were not 'modernist' at all. The mode carried with it an integral assessment of itself as the one, true form of literary expression, casting aside all previous attempts. Because of this, writers engaged with other preoccupations were marginalised. New Zealand's cultural nationalists helped entrench this idea, as it suited them to emphasise their own contribution as something new where nothing before had been truly worthy of the title 'literature'.

As a result, the *Phoenix* group saw the colonial writing world in a negative light, bolstered in some cases by disappointment at their lack of success overseas. To their minds, overseas publishing was preventing local literary growth, and making New Zealanders exiles in their own country. The cultural nationalists, many of them returning from overseas, came to dominate the literary scene in the late 1930s and 1940s. They promoted local initiatives and the fostering of an 'essential New Zealandness' in literature, and they dismissed the many works that had been published under the auspices of the colonial writing world, either because the writers were no longer in New Zealand or because, for them, overseas publishing did not count. In this way the role of the colonial writing world in the creation of New Zealand literature was obscured from view.

Of course, the idea of creating writing distinctive to New Zealand was not invented by the *Phoenix* group. Blanche Baughan was a writer firmly placed by Allen Curnow in the earlier set of writers: in the struggle of 'rata blossoms vs. reality' she was associated with the former.[20] In 1912, however, she published 'Café au Lait' in the volume of short stories *Brown Bread from a Colonial Oven*. In this story Baughan metaphorically emphasised the growth of an unselfconscious new literature in the new country, though of course its roots were unmistakably in the old one: 'The old bush that bore it came of stock that had crossed the ocean more than half a century before; but what did this little bough care about that? – its blossoms were new this year.'[21] Writing about the project of a distinctive national culture was nothing new. Jessie Mackay's earliest book of poems, published in 1889, included in the introduction her hope for 'the dawning of a national spirit'.[22] As Charlotte Elder mentions, Ursula Bethell used the New Zealand condition to provide contrast in her work as she juxtaposed the exotic and the native, often achieving a peaceful synthesis.[23] An example is one of her most famous poems, 'The long harbour', from *Time and Place*. In this she wrote of the 'blackbird, happy colonist,' and the 'blacker, sweeter-fluted tui' that 'echo / either the other's song'.[24] This was not a concern invented by the *Phoenix* group, but by their predecessors within the colonial writing world who loved New Zealand as their home within the wider British Empire.

Women like Baughan and Mackay were not at the forefront of the *Phoenix* group's new world order, although they contributed greatly to writing in New Zealand. The cultural nationalist model was narrowly focused on a masculine definition of the quintessential New Zealander. Women writers were to a large extent disenfranchised, and disappeared from the forefront of the writing community. This was encouraged by the misogynistic (or at least belittling) attitudes of the cultural nationalists themselves. Bethell's poetry addressed the difficulty of writing about New Zealand, and as a result she was adopted as a forerunner by Curnow. Even she did not escape this literary oppression, however, as when D'Arcy Cresswell reviewed her book of verse, *Time and Place*, in *Tomorrow*. He praised the work, but was critical that she sometimes attempted 'too much intellectually', as 'it is the men who must matter in the long run, of course'.[25] The sidelining of women writers was not reflected in the amount of material actually published by women, as this was consistent throughout the period.[26]

The champions of these women were the bookmen of the previous generation, who were now represented as holding back the development of New Zealand literature. The amount of control they had over publishing in New Zealand made it seem to Denis Glover that Mulgan, Marris and Schroder were the men 'who hold within their hand / the literary of the land'.[27]

The previous generation's approach might have looked limited, but this was because the *Phoenix* group was ignoring the much wider spectrum of opportunities made possible by the colonial writing world. As a result, those who insisted on a cultural nationalist approach were actually 'remarkably ignorant' of their own country's literature and what had gone before.[28] Patrick Evans claims that Curnow's espousals were an attempt to write his own version of literary history with himself occupying the central role, describing it as a 'story told by a particular group of people who had placed themselves at the beginning of things in order to enhance their own importance'.[29] Mark Williams' response to Evans' *Penguin History of New Zealand Literature* finds this to be justified because 'Brasch, Curnow, Glover and Mason were vastly more talented than their predecessors, with the notable exception of Katherine Mansfield'. For Williams, what really makes this group of writers important is their 'concerted set of priorities', which led to a 'coherent effort by writers in this country to develop an intelligently local literature based on clear principles about how to proceed and towards what end'.[30] This is a fair assessment only if this very narrow view of the form and purpose of literature is taken – only writing contributing to the 'cause' of 'New Zealand literature' is worthy of discussion. This attitude ignores the transnational nature of writing and writers' lives in the early twentieth century, facilitated by the colonial writing world.

Although the cultural nationalists wanted to assert their own importance in the development of New Zealand literature, without the colonial writing world enabling literary conversations with Britain and allowing overseas

New Zealanders to stay in touch with the literary scene in New Zealand, their own contribution would never have come about. Although they would never have admitted it, the colonial writing world had fostered their own literary development. The efforts of Curnow and friends owed a great deal to the British literary tradition. At the same time, they themselves maintained close colonial world ties and were surprisingly interested in British literary developments as well as how their work was viewed by the British literati.

Similarly, the story of the colonial writing world is not just about New Zealand. Many other countries have their own 'expatriate myth', especially the other British settler colonies. South African and Canadian writers interacted with the metropolitan centre, though these countries faced additional complications due to the legacy of competing colonial powers and resulting linguistic and ethnic divisions. Literary histories of the United States have continued this dichotomy between nationalism at home and cosmopolitan writers abroad, which could benefit from empirical investigation.

The most obvious parallel can be drawn with Australia, and it is more than a comparison, as the two were firmly intertwined as members of the colonial writing world. The notion of necessary expatriatism still flourishes in Australia, and reference is often made to Victor Daley's 1900 poem on the subject:

> They leave us – artists, singers, all –
> When London calls aloud,
> Commanding to her Festival
> The gifted crowd.[31]

This poem contains the same melancholy sense of permanent desertion that is associated with the expatriation of writers. In the mid-1930s P.R. Stephensen (quoted by Peter Morton) wrote: 'From a national point of view our émigrés may be written off as a dead loss.'[32] This was a loss that would not be regained. For Nicholas Birns in *A Companion to Australian Literature since 1900*, the 'dilemma' of expatriation arose from the fact that it was expatriates who were the successes, and this success came about by their 'casting off their Australian identity as far as possible, or using it just as a marker that denoted the beginning of a journey'.[33]

Yet many Australian writers, like those associated with New Zealand, were fully involved with the colonial writing world from within and without

Australia. As with New Zealand, the concept of the colonial writing world is vital to any explanation of early Australian literature and the subsequent emergence of cultural nationalism. Henry Handel Richardson's status as an expatriate informs much of the response to her work, and her masterwork *The Fortunes of Richard Mahoney* has been interpreted as a chronicle of the inadequacies of her country by a 'self-loathing Australian'.[34] But Richard Mahoney is never at home anywhere and spends as much time feeling 'not at home' in England as in Australia. In fact, the book exemplifies the written expression of the colonial writing world and the permanent 'unhousedness' of people with connections to colonialism.

Even more broadly, the networks belonging to other colonial enterprises contain the same tropes, anxieties and possibilities, reflecting the 'unhousedness' of human civilisation since the massive turbulence unleashed by the advent of modernity and the Enlightenment, revealing the notion of literary expatriatism as exile to be vastly inadequate as a description of human experience. The experiences of New Zealand writers navigating the expanded British world demonstrate this well, but it is not a unique phenomenon. New Zealand, along with other self-conscious nations, has tended to overemphasise the importance of local distinctiveness in attempts to counter the homogenising effects of global connectedness, at the expense of many equally worthy artistic expressions and literary lives. As Bill Ashcroft says, once we 'distinguish the nation from the state we discover that mobility and border crossing are already features of the phenomenon we call the nation'.[35] This is a story about much more than New Zealand, and this is what cultural nationalism fails to recognise: that the answer to what it means to be a New Zealander – if there is an answer – cannot be found simply by looking within the country.

Notes

INTRODUCTION

1. A term coined by Gertrude Stein and popularised by Ernest Hemingway's use of it as the epigraph to *The Sun Also Rises* (New York: Scribner's, 1926), cited in 'The "Lost Generation"', British Library: www.bl.uk/onlinegallery/features/amliteuro/lostgen.html

2. Henry Lawson, 'Pursuing literature in Australia', *Bulletin*, no. 9, 21 January 1899.

3. Lawrence Jones, 'The novel', in *Oxford History of New Zealand Literature* (*OHNZL*), ed. Terry Sturm (Oxford: Oxford University Press, 1998), p. 135.

4. Patrick Buckridge, 'A kind of exile: Godfrey Blunden – an Australian in Paris', *Journal of Australian Studies*, vol. 26, no. 73, 2002, p. 111; Lydia Wevers, 'The short story', in *OHNZL*, ed. Terry Sturm (Oxford: Oxford University Press, 1998), p. 260.

5. Stephen Alomes, *When London Calls: The expatriation of Australian creative artists to Britain* (Cambridge: Cambridge University Press, 1999); Peter Morton, *Lusting for London: Australian expatriate writers at the hub of empire, 1870–1950* (New York: Palgrave Macmillan, 2011); Bruce Bennett and Anne Pender, *From A Distant Shore: Australian writers in Britain 1820–2012* (Clayton, Vic: Monash University Press, 2013).

6. Helen Bones, 'A dual exile? New Zealand and the colonial writing world, 1890–1945' (PhD thesis, University of Canterbury, 2011): http://hdl.handle.net/10092/5618

7. Terry Sturm, *An Unsettled Spirit: The life and frontier fiction of Edith Lyttleton (G.B. Lancaster)* (Auckland: Auckland University Press, 2003), p. 5.

8. 'Eileen Duggan', New Zealand Book Council: www.bookcouncil.org.nz/writer/duggan-eileen/

9. Duggan to Nettie Palmer, 1926, Duggan papers, MS Papers 801 2/2, Alexander Turnbull Library (ATL), Wellington.

10. Duggan to Nettie Palmer, 1926.

11. Katherine Mansfield to Sylvia Payne, 8 January 1907, in Anthony Alpers, *The Life of Katherine Mansfield* (Oxford: Oxford University Press, 1982), p. 43.

12. Katherine Mansfield, *Notebooks I*, ed. Margaret Scott, p. 86, in Jane Stafford, 'Fashioned intimacies: Maoriland and colonial modernity', *Journal of Commonwealth Literature*, vol. 37, no. 31, 2002, p. 32.

13. Jane Mander, letter to the *Triad*, 1909, in Rae McGregor, *The Story of a New Zealand Writer: Jane Mander* (Dunedin: University of Otago Press, 1998), p. 34.

14. Jane Stafford and Mark Williams, *Maoriland: New Zealand literature 1872–1914* (Wellington: Victoria University Press, 2006), p. 152.

15. Chris Hilliard, *The Bookmen's Dominion: Cultural life in New Zealand 1920–1950* (Auckland: Auckland University Press, 2006), p. 2.

16. Michele Leggott, 'Opening the archive: Robin Hyde, Eileen Duggan and the persistence of record', *Hecate*, vol. 20, no. 2, 1994, p. 193; Heather Murray,

'Celebrating our writers: 1936, 1951', *Journal of New Zealand Literature 10* (1992), pp. 99–114.

17. Lydia Wevers, *Reading on the Farm: Victorian fiction and the colonial world* (Wellington: Victoria University Press, 2010).

18. Isabel Maud Peacocke, writing as Isabel Cluett, 'Exodus of New Zealand writers', *All About Books*, 17 June 1930, p. 164.

19. Alomes, *When London Calls*, p. 2.

20. Peter Pierce, 'Australia's Australia', *The Cambridge History of Australian Literature* (Cambridge: Cambridge University Press, 2009), p. 137.

21. Geoffrey Serle, *From Deserts the Prophets Come: The creative spirit in Australia 1788–1972* (Melbourne: Heinemann, 1973), p. 126.

22. Morton, *Lusting for London*, pp. 2–3.

23. They include three exceptions to this rule: Martin Boyd, Patrick White and M.J. Hyland. Bennett and Pender, *From a Distant Shore*, p. 8.

24. John Arnold, 'Australian books, publishers and writers in England, 1900–1940', in Carl Bridge et al., *Australians in Britain: The twentieth-century experience* (Clayton, Vic: Monash University Press, 2009).

25. His figures are based on E. Morris Miller's bibliography (*Australian Literature: a bibliography to 1938, extended to 1950* (Sydney: Angus and Robertson, 1956)). Miller's list includes 'all who, as authors of books, have been connected with Australia, irrespective of whether or not they were born in this country or continue to reside here' (vii).

26. Azade Seyhan, *Writing Outside the Nation* (Princeton: Princeton University Press, 2001), p. 4.

27. Buckridge, 'A kind of exile', p. 111; 'Notes', p. 238.

28. Monte Holcroft, 'A professional expatriate', in *New Zealand's Heritage*, vol. 6, ed. Ray Knox (Wellington: Paul Hamlyn, c. 1973), p. 2210.

29. Sandra Coney, 'Riemke Ensing on women writers', *Broadsheet 22* (September 1974), p. 12.

30. 'Culture of New Zealand', Wikipedia: en.wikipedia.org/wiki/Culture_of_New_Zealand

31. Felicity Barnes, *New Zealand's London: A colony and its metropolis* (Auckland: Auckland University Press, 2012), pp. 117–22.

32. Limited to novels, short-story collections and books of verse, first editions only. Although New Zealanders did publish books in other languages during this time, the study was restricted to English for reasons of feasibility. See Bones, 'A dual exile?' for the full list. An online searchable version can be found at www.helenbones.com/NZpubsdata.html (note: the original list of 718 works contained a duplicate entry that has been removed in the online version and the figures in this book).

33. Franco Moretti, *Graphs, Maps and Trees: Abstract models for a literary history* (London: Verso, 2005), p. 4.

34. David Carter, 'Structures, networks, institutions: The new empiricism, book history and literary history', in *Resourceful Reading: The new empiricism, eresearch*

and Australian literary culture, eds Katherine Bode and Robert Dixon (Sydney: Sydney University Press, 2009), p. 43; Pierre Bourdieu, *The Field of Cultural Production: Essays on art and literature* (Cambridge: Polity Press, 1993).

35. Alan Lester, 'Historical geographies of British colonisation: New South Wales, New Zealand and the Cape in the early nineteenth century', in *Imperial Communication: Australia, Britain and the British Empire 1830–1850*, ed. Simon Potter (London: Menzies Centre, 2005), p. 97.

36. Tony Ballantyne, *Webs of Empire: Locating New Zealand's colonial past* (Wellington: Bridget Williams Books, 2012).

37. Bones, 'A dual exile?', p. 114.

38. Morton, *Lusting for London*, p. 188.

39. Terry Sturm, 'Scanlan, Ellen Margaret', Dictionary of New Zealand Biography (DNZB): www.teara.govt.nz/en/biographies/4s11/scanlan-ellen-margaret

40. David Lambert and Alan Lester, eds, *Colonial Lives across the British Empire: Imperial careering in the long nineteenth century* (Cambridge: Cambridge University Press, 2006), p. 1.

41. Sofia Eriksson, 'Observing the birth of a nation: British travel writing on Australia, 1870–1939' (PhD thesis, Macquarie University, 2011), p. 32.

42. Angela Woollacott, *Settler Society in the Australian Colonies* (Oxford: Oxford University Press, 2015), p. 12.

43. Allen Curnow, 'Introduction', *A Book of New Zealand Verse 1923–1945* (Christchurch: Caxton Press, 1945).

44. Curnow's brand of cultural nationalism was also associated with the poets Denis Glover, Charles Brasch, R.A.K. Mason and A.R.D. Fairburn, and prose writers Frank Sargeson and John Mulgan, although in reality the aims of this group were far from coherent. From the 1970s, feminist and Māori historians and representatives of other groups protested about their exclusion from this version of national identity. 1930s cultural nationalism was further deconstructed from the 1990s, by scholars such as Patrick Evans in the *Penguin History of New Zealand Literature* (Auckland: Penguin, 1990) and *The Long Forgetting* (Christchurch: Canterbury University Press, 2007) and Stuart Murray in *Never a Soul at Home* (Wellington: Victoria University Press, 1998).

45. Tony Ballantyne, 'On place, space and mobility in nineteenth-century New Zealand', *New Zealand Journal of History*, vol. 45, no. 1, 2011, p. 53.

46. Eileen Duggan, 'Shades of Maro of Toulouse', *More Poems* (Allen & Unwin: London, 1951), p. 17.

47. Evans, *Penguin History of New Zealand Literature*, p. 79.

48. Vincent O'Sullivan, '"Finding the pattern, solving the problem": Katherine Mansfield the New Zealand European', in *Katherine Mansfield: In from the margin*, ed. Roger Robinson (Baton Rouge: Louisiana State University Press, 1994), p. 13.

49. Sturm, *An Unsettled Spirit*, p. 5.

CHAPTER ONE

1.   Jane Mander, *The Story of a New Zealand River* (London: Bodley Head, 1920), p. 33.

2.   James Belich, *Paradise Reforged: A history of the New Zealanders from the 1880s to the year 2000* (Auckland: Penguin, 2001), p. 326.

3.   Alan Mulgan, 'The New Zealand novel', in *Annals of New Zealand Literature*, ed. Johannes Andersen (Wellington: New Zealand Authors' Week Committee, 1936), p. 9.

4.   Terry Sturm, 'Introduction', *Oxford History of New Zealand Literature (OHNZL)*, ed. Terry Sturm (Oxford: Oxford University Press, 1998), p. xi.

5.   MacDonald P. Jackson, 'Poetry: beginnings to 1945', in *OHNZL*, p. 406.

6.   Lydia Wevers, 'First, build your hut', *Pacific Highways. Griffith Review*, no. 43, 2013, p. 267.

7.   Samuel Butler, *A First Year in Canterbury Settlement* (London: Longman, Green, 1863), pp. 50; 66.

8.   Eric McCormick, *Letters and Art in New Zealand* (Wellington: Dept. of Internal Affairs, 1940), p. 129.

9.   R.A.K. Mason, Notebooks, MS 990/10, Hocken Collections (HC), Dunedin, in Rachel Barrowman, *Mason: The life of R.A.K. Mason* (Wellington: Victoria University Press, 2003), p. 47.

10.   Winnie Gonley, 'New Zealand life in contemporary culture' (MA thesis, University of New Zealand, 1932), p. 3.

11.   McCormick, *Letters and Art in New Zealand*, pp. 19–20.

12.   E.J. Wakefield, 'Advice to intending colonists', in *Life in a Young Colony: Selections from early New Zealand writing*, ed. Cherry Hankin (Christchurch: Whitcoulls, 1981), p. 39.

13.   Jane Stafford and Mark Williams, *Maoriland: New Zealand literature 1872–1914* (Wellington: Victoria University Press, 2006).

14.   Jock Phillips, 'Musings in Maoriland', *Historical Studies*, vol. 20, no. 81, 1983, p. 520.

15.   Other colonies are the subject of similar hyperbolic claims, which casts some doubt on this – they cannot all have been exceptional. For example, a 1953 survey concluded that 'Australia's national per capita expenditure on books – 21 shillings – remained the highest in the world'. Jason D. Ensor, 'Places of publication and the Australian book trade: A study of Angus & Robertson's London office, 1938–1970' (PhD thesis, Murdoch University, 2010), pp. 73–74.

16.   T.M. Hocken, *Contributions to the Early History of New Zealand* (London: S. Low, Marston and Company, Limited, 1898), p. 112, in Mary Ronnie, *Books to the People: A history of regional library services in New Zealand* (Wellington: New Zealand Library Association, 1993), p. 5.

17.   William Pember Reeves, *The Long White Cloud* (London: Horace Marshall & Son, 1898), p. 409.

18.   Howard McNaughton, *New Zealand Drama* (Boston: Twayne Publishers, 1981), p. 15.

19. Elizabeth Plumridge, 'The negotiation of circumstance: New Zealand women artists c. 1890–1914' (PhD thesis, Australian National University, 1985), pp. 108–09.
20. Maurice Hurst, *Music and the Stage* (Auckland: Charles Begg, 1944), p. 7.
21. Hurst, quoting 'a Dunedin historian', p. 7.
22. Alan Mulgan, *The Making of a New Zealander* (Wellington: Reed, 1958), p. 53.
23. Ngaio Marsh, *Black Beech and Honeydew* (London: Collins, 1966), p. 125, in Plumridge, 'The negotiation of circumstance', pp. 107–08.
24. Hurst, *Music and the Stage*, p. 62.
25. McNaughton, *New Zealand Drama*, p. 28.
26. Plumridge, 'The negotiation of circumstance', p. 100.
27. 'Results of a census of the Dominion of New Zealand', Statistics New Zealand: www3.stats.govt.nz/historic_publications/1911-census/1911-results-census.html#d50e448066Census
28. 'Tempo', 'Music Notes', *Star* (Christchurch), 26 December 1905, p. 4.
29. Guy H. Scholefield, *Newspapers in New Zealand* (Wellington: Reed, 1958), p. 23.
30. Anna Rogers and Max Rogers, *Turning the Pages: The story of bookselling in New Zealand* (Auckland: Reed, 1993), p. 2.
31. James Belich, *Making Peoples* (Auckland: Penguin, 1996), p. 393; Lydia Wevers, *Reading on the Farm: Victorian fiction and the colonial world* (Wellington: Victoria University Press, 2010), p. 29. The average illiteracy rate in Britain in the second half of the nineteenth century was 25 per cent, according to David Vincent: 'A study of British literacy indicates that rates were indeed similar: in the sample of registration districts undertaken for this study, literate and illiterate England were almost exactly balanced at the end of the 1830s. During the subsequent seventy-five years, illiteracy fell to 1 per cent, leaving an average for the period of 25 per cent.' David Vincent, *Literacy and Popular Culture: England, 1750–1914* (Cambridge [England]; New York: Cambridge University Press, 1989), p. 22. This is a measure of 'innominacy', however, meaning being unable to sign one's name (measured using marriage records). Belich says New Zealand in 1858 was 12 per cent 'innominate' 'compared with 18–31 per cent in the New Zealand-prone counties [e.g. Kent] of England in the 1860s'. Belich, *Making Peoples*, p. 393.
32. Reeves, *The Long White Cloud*, p. 409.
33. A.G. Stephens, 'Canterbury bells', *Bulletin*, 1 December 1900, quoted in Theresia Marshall, 'New Zealand literature in the Sydney *Bulletin*' (PhD thesis, University of Auckland, 1995), p. 55.
34. Alan Preston, 'Bookselling', in *Book and Print in New Zealand: A guide to print culture in Aotearoa*, eds Penny Griffith, Ross Harvey and Keith Maslen (Wellington: Victoria University Press, 1997), p. 157.
35. Dulcie Needham-Gillespie, 'The colonial and his books' (PhD thesis, Victoria University, 1971), p. 127.
36. Although Wevers says there is no firm evidence of the latter. Wevers, *Reading on the Farm*, p. 29.
37. Anthony Trollope, *Australia and New Zealand*, vol. 2 (London: Chapman & Hall, 1873), p. 336.

38. J.E. Traue, 'The public library explosion in colonial New Zealand', *Libraries and the Cultural Record*, vol. 42, no. 2, 2007, pp. 151–64.

39. W.B. Sutch, 'Libraries for all', *Tomorrow*, vol. 2, no. 1, 1935, p. 5.

40. Maxine Rochester, *The Revolution in New Zealand Librarianship: American influence as facilitated by the Carnegie Corporation of New York in the 1930s*, Occasional Papers Series 50 (Halifax, Nova Scotia: Dalhousie University, 1990), p. 8.

41. W.J. McEldowney, *The New Zealand Library Association 1910–1960 and its Part in New Zealand Library Development* (Wellington: New Zealand Library Association, 1962), p. 6. Statistics are from the New Zealand Department of Censuses and Statistics, '24: Census of Public Libraries', *Vol XVII: General Report, Population Census* (Wellington: Department of Censuses and Statistics, 1926), p. 97.

42. Rochester, *The Revolution in New Zealand Librarianship*, p. 6.

43. Chris Hilliard, *The Bookmen's Dominion: Cultural life in New Zealand 1920–1950* (Auckland: Auckland University Press, 2006), p. 17.

44. Traue, 'The public library explosion', pp. 152–53.

45. Traue, p. 152.

46. Or, with regards to Australia, the difference results from the fact that a higher proportion of New Zealanders lived in small communities, each with its own small library. Australia was one of the most 'metropolitanised' societies in the world, with a higher proportion of people living in big cities with fewer but larger libraries.

47. A commentator with the alias 'New Zealander' in the *Publisher's Gazette*, quoted in 'Among the Books', *Dominion*, 30 January 1909.

48. Robin Winks, *These New Zealanders* (Christchurch: Whitcombe & Tombs, 1954), p. 122.

49. Preston, 'Bookselling', p. 157.

50. Stanley Unwin, 'English books abroad', in *The Book World*, ed. Basil Blackwell (London: Thomas Nelson & Sons, 1935), p. 173.

51. Constance A. Barnicoat, 'The reading of the colonial girl', *Nineteenth Century and After: A monthly review*, vol. 60, no. 358, 1906, p. 944.

52. McCormick, *Letters and Art in New Zealand*, p. 51.

53. Dennis McEldowney, 'Publishing, patronage and literary magazines', in *OHNZL*, p. 633.

54. This was the second book printed in New Zealand. The first was produced by the Reverend W. Yate and was also a catechism in Māori. Johannes Andersen, 'Early printing in New Zealand', in *A History of Printing in New Zealand, 1830–1940*, ed. R.A. Mackay (Wellington: Wellington Club of Printing House Craftsmen, 1940), p. 6.

55. Rogers and Rogers, *Turning the Pages*, p. 2.

56. New Zealand Department of Censuses and Statistics, *The New Zealand Official Yearbook, 1934* (Wellington: Government Printer, 1933), p. 239.

57. Ross Harvey, 'Newspapers', in Griffith, Harvey and Maslen, *Book and Print in New Zealand*, p. 130.

58. Patrick Evans, *Penguin History of New Zealand Literature* (Auckland: Penguin, 1990), p. 25.
59. Monte Holcroft, 'A professional expatriate', in *New Zealand's Heritage*, vol. 6, ed. Ray Knox (Wellington: Paul Hamlyn, c. 1973), p. 2210.
60. Keith Sinclair, *Distance Looks Our Way* (Auckland: Paul's Book Arcade, 1961), p. 33.
61. Evans, *Penguin History of New Zealand Literature*, p. 41.
62. Tony Ballantyne, 'On place, space and mobility in nineteenth-century New Zealand', *New Zealand Journal of History*, vol. 45, no. 1, 2011, p. 63.
63. See, for example, David Lambert and Alan Lester, eds, *Colonial Lives across the British Empire: Imperial careering in the long nineteenth century* (Cambridge: Cambridge University Press, 2006).
64. James Belich, *Replenishing the Earth* (Oxford: Oxford University Press, 2011), p. 9.
65. Janet Wilson, 'Constructing the metropolitan homeland: The literatures of the white settler societies of New Zealand and Australia', in *Comparing Postcolonial Diasporas*, eds Michelle Keown, David Murphy and James Procter (Basingstoke: Palgrave Macmillan, 2009), p. 130.
66. Wevers, *Reading on the Farm*, p. 19.
67. Peter Gibbons, 'The far side of the search for identity', *New Zealand Journal of History*, vol. 37, no. 1, 2003, p. 44.
68. John Eddy and Deryck Schreuder, *The Rise of Colonial Nationalism: Australia, New Zealand, Canada and South Africa first assert their identities* (Sydney: Allen & Unwin, 1988), p. 31.
69. Felicity Barnes, 'New Zealand's London: The metropolis and New Zealand's culture, 1890–1940' (PhD thesis, University of Auckland, 2008), pp. 2–3.
70. Felicity Barnes, *New Zealand's London: A colony and its metropolis* (Auckland: Auckland University Press, 2012), p. 13.
71. Belich, *Paradise Reforged*, p. 69.
72. 'History of Cable Bay Station', Cable Bay Holiday Park: www.cablebayfarm.co.nz/history2.html
73. Wevers, *Reading on the Farm*, p. 143.
74. Angela Woollacott, *Settler Society in the Australian Colonies* (Oxford: Oxford University Press, 2015), p. 16.
75. E.J. Wakefield, 'Advice to intending colonists', p. 39.
76. G.R. Gilbert, 'A reading writing man', unpublished manuscript, MS 957, Macmillan Brown Library, Christchurch, p. 49.
77. Sydney J. Shep, 'The printers' web: New tools to crack old chestnuts', in *Advancing Digital Humanities: Research, methods, theories*, eds Paul Longley Arthur and Katherine Bode (Basingstoke: Palgrave Macmillan, 2014), p. 69.
78. Hugh Price, 'Educational publishing', in *Book and Print in New Zealand*, eds Griffith, Harvey and Maslen, p. 145.
79. Richard Nile and David Walker, 'The "Paternoster Row Machine" and the Australian book trade, 1890–1945', in *A History of the Book in Australia 1891–*

1945: A national culture in a colonised market, eds Martyn Lyons and John Arnold (St Lucia, Qsld: University of Queensland Press, 2001), p. 9.

80. Nile and Walker, p. 7.
81. Martyn Lyons, 'Britain's largest export market', in *A History of the Book in Australia*, eds Lyons and Arnold, pp. 22–23.
82. Luke Trainor, 'Colonial editions', in *Book and Print in New Zealand*, eds Griffith, Harvey and Maslen, p. 113.
83. Endnote, in Harry Vogel, *A Maori Maid* (London: Macmillan, 1898), p. 402.
84. Trainor, 'Colonial editions', p. 114. For a detailed discussion of the prices of colonial editions see Graeme Johanson, *Colonial Editions in Australia, 1843–1972* (Wellington: Elibank Press, 2000), pp. 159–210.
85. Trainor, 'Colonial editions', p. 111.
86. Lyons, 'Britain's largest export market', p. 24.
87. Lyons, pp. 24–25.
88. Jock Phillips, 'Of verandahs and fish and chips and footie on Saturday afternoon', *New Zealand Journal of History*, vol. 24, no. 2, 1990, p. 119.
89. Keith Sinclair, *A History of New Zealand* (Harmondsworth, Middlesex: Penguin, 1959), p. 221.
90. Eddy and Schreuder, *The Rise of Colonial Nationalism*, p. 6.
91. Hall was New Zealand premier from 1879 to 1882. John Hall to George Williamson Hall, Private Letter Book, 17 December 1885, p. 304, Hororata Collection, in Jean Garner, *By His Own Merits* (Hororata: Dryden Press, 1995), p. 199.
92. Ormond Edward Burton, *The New Zealand Division* (Auckland: Clark & Matheson, 1936), pp. 9 and 10.
93. H.A. Talbot-Tubbs, 'Introductory', *New Zealand Illustrated Magazine*, vol. 1, no. 1, 1899, p. 5.
94. Phillips, 'Musings in Maoriland', p. 527.
95. Stafford and Williams, *Maoriland*, p. 11.
96. Edith Lyttleton, *Promenade* (London: John Lane, 1938), p. 98.
97. Miles Fairburn, 'Is there a good case for New Zealand exceptionalism?' *Thesis Eleven*, no. 92, 2008, p. 45.
98. Hilliard, *The Bookmen's Dominion*, p. 13.
99. Mander, *The Story of a New Zealand River*, p. 34.

CHAPTER TWO

1. Edith Searle Grossmann, *The Heart of the Bush* (London: Sands, 1910), p. 88.
2. Andrew Mason, 'R.A.K. Mason', in *The Oxford Companion to New Zealand Literature (OCNZL)*, eds Roger Robinson and Nelson Wattie (Oxford: Oxford University Press, 1998), p. 366.
3. 'Another, less romantic version has Mason at home in Ellerslie bundling the *Beggars* into a fire in the washhouse copper.' Rachel Barrowman, *Mason: The life of R.A.K. Mason* (Wellington: Victoria University Press, 2003), p. 13.

4. Dennis McEldowney, 'Publishing, patronage and literary magazines', in *Oxford History of New Zealand Literature (OHNZL)*, ed. Terry Sturm (Oxford: Oxford University Press, 1998), pp. 641–43.

5. Derek Challis and Gloria Rawlinson, *The Book of Iris* (Auckland: Auckland University Press, 2002), p. 183.

6. Eileen Duggan to Nettie Palmer, 1935, MS Papers 0801 2/5, ATL.

7. Ian Dougherty, *Books and Boots: The story of New Zealand publisher, writer and long distance walker, Alfred Hamish Reed* (Dunedin: University of Otago Press, 2005), p. 69.

8. Challis and Rawlinson, *The Book of Iris*, p. 186.

9. Nancy Swarbrick, 'Kenny, Alice Annie', Dictionary of New Zealand Biography (DNZB): www.teara.govt.nz/en/biographies/3k10/kenny-alice-annie

10. Stephen Hamilton, 'Montague Harry Holcroft, 1902–1993', *Kōtare 2008: Special Issue – Essays in New Zealand literary biography series two: 'Early male prose writers'* (Wellington: Victoria University, 2008): www.nzetc.org/tm/scholarly/tei-Whi072Kota-t1-g1-t17.html

11. Jane Mander, 'N.Z. Writing', manuscript of a radio talk, c. 1932, Mander papers, NZMS 535, APL.

12. Robin Hyde in 1931 bemoaned living in 'a country where a writer of verse can consider him or herself overpaid if ten and sixpence is proffered for a contribution to any of the newspapers'. 'A poetaster on poets', *Observer*, 5 March 1931, in Challis and Rawlinson, *The Book of Iris*, p. 181. The median yearly income for 1926 (there was no census in 1931 due to the Napier earthquake) was £235, thus 10 shillings and sixpence represents just under an average day's wages. New Zealand Department of Censuses and Statistics, Incomes (Wellington: Department of Censuses and Statistics, 1926).

13. 'Current literature', *New Zealand Herald*, 2 April 1910, p. 4 (supplement).

14. Reginald O'Neill, *The Press, 1861–1961: The story of a newspaper* (Christchurch: Christchurch Press, 1963), p. 182.

15. O'Neill, p. 121.

16. See note 25 – there was a high level of local literary content in the *Press* in the 1920s.

17. Dennis McEldowney, 'Duff, Oliver', DNZB: www.teara.govt.nz/en/biographies/4d22/duff-oliver

18. Eileen Duggan, 'Foreword', *New Zealand Bird Songs* (Wellington: Harry T. Tombs, 1929).

19. A.R.D. Fairburn to Geoffrey de Montalk, 15 June 1927, Letters from A.R.D. Fairburn, MS Papers 2461/3, ATL.

20. Winifred Tennant to Pat Lawlor, 28 April 1936, Lawlor papers, 77-067 5/2, ATL.

21. Eileen Duggan to Nettie Palmer, 1930, MS Papers 801 2/3, ATL.

22. Eileen Duggan, testimonial regarding Alan Mulgan, c. 1936, Mulgan papers, MS Papers 0224-16, ATL.

23. Chris Hilliard, *The Bookmen's Dominion: Cultural life in New Zealand 1920–1950* (Auckland: Auckland University Press, 2006).

24. Charlotte Elder, 'An annotated edition of the correspondence between Ursula Bethell and John Schroder' (MA thesis, Victoria University, 1999), p. 15.

25. From a systematic study of these newspapers. In 1916 Schroder's literary section in the *Sun* took up half a page (out of 12). By 1925 the 'Among the Books' section was nearly a whole page, and usually included at least two original poems by New Zealanders. This was not due to a large increase in the size of the paper, as by 1925 the paper had hardly grown at all on weekdays, fluctuating between 12 and 16 pages (24 on Saturdays). When Schroder left for the *Press* in 1929, the number of original poems published in the *Sun* dropped off markedly, and by 1934 was almost back to pre-Schroder levels. By this time, too, the literary column had shrunk back to half a page, with the size of the paper remaining relatively unchanged. The literary page of the *Christchurch Press* had a similar high point, correlating with the reign of influential editors in the 1920s.

26. McEldowney, 'Publishing, patronage and literary magazines', p. 638.

27. McEldowney, p. 643.

28. Pat Lawlor, Draft of 'N.Z. Writing: A survey' (c. 1962), p. 3, 77-067 7/2, ATL.

29. Gregory Andrew Keith Baughen, 'C.N. Baeyertz and the Triad 1893–1915' (BA[Hons] thesis, University of Otago, 1980), p. 14.

30. Rae McGregor, *The Story of a New Zealand Writer: Jane Mander* (Dunedin: University of Otago Press, 1998), p. 34.

31. Judith Wild, 'The literary periodical in New Zealand' (MA thesis, Victoria University College, 1951), p. 17.

32. Charles Baeyertz, *Triad*, vol. 20, no. 10, January 1913, p. 1.

33. Robin Hyde, *Journalese* (Auckland: National Printing Company, 1934), p. 21.

34. McEldowney, 'Publishing, patronage and literary magazines', p. 641.

35. Jane Mander to Monte Holcroft, 17 May 1934, Holcroft papers, MS Papers 1186/16, ATL.

36. Paul Millar, *No Fretful Sleeper: A life of Bill Pearson* (Auckland: Auckland University Press, 2010), p. 41.

37. Riemke Ensing, 'Rawlinson, Gloria Jasmine', DNZB: www.teara.govt.nz/en/biographies/4r8/rawlinson-gloria-jasmine

38. Noel Hoggard, *The Inky Way: An essay into autobiography* (Wellington: Handcraft Press, 1940), pp. 12–13.

39. Lydia Wevers, 'First, build your hut', *Pacific Highways. Griffith Review*, no. 43, 2013, pp. 261–67.

40. J.E. Traue, 'Submerged below the codex line: New Zealand's neglected nineteenth century serial novels', *Journal of New Zealand Studies*, no. 20, 2015, pp. 1, 6.

41. From my data: books published in New Zealand by New Zealand authors from 1890–1935. See Helen Bones, 'A dual exile? New Zealand and the colonial writing world, 1890–1945' (PhD thesis, University of Canterbury, 2011): http://hdl.handle.net/10092/5618, Appendix A. This excludes the 120 books published by Fergus Hume, as do all the figures where indicated. Because of Hume's unusually prolific output, he is considered an outlier whose inclusion would distort the statistics.

42. 'Full of envy of the production of *Phoenix* and the establishment of the Auckland University College Students' Association Press – dreadful mouthful – I thought it was time that Canterbury did something of the sort.' Denis Glover, *Hot Water Sailor & Landlubber Ho!* (Auckland: Collins, 1981), p. 82.

43. Robert Chapman, 'Fiction and the social pattern', *Landfall*, vol. 7, no. 1, March 1953, p. 31.

44. Eileen Duggan, 'Heralds', *Poems* (London: Allen and Unwin, 1937), p. 13.

45. Felicity Barnes, *New Zealand's London: A colony and its metropolis* (Auckland: Auckland University Press, 2012), p. 9.

46. Mary Scott, *Days That Have Been* (Auckland: Blackwood & J. Paul, 1966), p. 177.

47. Eileen Duggan to Nettie Palmer, 1924, MS Papers 801 2/2, ATL.

48. Duggan to Palmer, 1930, MS Papers 801 2/3, ATL.

49. Fairburn to de Montalk, 21 July 1936, MS Papers 2461/4, ATL.

50. Challis and Rawlinson, *The Book of Iris*, p. 105.

51. Challis and Rawlinson, p. 186.

52. 'R.A.K. Mason on Rex Fairburn', 1957, transcript, Auckland University Library, pp. 15–16, in Barrowman, *Mason*, p. 47.

53. James McNeish, *Dance of the Peacocks: New Zealanders in exile at the time of Hitler and Mao Tse-tung* (Auckland: Vintage, 2003), p. 21.

54. Charles Brasch, *Indirections, A Memoir* (Wellington: Oxford University Press, 1980), in Jill Trevelyan, '"Perfectly fairy-godmotherish": The friendship of Toss Woollaston and Ursula Bethell', *Kōtare*, vol. 4, no. 1, 2001: http://ojs.victoria.ac.nz/kotare/article/view/730

55. Toss Woollaston, *Sage Tea* (Wellington: Te Papa Press, 2001), p. 216.

56. Woollaston, p. 222.

57. Peter Simpson, *Bloomsbury South: The arts in Christchurch 1933–1953* (Auckland: Auckland University Press, 2016).

58. Betty Gilderdale, 'Peacocke, Inez Isabel Maud', DNZB: www.teara.govt.nz/en/biographies/4p6/peacocke-inez-isabel-maud. Though Hyde said the 'actual production or appreciation of literature comes a very, very meek second to chatting over cups of tea'. Hilliard, *The Bookmen's Dominion*, pp. 24–25.

59. Stephen Hamilton, 'New Zealand English language periodicals of literary interest active 1920s–1960s' (PhD thesis, University of Auckland, 1995), pp. 557–58, in Hilliard, *The Bookmen's Dominion*, p. 24.

60. *New Zealand Illustrated Magazine*, June 1900, p. 718, in Theresia Marshall, 'New Zealand literature in the Sydney *Bulletin*' (PhD thesis, University of Auckland, 1995), p. 67.

61. 'The Editor and his contributors', *The New Zealand Illustrated Magazine*, January 1903, p. 260.

62. Hyde to Schroder, 16 May 1928, in Challis and Rawlinson, *The Book of Iris*, p. 109.

63. Valerie Laura, 'Bethell, Mary Ursula', DNZB: www.teara.govt.nz/en/biographies/4b29/bethell-mary-ursula

64. 'The minute book records no sense of incongruity at such an organisation's being founded by a man.' Hilliard, *The Bookmen's Dominion*, p. 25.

65. Denis Glover, 'Pointers to Parnassus: A consideration of the morepork and the muse', *Tomorrow*, no. 2, 1935.

66. Glover, 'Pointers to Parnassus', quoted in Lawrence Jones, *Picking Up the Traces: The making of a New Zealand literary culture 1932–1945* (Wellington: Victoria University Press, 2003), p. 53.

67. Hilliard, *The Bookmen's Dominion*, p. 47.

68. Anne French, 'Georgians and New Zealand Georgians: A study of Eileen Duggan and R.A.K. Mason, and New Zealand poetry of the twenties and thirties in the context of Georgian poetry in England' (MA thesis, Victoria University, 1979), p. 2.

69. F.W. Neilsen Wright, *Theories of Style in the Schroder-Marris School of Poets in Aotearoa: An essay in formal stylistics with particular reference to the poets Eileen Duggan, Robin Hyde and Ruth Gilbert* (Wellington: Political and Cultural Booklets, 2001), p. 6.

70. 'Books and authors', *Dominion*, 23 January 1909, p. 9.

71. Grossmann, *The Heart of the Bush*, p. 40.

72. Grossmann, p. 66.

73. Jane Stafford and Mark Williams, *Maoriland: New Zealand literature 1872–1914* (Wellington: Victoria University Press, 2006), p. 193.

74. Patrick Evans, *Penguin History of New Zealand Literature* (Auckland: Penguin, 1990), p. 76.

75. R.A.K. Mason, 'Why We Can't Write For Nuts', MS 1134/1, HC, in Barrowman, *Mason*, p. 94.

76. Glover, *Hot Water Sailor*, p. 94.

77. Allen Curnow, 'Introduction', *A Book of New Zealand Verse 1923–1945* (Christchurch: Caxton Press, 1945), p. 17.

78. Jessie Mackay, 'Concerning New Zealand letters', *Art in New Zealand*, March 1929, p. 163.

79. Eileen Duggan, article on Jessie Mackay, 77-067 3/6, ATL.

80. Eileen Duggan, 'Shades of Maro of Toulouse', *More Poems* (London: Allen & Unwin, 1951), p. 17.

81. Robin Hyde, *Journalese* (Auckland: National Printing Company, 1934), p. 191.

82. Challis and Rawlinson, *The Book of Iris*, p. 153.

83. Monte Holcroft, *Discovered Isles: A trilogy* (Christchurch: Caxton Press, 1950), p. 33.

84. Peter Gibbons, 'The far side of the search for identity', *New Zealand Journal of History*, vol. 37, no. 1, 2003, p. 38.

85. Ian Wedde, 'Introduction', *The Penguin Book of New Zealand Verse* (Auckland: Penguin, 1985), p. 33.

86. Wedde, p. 37.

87. Kai Jensen, *Whole Men* (Auckland: Auckland University Press, 1996), p. 43.

88. For example, Glover's more rugged 'personae' who appeared in his poems: Harry, Arawata Bill and Mick Stimson. John Newton, 'Colonialism above the snowline', *Journal of Commonwealth Literature*, vol. 34, no. 85, 1999, pp. 89–90.

89. A.R.D. Fairburn to Denis Glover, 17 August 1934, Glover Papers, MS Papers 418/15, ATL.

90. There were women writers associated with the *Phoenix* group, such as Jean Alison and Elsie Locke, as well as a multitude of women writers at this time, but they 'seemed to melt away', according to Evans, *Penguin History of New Zealand Literature*, p. 83.

91. E.g. Guy Scholefield and Johannes Andersen occupied several roles. Hilliard, *The Bookmen's Dominion*, p. 20.

92. Eric McCormick, *Letters and Art in New Zealand* (Wellington: Dept. of Internal Affairs, 1940), p. 125.

CHAPTER THREE

1. Bruce Nesbitt, 'Aspects of literary nationalism in Australia and New Zealand with special reference to the *Bulletin*, 1880–1900' (PhD thesis, Australian National University, 1968).

2. Peter Kirkpatrick, *The Sea Coast of Bohemia: Literary life in Sydney's roaring twenties* (Perth: API Network, 2007), p. 32.

3. Jock Phillips, 'Musings in Maoriland – or was there a *Bulletin* school in New Zealand?', *Historical Studies*, vol. 20, no. 81, 1983, p. 522.

4. Theresia Marshall, 'New Zealand literature in the Sydney *Bulletin*' (PhD thesis, University of Auckland, 1995), p. 13.

5. Edith Lyttleton to Frederick de la Mare, 24 August 1934, in Frederick de la Mare, *G.B. Lancaster 1873–1945: A tribute* (Hamilton: Waikato Times, 1945), p. 14.

6. Lydia Wevers, 'Books: Are New Zealand and Australia part of the same literary community?' in *New Zealand and Australia: Where are we going?*, Papers presented at the seminar arranged by the New Zealand Institute of International Affairs at Victoria University, Wellington, on 4 July 2001, ed. Bruce Brown (Wellington: New Zealand Institute of International Affairs, 2001), p. 80.

7. Terry Sturm, 'The neglected middle distance: Towards a history of transTasman literary relations', *Ariel*, vol. 16, no. 4, 1985, p. 30.

8. Peter Hempenstall, Philippa Mein Smith and Shaun Goldfinch, *Remaking the Tasman World* (Christchurch: Canterbury University Press, 2008), p. 19.

9. G.R. Hawke, *The Making of New Zealand: An economic history* (Cambridge: Cambridge University Press, 1985), p. 151.

10. Hempenstall, Mein Smith and Goldfinch, *Remaking the Tasman World*, p. 31.

11. Pat Lawlor, Draft of 'New Zealand Writing: A survey', c. 1962, 77-067 7/2, ATL.

12. McCormick to Heenan, 2 October 1940, Heenan papers, MS Papers 1132-134, ATL, in Chris Hilliard, *The Bookmen's Dominion: Cultural life in New Zealand 1920–1950* (Auckland: Auckland University Press, 2006), p. 102.

13. Curnow to Alan Mulgan, 10 February 1948, Mulgan papers, MS Papers 244-15, ATL, in Hilliard, *The Bookmen's Dominion*, p. 103.

14. Glover to Mulgan, 20 July 1948, MS Papers 0224-15, ATL.

15. Allen Curnow, 'Modern Australian Poetry', *Landfall*, vol. 1, no. 2, 1947, p. 142.

16. In 1930 Duggan wrote to Nettie Palmer, saying that Fairburn 'used to have a blind spot on Australian literature but I see he was in the Christmas *Bulletin*'. Duggan to Palmer, Duggan papers, 1930, MS Papers 801 2/3, ATL.

17. Pat Lawlor to Hector Bolitho, 9 May 1966, 77-067 1/5, ATL.

18. Jason D. Ensor, 'Places of publication and the Australian book trade: A study of Angus & Robertson's London office, 1938–1970' (PhD thesis, Murdoch University, 2010), p. 151.

19. *Auckland Star*, 27 October 1928 (supplement), p. 2.

20. Marshall, 'New Zealand literature in the Sydney *Bulletin*', p. 12.

21. 'Answers to correspondents', *Bulletin*, 27 April 1922, p. 44.

22. Nelle Scanlan, *Road to Pencarrow* (London: Robert Hale, 1963), p. 121.

23. Marshall, 'New Zealand literature in the Sydney *Bulletin*', p. 249.

24. Jane Stafford and Mark Williams, *Maoriland: New Zealand literature 1872–1914* (Wellington: Victoria University Press, 2006), p. 153.

25. Scanlan, *Road to Pencarrow*, p. 121.

26. Stuart Lee, 'Stephens, Alfred George (1865–1933)', Australian Dictionary of Biography (ADB): http://adb.anu.edu.au/biography/stephens-alfred-george-8642

27. E.g. on Jessie Mackay, 'Reactions', *The Bookfellow*, 1 July 1913, p. 154; 'Trade reports', *The Bookfellow*, 1 April 1931, pp. xviii–xix.

28. Phillips, 'Musings in Maoriland', p. 522, referring to Arthur H. Adams, *Tussock Land* (London: T. Fisher Unwin, 1904), p. 8.

29. Isabel Maud Peacocke to A.G. Stephens, 20 March 1910, Box 4, MLMSS 4937, SLNSW.

30. A.G Stephens, Autobiographies of Australian and New Zealand authors, Box 28, MLMSS 4937, SLNSW.

31. Stafford and Williams, *Maoriland*, p. 147.

32. Andrew Nash, 'Literary culture and literary publishing in inter-war Britain: A view from Chatto & Windus', in *Literary Cultures and the Material Book*, eds Simon Eliot, Andrew Nash and Ian Willison (London: British Library, 2007), p. 331.

33. Deana Heath, 'Literary censorship, imperialism and the White Australia policy', in *A History of the Book in Australia 1891–1945: A national culture in a colonised market*, eds Martyn Lyons and John Arnold (St Lucia, Qsld: University of Queensland Press, 2001), p. 69.

34. Jessie Mackay to Lawlor, 1 April 1937, 77-067 3/6, ATL, quoted in Hilliard, *The Bookmen's Dominion*, p. 7.

35. Nettie Palmer, 'Jessie Mackay', undated [c. 1930] clipping from the Red Page of the *Bulletin*, Lawlor papers, 77-067 3/6, ATL, in Hilliard, *The Bookmen's Dominion*, p. 9.

36. 'Australian and New Zealand literary societies', *All About Books*, 20 January 1930, p. 33; 15 September 1930, p. 247.

37. Jessie Mackay to A.G. Stephens, 3 May 1910, Box 4, MLMSS-4937, SLNSW.

38. Graeme Johanson, *Colonial Editions in Australia, 1843–1972* (Wellington: Elibank Press, 2000), p. 5.

39. Hilliard, *The Bookmen's Dominion*, p. 33.

40. Hilliard, p. 33.
41. Hugh Price, 'Educational publishing', in *Book and Print in New Zealand*, eds Griffith, Harvey and Maslen, p. 144.
42. Ian F. McLaren, *Whitcombe's Story Books: A trans-Tasman survey* (Parkville: University of Melbourne Library, 1984), p. vii.
43. See Philippa Mein Smith, 'Mapping Australasia', *History Compass*, no. 7, 2009, p. 3.
44. Agnieszka Sobocinska and Richard White, 'Travel and connections', in *Cambridge History of Australia: Volume 2 – The Australian Commonwealth*, eds Alison Bashford and Stuart Macintyre (Melbourne: Cambridge University Press, 2013), p. 478.
45. Robert Lee, *Transport: An Australian history* (Sydney: University of New South Wales Press, 2010), p. 159.
46. Mein Smith, 'Mapping Australasia', p. 19.
47. Nigel Prickett, 'Trans-Tasman stories: Australian Aborigines in New Zealand sealing and shore whaling', in *Islands of Inquiry: Colonisation, seafaring and the archaeology of maritime landscapes (Volume 29 of Terra Australis)*, eds Geoffrey Clark, Sue O'Connor and Bryan Leach (Canberra: Australian National University EPress, 2008), p. 362, quoting Belich, *Making Peoples*, p. 134.
48. In the 1870s mail took five-and-a-half days to reach Auckland from Sydney. Howard Robinson, *A History of the Post Office in New Zealand* (Wellington: Government Printer, 1964), p. 130. In 1908 the journey from Sydney to Auckland or Wellington took five days, and by 1918 just four days. Mein Smith, 'Mapping Australasia', p. 19.
49. In a letter to Palmer from 1924 Duggan confesses to not knowing much about Australian literature but says she has 'seen [Palmer's] name in the book-lists'. 1924, MS Papers 801 2/2, ATL.
50. Duggan to Nettie Palmer, 1924, MS Papers 801 2/2, ATL.
51. Duggan to Palmer, 1930, MS Papers 801 2/3, ATL.
52. Duggan to Palmer, 1927.
53. Duggan to Palmer, 1928.
54. Duggan to Palmer, 1926.
55. Jean Devanny, *Point of Departure* (St Lucia, Qld: University of Queensland Press, 1986).
56. Heather Roberts, 'Devanny, Jean', DNZB: www.teara.govt.nz/en/biographies/4d13/devanny-jean
57. Devanny, *Point of Departure*.
58. Hector Bolitho, *My Restless Years* (London: Parrish, 1962), p. 79.
59. Sturm, 'The neglected middle distance', p. 40.
60. Rollo Arnold, 'The dynamics and quality of trans-Tasman migration 1885–1910', *Australian Economic History Review*, vol. 26, no. 1, 1986, pp. 1–2, in Hempenstall, Mein Smith and Goldfinch, *Remaking the Tasman World*, p. 144.
61. Hayden Glass and Wai Kin Choy, 'Brain drain or brain exchange?', Treasury Working Paper 01/22: www.treasury.govt.nz/publications/research-policy/wp/2001/01-22/twp01-22.pdf

62. Jock Phillips, 'History of immigration – Depression: 1885 to 1900', Te Ara – the Encyclopedia of New Zealand: www.teara.govt.nz/en/history-of-immigration/10
63. Rosemary Baird, 'Across the Tasman: Narratives of New Zealand migrants to and from Australia, 1965–95' (PhD thesis, University of Canterbury, 2012), p. 52.
64. Labour and Immigration Research Centre, 'Permanent and long term migration: The big picture', Ministry of Business, Innovation and Employment: www.mbie. govt.nz/publications-research/research/migration/plt-migration.pdf
65. 'International travel and migration: December 2015', Statistics New Zealand: www. stats.govt.nz/browse_for_stats/population/Migration/IntTravelAndMigration_ HOTPDec15/Tables.aspx
66. 'Migration trends 2015/2016', Ministry of Business, Innovation and Employment: www.mbie.govt.nz/publications-research/research/migrants---monitoring/ migration-trends-and-outlook-2015-16.pdf
67. Helen Bones, 'A dual exile? New Zealand and the colonial writing world, 1890–1945' (PhD thesis, University of Canterbury, 2011): http://hdl.handle. net/10092/5618, pp. 68–69.
68. Bertha Lawson, *My Henry Lawson* (Sydney: Frank Johnson, 1943), p. 57, in Bill Pearson, *Henry Lawson Among Maoris* (Wellington: Reed, 1968), p. 82.
69. Pearson, *Henry Lawson Among Maoris*, p. 107.
70. Mary Louise Ormsby, 'Wilson, Anne', DNZB: www.teara.govt.nz/en/ biographies/2w27/wilson-anne
71. Steven Loveridge, 'The "other" on the other side of the ditch? The conception of New Zealand's disassociation from Australia', *Journal of Imperial and Commonwealth History*, vol. 44, no. 1, 2016, p. 81.
72. B.G. Andrews and Martha Rutledge, 'Morton, Frank (1869–1923)', ADB: http:// adb.anu.edu.au/biography/morton-frank-7667
73. Hilliard, *The Bookmen's Dominion*, p. 4.
74. Hilliard, p. 35.
75. 'Written in Australia', *Maoriland and Other Verses* (Sydney: Bulletin Newspaper Company, 1899).
76. For instance, writing for the *Sydney Morning Herald* in 1905 he discusses the perspective of 'the Australian visitor to London', presumably meaning himself ('The London stage', *Sydney Morning Herald*, 26 August 1905, p. 8), and for a London paper in 1902, 'A New Zealander's impressions', *Daily Mail*, reprinted in the *Broadford Courier and Reedy Creek Times*, 28 August 1902, p. 6.
77. Kirstine Moffat, 'Arthur. H Adams, 1872–1935', *Kōtare*, vol. 7, no. 3, 2008, p. 80.
78. 'The *Triad*', *The Land* (Sydney), 29 December 1916, p. 12.
79. Patrick Evans, *Penguin History of New Zealand Literature* (Auckland: Penguin, 1990), p. 44.
80. Hilliard, *The Bookmen's Dominion*, p. 25.
81. Pat Lawlor, *Confessions of a Journalist* (Auckland: Whitcombe & Tombs, 1935), p. 221.
82. Douglas Stewart to Alan Mulgan, 20 Feb c. 1940, MS Papers 224-15, ATL.
83. Sturm, 'The neglected middle distance', p. 41.

84. B.G. Andrews and Ann-Mari Jordens, 'Adams, Arthur Henry (1872–1936)', ADB: http://adb.anu.edu.au/biography/adams-arthur-henry-4969
85. Moffat, 'Arthur H. Adams', pp. 73, 80.
86. Marshall, 'New Zealand literature in the Sydney *Bulletin*', p. 305.
87. James Belich, *Paradise Reforged: A history of the New Zealanders from the 1880s to the year 2000* (Auckland: Penguin, 2001), p. 51.
88. David Carter, 'Good readers and good citizens: Literature, media and the nation', *Australian Literary Studies*, vol. 19, no. 2, 1999, p. 138.

CHAPTER FOUR

1. Mary Scott, *The Unwritten Book* (Wellington: Reed, 1957), p. 143.
2. Lydia Wevers, 'Scott, Mary Edith', Dictionary of New Zealand Biography (DNZB): www.teara.govt.nz/en/biographies/4s14/scott-mary-edith
3. Mary Scott, *Days that Have Been* (Auckland: Blackwood & J. Paul, 1966), p. 165; Scott, *The Unwritten Book*, p. 143.
4. See Helen Bones, 'A dual exile? New Zealand and the colonial writing world, 1890–1945' (PhD thesis, University of Canterbury, 2011): http://hdl.handle.net/10092/5618, Appendix A. These figures exclude the work of Fergus Hume.
5. Terry Sturm, 'Attila of the Antipodes; or, the mad hatter's tea-party: The publishing history of Edith Lyttleton (G.B. Lancaster) in the 1930s', in *A Book in the Hand: Essays on the history of the book in New Zealand*, eds Penny Griffith, Peter Hughes and Alan Loney (Auckland: Auckland University Press, 2000), p. 85.
6. Dennis McEldowney, 'Publishing, patronage and literary magazines', in *Oxford History of New Zealand Literature* (*OHNZL*), ed. Terry Sturm (Oxford: Oxford University Press, 1998), pp. 651–53.
7. Pat Lawlor, Draft of 'New Zealand Writing: A survey', 77-067 7/2, ATL.
8. John Barnes, '"Heaven forbid that I should think of treating with an English publisher": The dilemma of literary nationalists in federated Australia', in *Literary Cultures and the Material Book*, eds Simon Eliot, Andrew Nash and Ian Willison (London: The British Library, 2007), p. 406. Stephens turned out to be wrong, as it sold 4000 copies, mostly in Australia.
9. Jane Mander, 'N.Z. authors and English publishers', Talk for Authors' Week, p. 1, NZMS 535, APL.
10. From the figure cited in Chapter 2, note 12. It is not clear whether Mander is referring to British or New Zealand pounds here, but at least until 1930 they were more or less the same. In 1931 UK£100 = NZ£125, as 'in the late 1920s, the rate of exchange between Britain and New Zealand diverged from the parity which had long been customary'. G.R. Hawke, *The Making of New Zealand: An economic history* (Cambridge: Cambridge University Press, 1985), p. 151.
11. C.R. Allen, letter to Pat Lawlor, 9 May 1934, 77-067 7/2, ATL.
12. Martyn Lyons, 'Britain's largest export market', in *A History of the Book in Australia 1891–1945: A national culture in a colonised market*, eds Martyn Lyons and John Arnold (St Lucia, Qsld: University of Queensland Press, 2001), p. 24.

13. Lyons, pp. 24–25.

14. Luke Trainor, 'Colonial editions', in *Book and Print in New Zealand: A guide to print culture in Aotearoa*, eds Penny Griffith, Ross Harvey and Keith Maslen (Wellington: Victoria University Press, 1997), p. 116.

15. Eileen Duggan, letter to Stanley Unwin, 27 October 1948, Allen & Unwin papers, AUC 345/10, University of Reading Special Collections (URSC).

16. Ursula Bethell to Frank Sidgwick, 5 December 1929, Sidgwick & Jackson papers, MSS 142, fols. 84–85, BLSC, Oxford.

17. Geoffrey de Montalk to Lawlor, 10 July 1930, 77-067 3/1, ATL.

18. Janet McCallum, 'Rollett, Hilda', DNZB: www.teara.govt.nz/en/biographies/3r26/rollett-hilda

19. Terry Sturm, *An Unsettled Spirit: The life and frontier fiction of Edith Lyttleton (G.B. Lancaster)* (Auckland: Auckland University Press, 2003), p. 2.

20. She wrote regularly for the *New Zealand Tablet* 'by way of serving her Catholic faith'. Frank McKay, *Eileen Duggan* (Wellington: Oxford University Press, 1977), p. 5.

21. Hector Bolitho, *My Restless Years* (London: Parrish, 1962), p. 67.

22. W.M. Roger Louis, 'Introduction', *The Oxford History of the British Empire: Volume IV: The twentieth century* (Oxford: Oxford University Press, 1999), p. 16.

23. Louis, p. 16.

24. Sturm, *An Unsettled Spirit*, p. 2.

25. Sturm, p. 1.

26. Lydia Wevers says, 'Virtually everything was published in the United Kingdom, and there was almost no direct interaction with the United States despite huge literary similarities.' Wevers, 'Books: Are New Zealand and Australia part of the same literary community?', in *New Zealand and Australia: Where are we going?* Papers presented at the seminar arranged by the New Zealand Institute of International Affairs at Victoria University, Wellington, on 4 July 2001, ed. Bruce Brown (Wellington: New Zealand Institute of International Affairs, 2001), p. 73.

27. James Belich, *Paradise Reforged: A history of the New Zealanders from the 1880s to the year 2000* (Auckland: Penguin, 2001), p. 53.

28. Felicity Barnes, *New Zealand's London: A colony and its metropolis* (Auckland: Auckland University Press, 2012), p. 8.

29. Martyn Lyons, 'Britain's largest export market', in *A History of the Book in Australia 1891–1945*, eds Lyons and Arnold, p. 22.

30. Lyons, p. 10.

31. Lyons, p. 10.

32. A.G. Stephens to Joseph Furphy, 22 May 1897, in John Barnes, *The Writer in Australia* (Melbourne: Oxford University Press, 1969), p. 119.

33. Stanley Unwin, letter to Eileen Duggan, 31 March 1931, AUC 110/13, URSC.

34. Edward Dyson, 'The Australian Author and his Publisher', qMS-0100, Australian Mss. V.III, ATL, quoted in Luke Trainor, 'New Zealand writers seeking overseas publishers, 1870–1914: Some issues of nation and empire', *Script & Print 29*, nos. 1–4, 2005, p. 320.

35. Belich, *Paradise Reforged*, p. 69.

36. Howard Robinson, *A History of the Post Office in New Zealand* (Wellington: Government Printer, 1964), p. 141.

37. Tony Ballantyne, 'Mobility, empire, colonisation', *History Australia*, vol. 11, no. 2, 2014, p. 8.

38. Peter Whiteford, '"Food parcels and fond hopes": Some correspondence of Walter de la Mare', *Kōtare*, vol. 4, no. 1, 2001, p. 56.

39. Phillip Wilson, *William Satchell* (New York: Twayne Publishers 1968), p. 38.

40. Sturm, *An Unsettled Spirit*, p. 97.

41. Lyttleton, letter to Hitchcock, 21 February 1933, MS Papers 8649/31, ATL.

42. Edith Lyttleton to F.A. Jones, 16 June 1933, MS Papers 8649/31, ATL.

43. Sturm, *An Unsettled Spirit*, p. 208.

44. Jane Mander to Monte Holcroft, 26 June 1934, MS Papers 1186/6, ATL.

45. Duggan to Palmer, 1936, MS Papers 801 2/5, ATL.

46. In one article Trainor mentions that it was very difficult for writers to publish ethnography and history in the United Kingdom without contacts to place their manuscripts, and to 'see their manuscripts through the press, for the prospect of sending proofs to Australia and getting them back was daunting'. Luke Trainor, 'British publishers and cultural imperialism: History and ethnography in Australasia 1870–1930', *Bibliographical Society of Australia and New Zealand Bulletin*, vol. 20, no. 2, 1996, p. 101.

47. Papers of Sidgwick & Jackson, MSS 142, BLSC.

48. Peter Whiteford, 'Secrets of Felicity: Letters of Ursula Bethell', New Zealand Electronic Poetry Centre: www.nzepc.auckland.ac.nz/authors/bethell/letters03.asp

49. Monte Holcroft, *Mary Ursula Bethell* (Wellington; New York: Oxford University Press, 1975), p. 20.

50. Denys Trussell, *Fairburn* (Auckland: Auckland University Press, 1984), p. 83.

51. Winnie Davin to Dan Davin, 17 May 1944, Anna Davin (private collection), London.

52. T. Fisher Unwin to Angus & Robertson, 15 January 1897, ML MSS 314/85/2, SLNSW.

53. Ursula Bethell to J. Sidgwick, 4 November 1929, MSS 142, fol. 75, BLSC.

54. Frank Sidgwick to Arthur Mayhew, 29 May 1929, Bethell papers, MS 558, MBL.

55. Frank Sidgwick to Ursula Bethell, 20–21 December 1929, MS 558, MBL.

56. Monte Holcroft, Notebook, from 1923, MSX-0253, ATL. Statistics are from 1925 entries.

57. From census data – see Chapter Two, note 12.

58. Frank Sargeson, *More than Enough* (1975), reprinted in Frank Sargeson, *Sargeson* (Auckland: Penguin, 1981), p. 172.

59. Luke Trainor, 'New Zealand writers seeking overseas publishers, 1870–1914: some issues of nation and empire', *Script & Print*, 29, no. 1–4 (2005), pp. 317–18.

60. R.A.K. Mason, written on the back of a letter from the Seddon Memorial Technical College, 19 September 1923, MS 990/15/1, HC, Dunedin, in Rachel Barrowman, *Mason: The life of R.A.K. Mason* (Wellington: Victoria University Press, 2003), p. 39.

61. Barrowman, *Mason*, p. 58.
62. Edith Lyttleton to Mr Skinner, 18 February 1933, AUC 37/6, URSC.
63. Nelle Scanlan, *Road to Pencarrow* (London: Robert Hale, 1963), p. 181.
64. Jane Mander, 'A London letter: Another N.Z. writer', *Sun*, 20 February 1925.
65. Alan Mulgan, 'Letters in NZ', no date, typescript, MS Papers 0224-31, ATL; 'Difficulties of the New Zealand novelist', *Art in New Zealand*, December 1928.
66. Scanlan, *Road to Pencarrow*, p. 181.
67. Scanlan, p. 181.
68. Bones, 'A dual exile?', p. 88. Again, the work of Fergus Hume is omitted from this information. Hume's 120 books had virtually no New Zealand content.
69. Of those whose content is known; 73 per cent had at least some New Zealand content.
70. 'The Butler cult at home', *Press*, 10 March 1925.
71. 'Women's Forum – the fiction market', *Auckland Star*, 12 November 1932, NZMS 535, Folder 9, box 1, APL.
72. Going by Luke Trainor's rejection rate of 92 per cent, that would give a total of 1625 submissions for 130 successes. Trainor, 'New Zealand writers seeking overseas publishers, 1870–1914', pp. 317–18.
73. Jane Stafford and Mark Williams, *Maoriland: New Zealand literature 1872–1914* (Wellington: Victoria University Press, 2006), p. 35.
74. Barnes, '"Heaven forbid that I should think of treating with an English publisher"', p. 408.
75. Patrick Evans, *The Long Forgetting* (Christchurch: Canterbury University Press, 2007), p. 62.
76. 'Noble savage', Encyclopedia Britannica: www.britannica.com/EBchecked/topic/416988/noble-savage
77. Stafford and Williams, *Maoriland*, p. 46.
78. Jock Phillips, 'Musings in Maoriland', *Historical Studies*, vol. 20, no. 81, 1983, p. 528.
79. Āpirana Ngata was a poet as well as a scholar and statesman, and Stafford and Williams devote a chapter to him.
80. Alfred Domett, *Ranolf and Amohia: A south sea day-dream* (London: Smith, Elder, 1872); Stafford and Williams, *Maoriland*, p. 36.
81. Nelson Wattie, 'Grace, Alfred Augustus', DNZB: www.teara.govt.nz/en/biographies/3g18/grace-alfred-augustus
82. Lawrence Jones, 'Chamier, George', DNZB: www.teara.govt.nz/en/biographies/2c15/chamier-george
83. William Satchell, *The Land of the Lost* (London: Methuen, 1902).
84. Patrick Brantlinger, *Rule of Darkness: British literature and imperialism, 1830–1914* (Ithaca: NY: Cornell University Press, 1988), p. 8, in Lydia Wevers, *Reading on the Farm: Victorian fiction and the colonial world* (Wellington: Victoria University Press, 2010), p. 196.
85. Robert Dixon, *Writing the Colonial Adventure: Race, gender, and nation in Anglo-Australian popular fiction, 1875–1914* (Cambridge: Cambridge University Press, 1995), pp. 1–2.

86. 'New chums': the surly Scottish station-master says, '"Englishman, eh? – Well, we no employ new chums here!"' Walter Smyth, *Jean of the Tussock Country* (London: Mills & Boon, 1928), p. 25.

87. Smyth, p. 20.

88. Isabel Maud Peacocke, *The Guardian* (London: Ward, Lock, 1920); Alice A. Kenny, *The Rebel* (Sydney: Macquarie Head Press, 1934).

89. F. Hellier, *Colonials in Khaki* (London: Murray & Evenden, 1916), p. 15.

90. Hellier, p. 51.

91. Raewyn Dalziel, 'Presenting the enfranchisement of New Zealand women abroad', in *Suffrage and Beyond: International feminist perspectives*, eds Caroline Daley and Melanie Nolan (Auckland: Auckland University Press, 1994).

92. Edith Searle Grossmann, *Hermione: A knight of the Holy Ghost* (London: Watts, 1908), p. 200.

93. Review of *Home Is Where the Heart Is*, *Times Literary Supplement* 1732, 11 April 1935, p. 246.

94. Review of *Ponga Bay*, *Times Literary Supplement* 1100, 15 February 1923, p. 110.

95. Review of *Tussock Land*, *Times Literary Supplement* 121, 5 June 1904, p. 140.

96. Review of *Heather of the South*, *Times Literary Supplement* 1187, 16 October 1924, p. 653.

97. Reproduced in the *Sun*, 3 January 1931.

98. Mason to Robert Graves, 17 March 1932, Correspondence re. *No New Thing*, MS 990/91, HC.

99. Jane Mander to Monte Holcroft, 23 December 1932, MS Papers 1186/6, ATL.

100. Jane Mander to Monte Holcroft, 9 May 1932, MS Papers 1186/6, ATL.

101. Terry Sturm, 'Anthony, Frank Sheldon', DNZB: www.teara.govt.nz/en/biographies/4a18/anthony-frank-sheldon

102. Prudence Cadey, *Broken Pattern* (London: Fenland Press, 1933), p. 79.

103. Cadey, p. 104.

104. Cadey, p. 258.

105. There are 118 New Zealand writers who published books between 1890 and 1945 for whom there is adequate biographical information to be included in my dataset (see Bones, 'A dual exile?', Appendix B). Of these writers, 53 stayed in New Zealand between 1890 and 1945, and 10 more left only for short trips lasting a year or less (for holidaying, sightseeing or visiting relatives).

CHAPTER FIVE

1. Dan Davin, *Cliffs of Fall* (London: Nicholson & Watson, 1945); Joan Stevens, *The New Zealand Novel 1860–1965* (Wellington: Reed, 1966), p. 65.

2. Stevens, *The New Zealand Novel 1860–1965*, p. 65.

3. James Bertram, *Flight of the Phoenix: Critical notes on New Zealand writers* (Wellington: Victoria University Press, 1985), p. 68.

4. Andrew Gurr, *Writers in Exile: The identity of home in modern literature* (Brighton: Harvester Press, 1981), pp. 18–19.

5. Gurr, p. 7.
6. Helen Bones, 'A dual exile? New Zealand and the colonial writing world, 1890–1945' (PhD thesis, University of Canterbury, 2011): http://hdl.handle.net/10092/5618, Appendix B.
7. Eric McCormick, *Letters and Art in New Zealand* (Wellington: Dept. of Internal Affairs, 1940), p. 130.
8. McCormick, p. 105.
9. James Smithies, 'Modernism or exile? E.H. McCormick and "Letters and Art in New Zealand"', *Journal of Commonwealth Literature*, vol. 39, no. 3, 2004, p. 101.
10. Jane Mander to Monte Holcroft, 9 November 1931, MS Papers 1186/16, ATL.
11. Roslyn Russell, *Literary Links: Celebrating the literary relationship between Australia and Britain* (St. Leonards, NSW: Allen & Unwin, 1997), p. 84.
12. Drusilla Modjeska, *Exiles at Home: Australian women writers 1925–1945* (London: Sirius Books, 1981), p. 30.
13. Nelle Scanlan to Alan Mulgan, 9 December 1959, MS Papers 0224-11, ATL. The 1959 sales figure for Pencarrow was 30,700, and it was still selling.
14. McCormick, *Letters and Art in New Zealand*, p. 130.
15. Kirstine Moffat, 'Louisa Alice Baker, 1856–1926', *Kōtare*, vol. 7, no. 1, 2007, p. 12.
16. Heather Murray, 'Celebrating our writers: 1936, 1951: Part 1: 1936', *Journal of New Zealand Literature*, no. 10, 1992.
17. Aorewa McLeod, 'A home in this world: Why New Zealand women stopped writing', *Women's Studies Journal*, vol. 14, no. 2, 1998, p. 68.
18. Terry Sturm, 'Popular fiction', in *Oxford History of New Zealand Literature* (*OHNZL*), ed. Terry Sturm (Oxford: Oxford University Press, 1998), p. 587.
19. Heather Murray, 'Peacocke, Isabel Maud', in *The Oxford Companion to New Zealand Literature* (*OCNZL*), eds Roger Robinson and Nelson Wattie (Oxford: Oxford University Press, 1998), p. 434.
20. Review of *New Zealand in Evolution*, *Dominion*, 22 January 1910, p. 9.
21. Aorewa McLeod, 'Escott, Cicely Margaret', DNZB: www.teara.govt.nz/en/biographies/4e12/escott-cicely-margaret
22. Isabel Cluett (Maud Peacocke), 'Hector Bolitho – an outspoken criticism', *All About Books*, 18 June 1929, p. 221.
23. Tennant to Lawlor, 28 April 1936, 77-067 5/2, ATL.
24. Lawlor, 'The Heckling of Hector', c. 1929, 77-067 1/5, ATL.
25. A.A. Phillips, 'The cultural cringe', *Meanjin*, no. 4, 1950, p. 300.
26. W.F. Alexander, review of *Rose Lane* (play), *Evening Star*, 2 May 1936, in Heather Murray, 'Celebrating our writers', p. 105.
27. Alan Mulgan, Mulgan papers, ATL, in Phillip Wilson, *William Satchell* (New York: Twayne Publishers 1968), p. 41.
28. Ethel Wilson, 'Talk – on Mander', 1939, Mander papers, MS Papers 3404, ATL.
29. Rae McGregor, *The Story of a New Zealand Writer: Jane Mander* (Dunedin: University of Otago Press, 1998), p. 74.
30. James Bertram, *Dan Davin* (Auckland: Oxford University Press, 1983), pp. 3–4.
31. Bertram, p. 11.

32. Jean Devanny, *The Butcher Shop* (Auckland: Auckland University Press, 1981, first published 1926), p. 224.

33. James Courage to Brasch, 14 December 1947, Brasch papers, MS Papers 996-3/220, HC, Dunedin.

34. Isabel Cluett, 'Hector Bolitho – an outspoken criticism', *All About Books*, 18 June 1929, p. 221.

35. Isabel Cluett, 'Exodus of New Zealand writers', *All About Books*, 17 June 1930, p. 164.

36. Bill Pearson, Review, *Landfall*, vol. 18, no. 3, 1954, p. 227, in Paul Millar, *No Fretful Sleeper: A life of Bill Pearson* (Auckland: Auckland University Press, 2010), p. 202.

37. Cluett, 'Hector Bolitho – an outspoken criticism', p. 221.

38. Burn to Peter Fraser, 7 September 1937, Internal Affairs 1, 62/8; Oliver Duff to Joseph Heenan, 23 March 1938, Internal Affairs 1, 62/8/1, in Chris Hilliard, 'Island stories' (MA thesis, University of Auckland, 1997), p. 66.

39. McCormick, *Letters and Art in New Zealand*, p. 162.

40. Allen Curnow, 'Introduction', *A Book of New Zealand Verse 1923–1945* (Christchurch: Caxton Press, 1945), p. 21.

41. Curnow, p. 22.

42. Furphy to Stephens, 30 May 1897, in John Barnes, *The Writer in Australia* (Melbourne: Oxford University Press, 1969), p. 121.

43. Henry Lawson, *A Song of Southern Writers* (1892), in Martyn Lyons, 'Britain's largest export market', in *A History of the Book in Australia 1891–1945: A national culture in a colonised market*, eds Martyn Lyons and John Arnold (St Lucia, Qsld: University of Queensland Press, 2001), p. 25.

44. Dirk den Hartog, 'Australian male writers', in *Australian Cultural History*, eds Samuel Louis Goldberg and Francis Barrymore Smith (Cambridge: Cambridge University Press, 1988), p. 231.

45. John Barnes, '"Heaven forbid that I should think of treating with an English publisher": The dilemma of literary nationalists in federated Australia', in *Literary Cultures and the Material Book*, eds Simon Eliot, Andrew Nash and Ian Willison (London: The British Library, 2007), p. 409.

46. Barnes, p. 409.

47. Theresia Marshall, 'New Zealand literature in the Sydney *Bulletin*' (PhD thesis, University of Auckland, 1995), p. 43.

48. C.N. Connolly, 'Class, birthplace, loyalty: Australian attitudes to the Boer War', *Historical Studies*, vol. 18, no. 11, 1978, p. 230.

49. Barnes, '"Heaven forbid that I should think of treating with an English publisher"', p. 399.

50. From a poem by Jessie Mackay, 'The Ancient People', *From the Maori Sea* (Christchurch: Whitcombe & Tombs, 1908), pp. 17–18.

51. E.g. by Jane Stafford and Mark Williams, *Maoriland: New Zealand literature 1872–1914* (Wellington: Victoria University Press, 2006). Stafford and Williams describe the problems 'Maoriland' writers had when faced with unfamiliar surroundings, armed only with Victorian literary conventions.

52. Paul Eggert, *Biography of a Book: Henry Lawson's* While the Billy Boils (Sydney: Sydney University Press, 2013), p. 20.

53. Allen Curnow, 'Introduction', *Penguin Book of New Zealand Verse* (Harmondsworth: Penguin, 1960), p. 50.

54. A.W. Reed, *The Author–Publisher Relationship* (Wellington: Reed, 1946), p. 14, quoted in Luke Trainor, 'Imperialism, commerce and copyright: Australia and New Zealand, 1870–1930', *Bibliographical Society of Australia and New Zealand Bulletin*, vol. 21, no. 4, 1997, p. 204.

55. Terry Sturm, 'Anthony, Frank Sheldon', DNZB: www.teara.govt.nz/en/biographies/4a18/anthony-frank-sheldon

56. Terry Sturm, 'Introduction', in Frank Anthony, *Follow the Call* (Auckland: Auckland University Press, 1975).

57. McCormick, *Letters and Art in New Zealand*, p. 132.

58. Lydia Wevers, 'The short story', in *OHNZL*, ed. Terry Sturm (Oxford: Oxford University Press, 1998), p. 260.

59. Angela Smith, *Katherine Mansfield and Virginia Woolf: A public of two* (New York; Oxford: Clarendon Press, 1999), p. 48.

60. Vincent O'Sullivan, 'Katherine Mansfield: The exile of the mind', in *Flight from Certainty: The dilemma of identity and exile*, eds Anne Luyat and Francine Tolron (Amsterdam: Rodopi, 2001), p. 136.

61. Katherine Mansfield, May 1919, *Journal of Katherine Mansfield* (Auckland: Hutchinson, 1984), p. 157.

62. Malcolm Bradbury, 'Second countries: The expatriate tradition in American writing', *The Yearbook of English Studies*, no. 8, 1978, p. 15.

63. Peter Kalliney, *Modernism in a Global Context* (London; New York: Bloomsbury Academic, 2016), p. 3.

64. Asher Z. Milbauer, *Transcending Exile: Conrad, Nabokov, I.B. Singer* (Miami: Florida International University Press, 1985).

65. Gurr, *Writers in Exile*, p. 13.

66. Doris Eder, *Three Writers in Exile: Pound, Eliot and Joyce* (Troy, N.Y: Whitston, 1984), p. 89.

67. Bertram, *Dan Davin*, p. 4.

68. Patrick Buckridge, 'A kind of exile: Godfrey Blunden – an Australian in Paris', *Journal of Australian Studies*, vol. 26, no. 73, 2002, p. 111.

69. Bradbury, 'Second countries', pp. 18–19.

70. Fairburn to Montalk, 15 June 1927, Letters from Rex Fairburn, MS Papers 2461/3, ATL.

71. Frank Morton, 'These women writers. Under a handicap', *New Zealand Herald* supplement, 8 September 1923, p. 1.

72. James McNeish, *Dance of the Peacocks: New Zealanders in exile at the time of Hitler and Mao Tse-tung* (Auckland: Vintage, 2003), p. 66.

73. Madelaine Williams to Frances Hodgkins, 17 November 1919, in Elizabeth Plumridge, 'The negotiation of circumstance: New Zealand women artists c. 1890–1914' (PhD thesis, Australian National University, 1985), p. 60.

74. Piers Plowright, 'Alison Waley', *Independent*, 23 May 2001: www.independent.co.uk/news/obituaries/alison-waley-729143.html

75. Gillian Boddy, 'Mansfield, Katherine', DNZB: www.teara.govt.nz/en/biographies/3m42/mansfield-katherine

76. Andre Maurois, *Points of View: From Kipling to Graham Greene* (London: Frederick Muller, 1969), p. 322.

77. Maurois, p. 322.

78. Maurois, p. 323.

79. Dan Davin, *The Sullen Bell* (London: M. Joseph, 1956), p. 145.

80. Moffat, 'Louisa Alice Baker'.

81. Sturm, *An Unsettled Spirit*, p. 4.

82. A.R.D. Fairburn, 'To an expatriate', in *Penguin Book of New Zealand Verse*, ed. Allen Curnow (Harmondsworth: Penguin, 1960), p. 155.

CHAPTER SIX

1. Winnie Gonley, 'New Zealand life in contemporary culture' (MA thesis, University of New Zealand, 1932), p. 16.

2. Stuart Murray, Review of *Story of a New Zealand Writer*, *Landfall*, no. 197, 1999, p. 156.

3. James Bertram, 'Poetry comes of age', in *New Zealand's Heritage*, ed. Ray Knox (Wellington: Paul Hamlyn, 1971–73), p. 2400.

4. Eric McCormick, *Letters and Art in New Zealand* (Wellington: Dept. of Internal Affairs, 1940), p. 142.

5. She exhibited signs of despising colonials in general, saying in her journal during her 1907 camping trip in the North Island that 'it is splendid to see once again real English people – I am so sick and tired of the third-rate article – Give me the Maori and the tourist but nothing between'. Katherine Mansfield, *The Urewera Notebook*, ed. Ian A. Gordon (Oxford: Oxford University Press, 1978), p. 61.

6. She was particularly compelled to write about her childhood in New Zealand after the death of her brother in 1915. Anthony Alpers, *The Life of Katherine Mansfield* (Oxford: Oxford University Press, 1982), p. 183.

7. Ruth Mantz, *The Life of Katherine Mansfield* (London: Constable, 1933).

8. Ian A. Gordon, 'Introduction', in Mansfield, *The Urewera Notebook*, pp. 11–30.

9. Vincent O'Sullivan, *Long Journey to the Border* (Auckland: Penguin, 2003), p. 98.

10. Fairburn to Mason, 11 November 1930. Here he said: 'I know what it is, now, to be an exile.' He also mentioned that he felt less remote from home in England than he did in Wellington. In Lauris Edmond, ed., *The Letters of A.R.D. Fairburn* (Auckland: Oxford University Press, 1981).

11. Dora Wilcox, 'In London', *Verses from Maoriland* (London: George Allen, 1905).

12. Miles Fairburn, *The Ideal Society and its Enemies: The foundations of modern New Zealand society* (Auckland: Auckland University Press, 1989), p. 11.

13. Christchurch is a good example of this. D.W. Meinig describes this phenomenon in an American context. *The Shaping of America* (New Haven: Yale University

Press, 1986) is concerned with expansion out of New England, Pennsylvania and Virginia, and 'instant towns' 'mushrooming' on the frontier (p. 248).

14. Edith Searle Grossmann, *The Heart of the Bush* (London: Sands, 1910).

15. Nancy Keesing, *Australian Writers and Their Work: Douglas Stewart* (Sydney: Lansdowne Press, 1965), p. 9.

16. Brigid Magner, 'Trans-Tasman impostures', *Journal of the Association for the Study of Australian Literature*, January 2013, p. 174.

17. Helen Bones, 'A dual exile? New Zealand and the colonial writing world, 1890–1945' (PhD thesis, University of Canterbury, 2011): http://hdl.handle. net/10092/5618, Appendix B. Writers are classified based on the length and nature of their travel. This information was gathered from wherever available: *Oxford Companion to New Zealand Literature*, the *Dictionary of New Zealand Biography*, individual biographies, internet sources and the literary papers of authors in various archives.

18. Miles Fairburn, 'Is there a good case for New Zealand exceptionalism?' *Thesis Eleven*, no. 92, 2008, p. 33.

19. Bones, 'A dual exile?', p. 186.

20. Jane Mander, *The Passionate Puritan* (London: Lane, 1922), p. 198.

21. Stuart Murray, *Never a Soul at Home: New Zealand literary nationalism and the 1930s* (Wellington: Victoria University Press, 1998), p. 200.

22. J.G.A. Pocock, 'The antipodean perception', *The Discovery of Islands: Essays in British history* (Cambridge, UK: Cambridge University Press, 2005), p. 19.

23. Salman Rushdie, *Imaginary Homelands* (London: Viking, 1991), pp. 10–12.

24. Jessie Mackay, *Vigil* (Auckland: Whitcombe & Tombs, 1935).

25. F.M. Mackay, *New Zealand Writers and their Work: Eileen Duggan* (Wellington: Oxford University Press, 1977), p. 8.

26. Pocock, 'The antipodean perception', p. 11.

27. To use Benedict Anderson's phrase. Benedict Anderson, *Imagined Communities: Reflections on the origin and spread of nationalism* (London; New York: Verso, 2006).

28. For example, a review of *Locations of Literary Modernism: Region and nation in British and American modernist poetry* (edited by Alex Davis and Lee M. Jenkins) praises the authors' rejection of 'longstanding commonplaces' relating to the international nature of modernist writing in favour of 'the degree to which not only nationalism, but also more specific regional affiliations, have indeed shaped British and American modernism in profound ways'. Mark Morrisson, *Comparative Literature Studies*, vol. 39, no. 1, 2002, p. 82. But Jahan Ramazani complains that modernism is too tied to literary criticism within national frameworks: 'single-nation genealogies remain surprisingly entrenched'. 'A transnational poetics', *American Literary History*, vol. 18, no. 2, 2006, p. 332.

29. Patrick Williams, 'Simultaneous uncontemporaneities', in *Modernism and Empire*, eds Howard Booth and Nigel Rigby (Manchester: Manchester University Press, c. 2000), p. 25, cited in Andrzej Gąsiorek, *A History of Modernist Literature* (Chichester, West Sussex: Wiley Blackwell, 2015), p. 22.

30. Douglas Mao and Rebecca Walkowitz, 'The New modernist studies', *Publications of the Modern Language Association of America*, vol. 123, no. 3, 2008, p. 739.

31. Alan Mulgan, *Home: A New Zealander's adventure* (London: Longmans, Green, 1927), p. 8; McCormick, *Letters and Art in New Zealand*, p. 131.

32. Mulgan, *Home*, p. 48.

33. Bones, 'A dual exile?', Appendix B.

34. Pat Lawlor, Draft of 'New Zealand Writing: A survey', c. 1962, 77-067 7/2, ATL.

35. Elizabeth Webby, 'Lawson, William (Will) (1876–1957)', ADB: http://adb.anu.edu.au/biography/lawson-william-will-7122

36. Kirstine Moffat, 'Louisa Alice Baker, 1856–1926', *Kōtare*, vol. 7, no. 1, 2007, p. 12.

37. John Lee, '"A private history": Towards a biography of James Courage, expatriate New Zealand writer' (MA thesis, Victoria University, 2001), p. 11.

38. Angela Woollacott, *Settler Society in the Australian Colonies* (Oxford: Oxford University Press, 2015), p. 16.

39. Denis McLean, Review of *Dance of the Peacocks*, *New Zealand International Review*, no. 29, 2004.

40. Robert Holden, 'Wilcox, Mary Theodora Joyce (1873–1953)', ADB: http://adb.anu.edu.au/biography/wilcox-mary-theodora-joyce-7805

41. John Drew interview, 17 September 1995, in Gordon Ogilvie, *Denis Glover: His life* (Auckland: Godwit, 1999), p. 127.

42. Gordon Ogilvie, 'Glover, Denis James Matthews', DNZB: www.teara.govt.nz/en/biographies/4g11/glover-denis-james-matthews

43. Literae Humaniores: an undergraduate course focused on Classics.

44. James McNeish, *Dance of the Peacocks: New Zealanders in exile at the time of Hitler and Mao Tse-tung* (Auckland: Vintage, 2003), p. 38.

45. Paul Millar, *No Fretful Sleeper: A life of Bill Pearson* (Auckland: Auckland University Press, 2010), pp. 163, 167.

46. Terry Sturm, 'Scanlan, Ellen Margaret', DNZB: www.teara.govt.nz/en/biographies/4s11/scanlan-ellen-margaret

47. Janet McCallum and Paul Millar, 'Baume, Eric', in *OCNZL*, eds Roger Robinson and Nelson Wattie (Oxford: Oxford University Press, 1998), p. 44.

48. Roderick Cave, 'Printing in colonial New Zealand: An insular history?', in *A book in the hand: Essays on the history of the book in New Zealand*, eds Penny Griffith, Peter Hughes and Alan Loney (Auckland: Auckland University Press, 2000), p. 241.

49. 'Armistice Day – New Zealand in 1918', NZ History, Ministry for Culture and Heritage: https://nzhistory.govt.nz/war/armistice/nz-in-1918

50. A.A. Phillips, 'The cultural cringe', *Meanjin*, no. 4, 1950, p. 300.

51. Ruth Park, 'Some notes on my personal association with the writer Eve Langley, in 1940–42, Auckland, New Zealand', 1976, Ruth Park papers, 1938–1976, MLMSS 3128, SLNSW.

52. Martha Rutledge, 'Deamer, Mary Elizabeth Kathleen Dulcie (1890–1972)', ADB: http://adb.anu.edu.au/biography/deamer-mary-elizabeth-kathleen-dulcie-5928

53. Caroline Daley, *Leisure and Pleasure: Reshaping and revealing the New Zealand body 1900–1960* (Auckland: Auckland University Press, 2003), p. 171.

54. Martha Rutledge, 'Deamer, Mary Elizabeth Kathleen Dulcie'.

55. Raewyn Dalziel, 'The colonial helpmeet: Women's role and the vote in nineteenth-century New Zealand', *New Zealand Journal of History*, vol. 11, no. 2, 1977, p. 123.

56. Patrick Evans, *The Long Forgetting* (Christchurch: Canterbury University Press, 2007), p. 16.

57. Lawrence Jones, 'Puritanism', in *OCNZL*, p. 455.

58. Frank Sargeson autobiography, in Jones, 'Puritanism', p. 455.

59. Jones, 'Puritanism', p. 455.

60. Mander, *The Passionate Puritan*, p. 42.

61. Fairburn to de Montalk, 5 July 1927, Letters from Rex Fairburn, MS Papers 2461/3, ATL; de Montalk to R.A.K. Mason, 27 December 1927, Mason papers, MS Papers 592/11, HC.

62. Fairburn to de Montalk, 13 June 1927, MS Papers 2461/3, ATL.

63. Fairburn to Mason, 18 March 1930, Mason papers, MS 592/19, HC.

64. Denys Trussell, *Fairburn* (Auckland: Auckland University Press, 1984), p. 80.

65. Stephanie de Montalk, *Unquiet World* (Wellington: Victoria University Press, 2001), p. 98.

66. *Literature and the Arts, New Zealand* (University of California Press, 1947), in de Montalk, *Unquiet World*, p. 95.

67. Aorewa McLeod, 'A home in this world: Why New Zealand women stopped writing', *Women's Studies Journal*, vol. 14, no. 2, 1998, p. 68.

68. Rebecca Burns, 'Snapshot of a life reassessed: Edith Searle Grossmann', *Kōtare: New Zealand Notes and Queries* (Wellington: Victoria University Press, 2009).

69. Kirstine Moffat, 'Louisa Alice Baker, 1856–1926', *Kōtare*, vol. 7, no. 1, 2007, p. 12.

70. Derek Challis and Gloria Rawlinson, *The Book of Iris* (Auckland: Auckland University Press, 2002), p. 147.

71. Challis and Rawlinson, p. 147.

72. Robin Hyde to John Schroder, 23 October 1928, in Challis and Rawlinson, p. 121.

73. Challis and Rawlinson, p. 86.

74. New Zealand Department of Censuses and Statistics, *General Report, Population Census* (Wellington: Department of Censuses and Statistics, 1936).

75. Plus two writers using pseudonyms, whose gender is not known.

76. W.S. Broughton, 'Cresswell, Walter D'Arcy', DNZB: www.teara.govt.nz/en/biographies/4c42/cresswell-walter-darcy

77. Stephanie de Montalk, *Unquiet World*, pp. 97–98.

78. Kirstine Moffat, 'The puritan paradox: An annotated bibliography of puritan and anti-puritan New Zealand fiction, 1860–1940. Part 1: The puritan legacy', *Kōtare*, vol. 3, no. 1, 2000: http://ojs.victoria.ac.nz/kotare/article/view/627

79. Mary Scott, *Days that Have Been* (Auckland: Blackwood & J. Paul, 1966), p. 164.

80. Catherine Bishop, 'Women on the move: Gender, money-making and mobility in mid-nineteenth century Australasia', *History Australia*, vol. 11, no. 2, 2014, pp. 38–59.

81. Journeys abroad taken by New Zealand authors between 1890 and 1945 were sorted by the destination (United Kingdom, Australia and Other), the length of

the journey and the main activity during it (study, writing, journalistic work, travel/sightseeing/visiting relatives, war service or non-writing-related work). This is for the 65 authors for whom enough information was available and who went on trips overseas during this time period. Bones, 'A dual exile?', Table 4.3, p. 157.

82. Ronda Cooper, 'Guthrie-Smith, William Herbert', DNZB: www.teara.govt.nz/en/biographies/3g27/guthrie-smith-william-herbert

83. Richard L.N. Greenaway, 'Burdon, Randal Mathews', DNZB: www.teara.govt.nz/en/biographies/4b49/burdon-randal-mathews

84. Mansfield's disgust with her parents is documented in Anthony Alpers's biography. Alpers, *The Life of Katherine Mansfield*, p. 41. In general her attitude was one of wishing to be no longer under their stifling jurisdiction.

85. Vincent O'Sullivan, '"Finding the pattern, solving the problem": Katherine Mansfield the New Zealand European', in *Katherine Mansfield: In from the margin*, ed. Roger Robinson (Baton Rouge: Louisiana State University Press, 1994), p. 24.

86. See Bones, 'A dual exile?', Appendix B.

87. James Courage, *The Call Home* (London: Jonathan Cape, 1956), p. 72.

88. Carl Walrond, 'Kiwis overseas – Staying in Britain', Te Ara – the Encyclopedia of New Zealand: www.teara.govt.nz/en/kiwis-overseas/3

CHAPTER SEVEN

1. Monte Holcroft, *The Way of a Writer* (Whatamongo Bay: Cape Catley, 1984), p. 118.

2. Holcroft, pp. 122, 128.

3. Holcroft, pp. 141–42.

4. Meg Tasker, '"When London calls" and Fleet Street beckons: Daley's poem, Reg's diary – what happens when it all goes "bung"?', in *Modern Mobilities: Australian–Transnational writing*, eds David Brooks and Elizabeth MacMahon (Blackheath, NSW: Brandl & Schlesinger, 2011), p. 107.

5. Stephanie de Montalk, *Unquiet World* (Wellington: Victoria University Press, 2001), p. 95.

6. Hector Bolitho, *My Restless Years* (London: Parrish, 1962), p. 79.

7. De Montalk, *Unquiet World*, p. 96.

8. Monte Holcroft, 'Who travels alone', *The Sun*, 8 March 1929.

9. W.S. Broughton, *A.R.D. Fairburn* (Wellington: Reed, 1968), p. 8.

10. Bolitho, *My Restless Years*, p. 89.

11. New liberal Charles Masterman spoke of the 'boost to leisure time' (and time where the light was good enough for reading by) that the electric train and gas stove (and gas lighting) were. Lucy Masterman, *C.F.G. Masterman* (1968), p. 83, in Philip Waller, *Writers, Readers and Reputations: Literary life in Britain, 1870–1918* (Oxford; New York: Oxford University Press, 2006), p. 47. Waller mentions improved printing methods on pp. 47–48.

12. Alvin Sullivan, *British Literary Magazines, V3: The Victorian and Edwardian age, 1837–1913* (Westport, Conn: Greenwood Press, 1983–1986), pp. 469–71.

13. Nelle Scanlan, *Ambition's Harvest* (London: Jarrold, 1935), p. 225.

14. Untitled transcript, 1935–38, Lyttleton family papers, paraphrased in Terry Sturm, *An Unsettled Spirit: The life and frontier fiction of Edith Lyttleton (G.B. Lancaster)* (Auckland: Auckland University Press, 2003), p. 118.

15. J.C. Beaglehole to his mother, 3–5 October 1926, New Zealand Electronic Text Centre: www.nzetc.org/tm/scholarly/metadata-tei-JCB-008.html

16. De Montalk, *Unquiet World*, p. 100.

17. Dan Davin, *The Sullen Bell* (London: M. Joseph, 1956), p. 99.

18. Douglas Glass to Mason, 11 April 1929, MS Papers 592/11, HC.

19. Douglas Glass to Mason, 28 April 1930, MS Papers 592/11, HC.

20. Fairburn to Mason, 22 December 1931, MS 592/020, HC.

21. Frank Sargeson, *Sargeson* (Auckland: Penguin, 1981), p. 117.

22. Kirstine Moffat, 'Arthur. H Adams, 1872–1935', *Kōtare*, vol. 7, no. 3, 2008, p. 80.

23. Broughton, *A.R.D. Fairburn*, p. 9.

24. Fairburn to Mason, 31 August 1931, MS Papers 592/20, HC.

25. Fairburn to Mason, 2 March 1932, MS Papers, 592/20, HC.

26. Charles Brasch, 'Introduction', *Such Separate Creatures* (Christchurch: Caxton Press, 1973), pp. 10–11, in John Lee, '"A private history": Towards a biography of James Courage, expatriate New Zealand writer' (MA thesis, Victoria University, 2001), p. 70.

27. James McNeish, *Dance of the Peacocks: New Zealanders in exile at the time of Hitler and Mao Tse-tung* (Auckland: Vintage, 2003), p. 78.

28. According to Mary Burgen, 'in the London area, phthisis (as the last stage of tuberculosis was then called) was the leading single cause of death for women in their late teens to twenties, accounting for more than 45 per cent of the fatalities in 1916'. This was the disease that ended Katherine Mansfield's life prematurely, and also, probably, Frank Anthony's. Tuberculosis is caused by airborne transmission of a bacillus from person to person, not one's environment, but the disease was considerably worsened by poor living conditions, pollution and overcrowding. Mary Burgen, *Illness, Gender and Writing: The case of Katherine Mansfield* (London: John Hopkins University Press, 1994), p. 124, in Angela Smith, *Katherine Mansfield and Virginia Woolf: A public of two* (New York; Oxford: Clarendon Press, 1999), p. 34.

29. Arnold Wall, 'London lost', *London Lost and Other Poems* (Auckland: Whitcombe & Tombs, 1922), p. 8.

30. David Lynn, *Love and Hunger* (London: Kangaroo Books, 1944), p. 3.

31. Mander to John A. Lee, 1934, APL, in Dorothea Turner, *Jane Mander* (New York: Twayne, 1972), p. 35.

32. Jane Mander to Monte Holcroft, 9 May 1932, MS Papers 1186/6, ATL.

33. A.G. Stephens, Autobiographies of Australian and New Zealand authors, Box 28, MLMSS 4937, SLNSW.

34. Eileen Duggan to Nettie Palmer, 1931, Duggan papers, MS Papers 801 2/3, ATL.

35. Fairburn protested to R.A.K. Mason that being heterosexual was a barrier to acceptance into London literary circles. Fairburn to Mason, 4 December 1931, MS 592/20, HC.

36. De Montalk to Mason, 19 July 1928, MS 592/11, HC.

37. De Montalk, *Unquiet World*, p. 100.

38. Isabel Maud Peacocke, *London Called Them* (London: Ward, Lock, 1946), p. 107.

39. Davin, *The Sullen Bell*, p. 100.

40. Arthur H. Adams, *Bulletin*, 1905 (although he had a book published in London by T. Fisher Unwin in 1904), in Theresia Marshall, 'New Zealand literature in the Sydney *Bulletin*' (PhD thesis, University of Auckland, 1995), p. 150.

41. Peacocke, *London Called Them*, p. 131.

42. Jane Mander to Monte Holcroft, 9 November 1931, MS Papers 1186/16, ATL.

43. Jane Mander, 'Modern authorship – conditions abroad: What the publishers want', *Auckland Star*, 27 October 1932.

44. Jane Mander, 'Talk to Lyceum Club', 8 June 1933, NZMS 535, APL.

45. *The Lyceum Club, London: A prospectus* (London, 1903), Bodleian Library Bookstack (5).

46. Nelle Scanlan wrote to Alan Mulgan in 1959: 'I was the first New Zealand writer to become a member of PEN in London. When my first book was published.' Nelle Scanlan to Alan Mulgan, Christmas Day, c. 1957, MS Papers 0224/11, ATL.

47. Drusilla Modjeska, *Exiles at Home: Australian women writers 1925–1945* (London: Sirius Books, 1981), p. 16.

48. Jane Mander, 'On making good: Colonials in London', Christchurch *Sun*, 4 December 1924, p. 8.

49. Curtice M. Hitchcock to Edith Lyttleton, Lyttleton papers, MS Papers 8649/31, ATL.

50. R.C.K. Ensor, 'The diffusion of ideas', in *Essays Mainly on the Nineteenth Century: Presented to Sir Humphrey Milford*, ed. G.F.J. Cumberlege (London; New York: Oxford University Press, 1948), p. 83, in Waller, *Writers, Readers and Reputations*, p. 117.

51. Arnold Bennett, *New Age*, 12 January 1911, in Arnold Bennett, *Books and Persons* (London: Chatto & Windus, 1917), pp. 289–90.

52. Waller, *Writers, Readers and Reputations*, p. 142.

53. Peacocke, *London Called Them*, p. 131.

54. Arnold Bennett, *New Age*, 12 January 1911, in Bennett, *Books and Persons*, p. 291.

55. Andrew Nash, 'Literary culture and literary publishing in inter-war Britain: A view from Chatto & Windus', in *Literary Cultures and the Material Book*, eds Simon Eliot, Andrew Nash and Ian Willison (London: British Library, 2007), p. 332.

56. Nash, 'Literary culture and literary publishing in inter-war Britain', p. 333.

57. Walter Besant, 'Literature as a career', *Review of Reviews*, August 1892, in Waller, *Writers, Readers and Reputations*, p. 32.

58. John Feather, *A History of British Publishing* (London; New York: Routledge, 1988), p. 178.

59. Agreement with Clara Cheeseman of Auckland, 8 April 1885, Richard Bentley & Son agreements (327), Add 46621, BL, London.

60. Miss Rosemary Rees v. Walter Melville, 1913–14, Society of Authors Archive, ff. 1–81, Vol. CCCCVII, Add. 56981, BL.

61. Elaine Aston and Ian Clarke, 'The dangerous woman of Melvillean melodrama', *New Theatre Quarterly*, vol. XII, no. 45, 1996, pp. 30–31.

62. Felicity Barnes, *New Zealand's London: A colony and its metropolis* (Auckland: Auckland University Press, 2012), p. 99.

63. Eric McCormick, *The Expatriate: A study of Frances Hodgkins* (Wellington: New Zealand University Press, 1954), p. 69.

64. Samira Ahmed, 'Arnold Bennett: The Edwardian David Bowie?', BBC News Online, 23 June 2014: www.bbc.com/news/entertainment-arts-27920331

65. Arnold Bennett, *The Truth About an Author* (London: Methuen, 1914), p. 2, in Peter Macdonald, *British Literary Culture and Publishing Practice, 1880–1914* (Cambridge; New York: Cambridge University Press, 1997), p. 68.

66. Gillian Boddy, 'Mansfield, Katherine', DNZB: www.teara.govt.nz/en/biographies/3m42/mansfield-katherine

67. Macdonald, *British Literary Culture and Publishing Practice, 1880–1914*, p. 17.

68. Waller, *Writers, Readers and Reputations*, p. 152.

69. Virginia Woolf, *A Room of One's Own* (Oxford: Oxford University Press, 1992), p. 9.

70. Angela Woollacott, *To Try Her Fortune in London* (Oxford: Oxford University Press, 2001), pp. 105–06.

71. Oxford English Dictionary Online: http://oed.com

72. Oxford English Dictionary Online

73. David Bevan, *Literature and Exile* (Amsterdam; Atlanta, GA: Rodopi, 1990), p. 3.

74. Vytautas Kavolis, 'Women writers in exile', *World Literature Today*, vol. 66, no. 1, 1992, p. 43.

75. Mander, 'On making good: Colonials in London'.

76. Mander, 'On making good: Colonials in London'.

77. McLeod, 'A home in this world', p. 68.

78. Monte Holcroft, 'Who travels alone', Christchurch *Sun*, 28 March 1929.

79. De Montalk, *Unquiet World*, p. 109.

80. Hector Bolitho, *My Restless Years* (London: Parrish, 1962), p. 95.

81. Hector Bolitho to Charles Prentice, 15 July 1927, Chatto & Windus papers, CW 25/3 (Folder One), URSC.

82. Bolitho to Prentice, 14 August 1927, CW 25/3, URSC.

83. Fairburn to Mason, 6 January 1932, MS 592/18, HC.

84. Bennett, *The Truth About an Author*, p. 79, in Macdonald, *British Literary Culture and Publishing Practice, 1880–1914*, pp. 68, 77.

85. Michael H. Black, 'D.H. Lawrence', Encyclopedia Britannica: www.britannica.com/biography/D-H-Lawrence

86. Tuppenny libraries operated on a 'pay as you read' system, as opposed to subscription libraries, where readers paid an annual fee. Nash, 'Literary culture and literary publishing in inter-war Britain', p. 340n.

87. Henry Scheurmier, ed., *The Book World* (London: Thomas Nelson, 1935), p. 201, in Nash, 'Literary culture and literary publishing in inter-war Britain', p. 326.

88. Nash, 'Literary culture and literary publishing in inter-war Britain', p. 325.

89. Macdonald, *British Literary Culture and Publishing Practice, 1880–1914*, p. 23.

90. Macdonald, p. 14.

91. Winnie Davin to Dan Davin, 29 December–2 January 1943–44, Anna Davin, private collection, London.

92. Robin Hyde, *Journalese* (Auckland: National Printing Company, 1934), p. 47.

CHAPTER EIGHT

1. Nelle Scanlan, *Road to Pencarrow* (London: Robert Hale, 1963), p. 136.

2. Alex Calder, *The Settler's Plot: How stories take place in New Zealand* (Auckland: Auckland University Press, 2013), p. 176.

3. Rae McGregor, *The Story of a New Zealand Writer: Jane Mander* (Dunedin: University of Otago Press, 1998), p. 90.

4. Kirstine Moffat, 'Edith Searle Grossmann, 1863–1931', *Kōtare*, vol. 7, no. 1, 2007, p. 22.

5. Ngaio Marsh, 'Expatriates', from An Encyclopaedia of New Zealand, ed. A.H. McLintock (1966), Te Ara – the Encyclopedia of New Zealand: www.teara.govt. nz/en/1966/expatriates/4

6. Jane Mander, *The Strange Attraction* (London: Bodley Head, 1923), p. 127.

7. Letter to *Triad*, 1909, in McGregor, *The Story of a New Zealand Writer*, p. 34.

8. Monte Holcroft to Ursula Bethell, 5 January 1934, C4, MS 558, MBL.

9. Keith Ovenden, *A Fighting Withdrawal: The life of Dan Davin* (Oxford: Oxford University Press, 1996), p. 108.

10. Fairburn to Mason, 5 November 1931, MS Papers 592/18, HC.

11. After he left New Zealand, Hume was based in London and then Essex (and briefly Melbourne) and published the vast majority of his novels in London. Note: this data is approximate and based on my best guess at the authors' whereabouts based on biographical and publishing data.

12. John Feather, *A History of British Publishing* (London; New York: Routledge, 1988), p. 141.

13. Mander to Holcroft, April 13 1933, MS Papers 1186/6, ATL.

14. Edith Lyttleton to the Society of Authors, London, 6 January 1933, MS Papers 8649/31, ATL.

15. Terry Sturm, *An Unsettled Spirit: The life and frontier fiction of Edith Lyttleton (G.B. Lancaster)* (Auckland: Auckland University Press, 2003), p. 120.

16. Tennyson complained that he got sent a verse 'for every three minutes' of his life. Cecil Lang and Edgar Shannon, eds, *The Letters of Alfred Lord Tennyson, iii* (Oxford: Clarendon Press, c. 1981–1990), p. 399, in Philip Waller, *Writers, Readers and Reputations: Literary life in Britain, 1870–1918* (Oxford; New York: Oxford University Press, 2006), p. 392.

17. Bolitho to G.K. Chesterton, 18 January 1935, G.K. Chesterton papers, Add. 73235 (134), BL.

18. Cresswell to T.E. Lawrence, 2 Sept 1930, CW 93/9, URSC.

19. W.S. Broughton, 'Cresswell, Walter D'Arcy', DNZB: www.teara.govt.nz/en/ biographies/4c42/cresswell-walter-darcy

20. Hector Bolitho to Chatto & Windus, received 11 November 1926, CW 25/3, URSC.

21. Waller, *Writers, Readers and Reputations*, p. 129.

22. Bolitho to Chatto & Windus, 6 January 1927, CW 25/3, URSC.

23. Felicity Barnes, *New Zealand's London: A colony and its metropolis* (Auckland: Auckland University Press, 2012), p. 113.

24. Escott to Harold Raymond at Chatto & Windus, 13 February 1936, CW 61/2, URSC.

25. Harold Raymond to Margaret Escott, 1 April 1936, CW 61/2, URSC.

26. Harold Raymond to Margaret Escott, 7 December 1936, CW 61/2, URSC.

27. 'Sons o' Men', *Times Literary Supplement*, 14 November 1904, p. 341.

28. Sturm, *An Unsettled Spirit*, p. 53.

29. 'New publications', *Evening Post*, 15 February 1908, p. 13.

30. Janet McCallum, 'Weston, Jessie', in *The Oxford Companion to New Zealand Literature* (*OCNZL*), eds Roger Robinson and Nelson Wattie (Oxford: Oxford University Press, 1998), p. 583.

31. Jane Mander, 'On making good: Colonials in London', Christchurch *Sun*, 4 December 1924, p. 8.

32. Arthur H. Adams, 'On going to London', *Bulletin*, 1905, in Theresia Marshall, 'New Zealand literature in the Sydney *Bulletin*' (PhD thesis, University of Auckland, 1995), p. 151.

33. Rhonda Bartle, 'John Brodie – New Plymouth's neglected author', Puke Ariki: http://pukeariki.com/Learning-Research/Taranaki-Research-Centre/Taranaki-Stories/Taranaki-Story/id/105/title/john-brodie-new-plymouths-neglected-author

34. Scanlan, *Road to Pencarrow*, p. 94.

35. Scanlan, pp. 94–96.

36. Robin Hyde, *Journalese* (Auckland: National Printing Company, 1934), p. 47.

37. Nelson Wattie, 'Watson, Henry Brereton Marriot', *OCNZL*, p. 577.

38. John A. Lee, 'John A Lee's Weekly', 24 April 1946, in Rowan Gibbs, 'The works of "David Lynn": New Zealand writer', *Kōtare*, vol. 1, no. 1, 1998: http://ojs.victoria. ac.nz/kotare/article/view/588#ftn7

39. Betty Gilderdale, 'Peacocke, Inez Isabel Maud', DNZB: www.teara.govt.nz/en/biographies/4p6/peacocke-inez-isabel-maud

40. This is from a table showing their literary productiveness in terms of the frequency of books produced per year. This is compared with their productivity in New Zealand. These figures show the number of years between 1890 and 1945 while the author was over 18 years of age. Non-full-time writers like Merton Hodge, William Hart-Smith and Randal Burdon are excluded, as is the exceptionally prolific Fergus Hume. Helen Bones, 'A dual exile? New Zealand and the colonial writing world, 1890–1945' (PhD thesis, University of Canterbury, 2011): http://hdl.handle.net/10092/5618, Table 4.4, p. 172.

41. Bones, 'A dual exile?', Table 4.5, p. 173.

42. John Barnes, '"Heaven forbid that I should think of treating with an English publisher": The dilemma of literary nationalists in federated Australia', in *Literary*

Cultures and the Material Book, eds Simon Eliot, Andrew Nash and Ian Willison (London: The British Library, 2007), pp. 405–06.

43. Barnes, p. 405.

44. Andrew Mason, 'Holcroft, Montague Harry', DNZB: www.teara.govt.nz/en/biographies/5h28/holcroft-montague-harry

45. Karim H. Karim, *The Definition of Visible Minority: A historical and cultural analysis* (Ottawa: Department of Canadian Heritage, 1996).

46. Jane Mander, 'London has a hot time', Auckland *Sun*, 28 August 1926, Mander Papers. NZMS 535, APL, in Barnes, *New Zealand's London*, p. 38.

47. Leonore Davidoff, *The Best Circles: Society etiquette and the season* (London: Cresset Library, 1986), p. 50; Angela Woollacott, *To Try Her Fortune in London* (Oxford: Oxford University Press, 2001), p. 49.

48. Barnes, *New Zealand's London*, p. 36.

49. Dan Davin, *The Sullen Bell* (London: M. Joseph, 1956), p. 23.

50. George Bull, 'Half a minute interviews: No. 11', *British-Australasian*, 22 March 1906, p. 7.

51. Frances Hodgkins to Rachel Owen Hodgkins, 13 April 1902, in Eric McCormick, *The Expatriate: A study of Frances Hodgkins* (Wellington: New Zealand University Press, 1954), p. 70.

52. Elizabeth Plumridge, 'The negotiation of circumstance: New Zealand women artists c. 1890–1914' (PhD thesis, Australian National University, 1985), p. 136.

53. *Lyttelton Times*, 9 January 1890, p. 3, in Plumridge, 'The negotiation of circumstance', pp. 136–37.

54. Tim Beaglehole, 'Beaglehole, John Cawte', DNZB: www.teara.govt.nz/en/biographies/5b16/beaglehole-john-cawte

55. John Mulgan to Alan Mulgan, October 1934, in James McNeish, *Dance of the Peacocks: New Zealanders in exile at the time of Hitler and Mao Tse-tung* (Auckland: Vintage, 2003), p. 87.

56. Rebecca Burns, 'Snapshot of a life reassessed: Edith Searle Grossmann', *Kōtare: New Zealand Notes and Queries* (Wellington: Victoria University Press, 2009): http://ojs.victoria.ac.nz/kotare/article/view/786. Also mentioned in Patrick Evans, *Penguin History of New Zealand Literature* (Auckland: Penguin, 1990), p. 36.

57. Edith Searle Grossmann, *Canterbury Times*, 29 August 1890, p. 49, in Plumridge, 'The negotiation of circumstance', p. 126.

58. Burns, 'Snapshot of a life reassessed'.

59. The judges' report read: 'We have received MSS. from Australia, South Africa, New Zealand, India, the Pacific Islands, and Canada— disappointingly few from Canada, by the way. For excellence, New Zealand unquestionably stands first, as our lists will show.' 'Encouragement of Australian writers in London', *Sydney Mail and New South Wales Advertiser*, 26 December 1906, p. 1626.

60. Carl Walrond, 'Kiwis overseas – Staying in Britain', Te Ara – the Encyclopedia of New Zealand: www.teara.govt.nz/en/kiwis-overseas/3

61. *British-Australasian*, 29 March 1906, p. 16.

62. 'Anglo New Zealand', *British-Australasian*, 10 May 1906, p. 17.
63. Mander, *Auckland Star*, 28 August 1926, in Felicity Barnes, *New Zealand's London*, p. 43.
64. Denis Glover, *Hot Water Sailor; & Landlubber Ho!* (Auckland: Collins, 1981), p. 153.
65. Scanlan, *Road to Pencarrow*, p. 176.
66. Plumridge, 'The negotiation of circumstance', p. 137.
67. 'Home: A New Zealander in England', *Press*, 8 January 1927.
68. Fairburn to Mason, 22 December 1931, MS 0592/20, HC.
69. Felicity Barnes, *New Zealand's London*, p. 36, quoting Cooke to Florrie, 23 July 1915, Ella Cooke Papers, 94/36, Auckland Institute and Museum Library.
70. C.W. Richmond to Emily E. Richmond, 22 September 1878, in Plumridge, p. 135. We may doubt whether all colonials were automatically blackballed, although some undoubtedly were.
71. Monte Holcroft, *Discovered Isles: A trilogy* (Christchurch: Caxton Press, 1950), p. 17.
72. Nelle Scanlan to her family, 28 November 1921, MS Papers 0232-6, ATL.
73. Scanlan to family, 2 November 1921, MS Papers 0232-6, ATL.
74. Jane Mander, Talk to the Lyceum Club, 8 June 1933, NZMS 535, APL.
75. Scanlan to Alan Mulgan, Christmas Day, c. 1959, MS Papers 0224-11, ATL.
76. Ross, *Around the World*, p. 73, in Felicity Barnes, *New Zealand's London*, p. 39.
77. Hector Bolitho, *My Restless Years* (London: Parrish, 1962), p. 94.
78. Vincent O'Sullivan, *Long Journey to the Border* (Auckland: Penguin, 2003), p. 145.
79. Dorothea Turner, *Jane Mander* (New York: Twayne, 1972), p. 23.
80. Baume to Lawlor, 14 September 1959, Lawlor papers, 77-067 1/5, ATL.
81. Keith Ovenden, 'Davin, Daniel Marcus', DNZB: www.teara.govt.nz/en/biographies/5d7/davin-daniel-marcus
82. W.S. Broughton, *A.R.D. Fairburn* (Wellington: Reed, 1968), p. 11.
83. Jane Mander, 'On making good'.
84. 'Alien', Sandra Kemp, Charlotte Mitchell and David Trotter, *The Oxford Companion to Edwardian Fiction* (Oxford; New York: Oxford University Press, c. 1997).
85. Rae McGregor, 'Mander, Mary Jane', DNZB: www.teara.govt.nz/en/biographies/4m34/mander-mary-jane
86. Jane Mander, 'Modern authorship – conditions abroad: What the publishers want', *Auckland Star*, 27 October 1932.
87. Geoffrey de Montalk to Fairburn, 5 April 1929, Fairburn papers, MS Papers 1128/10, ATL.
88. Janet McCallum, 'Baker, Louisa Alice', DNZB: www.teara.govt.nz/en/biographies/3b4/baker-louisa-alice
89. Felicity Barnes, *New Zealand's London*, p. 119.
90. Hector Bolitho to Pat Lawlor, 20 September 1966, 77-067 1/4, ATL.
91. Eric Baume to Lawlor, 14 September 1959, 77-067 1/5, ATL.

92. McCormick, *The Expatriate*, p. 121.

93. 'Death of an Australian poet', *British-Australasian*, 11 January 1906, p. 18.

94. *British-Australasian*, 25 January 1906, p. 18.

95. *New Zealand News*, 28 January 1930, in de Montalk, *Unquiet World*, p. 102.

96. 'New Zealanders in London', *Press*, 12 February 1929, p. 15.

97. Meg Tasker, '"When London calls" and Fleet Street beckons: Daley's poem, Reg's diary – what happens when it all goes "bung"?', in *Modern Mobilities: Australian-transnational writing*, eds David Brooks and Elizabeth MacMahon (Blackheath, N.S.W.: Brandl & Schlesinger, 2011), p. 107.

98. Actually she was born in South Africa.

99. Jane Mander, 'Post-war N.Z. Novelists', transcript of a radio talk, c. 1932, p. 21, NZMS 535, APL.

100. Olaf Ruhen to Pat Lawlor, 3 February 1963, 77-067 4/4, ATL.

101. Patrick Sandbrook, '"Not easily put on paper": Robin Hyde's *The Godwits Fly*', in *A Book in the Hand: Essays on the history of the book in New Zealand*, eds Penny Griffith, Peter Hughes and Alan Loney (Auckland: Auckland University Press, 2000), p. 128.

CONCLUDING THOUGHTS

1. Fairburn to Mason, 6 January 1932, MS Papers 592/18, HC.

2. Frank Sargeson, *Sargeson* (Auckland: Penguin, 1981), p. 63.

3. Denys Trussell, *Fairburn* (Auckland: Auckland University Press, 1984), p. 100.

4. James Bertram, *Dan Davin* (Auckland: Oxford University Press, 1983), p. 5.

5. Philip Steer, 'James Courage, 1903–1953', *Kōtare*, vol. 7, no. 2, 2008: http://ojs.victoria.ac.nz/kotare/article/view/674

6. *Evening Post*, 4 August 1909.

7. Denis Glover, *Hot Water Sailor; & Landlubber Ho!* (Auckland: Collins, 1981), p. 173.

8. Sargeson, *Sargeson*, p. 63.

9. Katherine Mansfield, Journal, in Anthony Alpers, *The Life of Katherine Mansfield* (Oxford: Oxford University Press, 1982), p. 195.

10. Bertram, *Dan Davin*, p. 5.

11. Monte Holcroft, *The Deepening Stream* (Christchurch: Caxton Press, 1940), p. 12.

12. Jane Mander, letter to Pat Lawlor, 12 May, the year not given but internal evidence points to 1931, in Dorothea Turner, *Jane Mander* (New York: Twayne, 1972), p. 31.

13. Mulgan to his mother, in Vincent O'Sullivan, *Long Journey to the Border* (Auckland: Penguin, 2003), p. 128.

14. Gordon Ogilvie, *Denis Glover: His life* (Auckland: Godwit, 1999), p. 209.

15. From 1934 the firm known as A.H. & A.W. Reed began publishing occasional novels and works of poetry (20 between 1934 and 1945) but they were initially better known for non-fiction.

16. Noel Waite, *Adventure and Art: The Caxton Press* (Wellington: National Library of New Zealand, 1998), p. 5.

17. Andrzej Gąsiorek, *A History of Modernist Literature* (Chichester, West Sussex: Wiley Blackwell, 2015), p. 8.

18. Gąsiorek, p. 4.

19. Allen Curnow, *A Book of New Zealand Verse 1923–1945* (Christchurch: Caxton Press, 1945), p. 17.

20. Allen Curnow, 'Rata blossoms or reality', *Look Back Harder: Critical writings 1935–1984* (Auckland: Auckland University Press, 1987), p. 11, in Jane Stafford and Mark Williams, *Maoriland: New Zealand literature 1872–1914* (Wellington: Victoria University Press, 2006), p. 223.

21. Blanche Baughan, 'Café au Lait', in *New Zealand Short Stories*, ed. O.N. Gillespie (London: Dent, 1930), pp. 38, 48–49.

22. Jessie Mackay, *The Spirit of the Rangatira and Other Ballads* (Melbourne: Robertson, 1889).

23. Charlotte Elder, 'An annotated edition of the correspondence between Ursula Bethell and John Schroder' (MA thesis, Victoria University, 1999), p. 22.

24. Ursula Bethell, 'The long harbour', *Time and Place* (Christchurch: Caxton Press, 1936).

25. Elder, 'An annotated edition of the correspondence between Ursula Bethell and John Schroder', p. 14.

26. The percentage of books published by women remained in the vicinity of 50 per cent between 1920 and 1940 (if Fergus Hume's contribution is not included in the calculation), though it did drop to 38 per cent between 1940 and 1944.

27. Denis Glover, *The Arraignment of Paris* (Christchurch: Caxton Press, 1937).

28. Keith Sinclair mentions this in *A Destiny Apart* (Wellington: Allen & Unwin, 1986), p. 246, according to Patrick Evans, *Penguin History of New Zealand Literature* (Auckland: Penguin, 1990), p. 78.

29. Evans, *Penguin History of New Zealand Literature*, p. 8.

30. Mark Williams, 'Repetitious beginnings: New Zealand literary history in the late 1980s', *Journal of New Zealand Literature*, no. 7, 1989, p. 73.

31. Victor Daley, 'When London calls', *Bulletin*, 8 December 1900, p. 15.

32. P.R. Stephensen, *The Foundations of Culture in Australia: An essay towards national self respect [1935–36]*, pp. 123–24, in Peter Morton, *Lusting for London: Australian expatriate writers at the hub of empire, 1870–1950* (New York: Palgrave Macmillan, 2011), p. 196.

33. Nicholas Birns, 'Introduction', in *A Companion to Australian Literature Since 1900*, eds Nicholas Birns and Rebecca McNeer (Rochester, N.Y.: Camden House, 2007), pp. 2–3.

34. Peter Craven, 'No success like failure', introduction to Henry Handel Richardson, *The Fortunes of Richard Mahoney* (Melbourne: Text Publishing Company, 2012), p. xvi.

35. Bill Ashcroft, 'Australian transnation', *Southerly*, vol. 71, no. 1, 2011, p. 18.

Bibliography

PRIMARY SOURCES

Manuscript sources

Alexander Turnbull Library (ATL), Wellington
Duggan, Eileen, Papers, MS Papers 0801.
Fairburn, A.R.D., Papers, MS Papers 1128.
Glover, Denis, Papers, MS Papers 418.
Heenan, Joseph, Papers, MS Papers 1132.
Holcroft, Monte, Papers, MS Papers 1186.
Holcroft, Monte, Notebooks, MSX-0253.
Lawlor, Patrick Anthony, Papers, Ref. 77-067.
Lyttleton, Edith, Papers, MS Papers 8649.
Mander, Jane, Papers, MS Papers 3404.
de Montalk, Geoffrey, Letters from Rex Fairburn, MS Papers 2461.
Mulgan, Alan, Papers, MS Papers 0224.
Scanlan, Nelle, Papers, MS Papers 0232.

Hocken Collections (HC), Dunedin
Mason, R.A.K., Papers, MS Papers 592.
Brasch, Charles, Papers, MS Papers 996.

Macmillan Brown Library (MBL), Christchurch
Bethell, Ursula, Papers, MS 558.
Gilbert, G.R., Papers, MS 957.

Auckland Public Library (APL)
Mander, Jane, Papers, NZMS 535.
Mulgan, Alan, Papers, NZMS 748.

State Library of New South Wales (SLNSW)
Park, Ruth, Papers, 1938–1976, MLMSS 3128.
Stephens, A.G., Papers, MLMSS 4937.
Angus & Robertson, Papers, MLMSS 314.

Bodleian Library Special Collections (BLSC), Oxford
Sidgwick and Jackson, Papers, MSS 142 (Ursula Bethell) and MSS 252 (William
    Satchell).

Oxford University Press Archives
Mulgan, John, personal file, Ref. CPGE 383.

University of Reading Special Collections (URSC)
Allen & Unwin, Papers, AUC.
Chatto & Windus, Papers, C/W.

British Library Additional Manuscripts (BL), London

Richard Bentley & Son, Papers, Add. 46621, f. 327 (agreement with Clara Cheeseman). Chesterton, G.K., Correspondence, Add. 73235, f. 134 (letters from Hector Bolitho). Society of Authors Archive, Add. 56981, ff. 1-81 (Rosemary Rees vs. Walter Melville).

Literary periodicals and newspapers

All About Books for Australian and New Zealand Readers
Art in New Zealand
Auckland Star
British-Australasian (or *British-Australian and New Zealander*)
Bulletin (Sydney)
Daily Mail (United Kingdom)
Dominion
Evening Post (Wellington)
Land (Sydney)
Landfall
Lyttelton Times
New Zealand Herald
New Zealand Illustrated Magazine
New Zealand Listener
Phoenix
Press (Christchurch)
Star (Christchurch)
Sun (Auckland)
Sun (Christchurch)
Sydney Morning Herald
Times Literary Supplement
Tomorrow
Triad

Novels, poetry and memoirs

Adams, Arthur H., *Maoriland and Other Verses* (Sydney: Bulletin Newspaper Company, 1899)
——, *Tussock Land* (London: T. Fisher Unwin, 1904)
Baughan, Blanche, 'Café au Lait', in O.N. Gillespie (ed.), *New Zealand Short Stories* (London: Dent, 1930)
Bennett, Arnold, *Books and Persons: Being comments on a past epoch, 1908–1911* (London: Chatto & Windus, 1917)
Bethell, Ursula, *Time and Place* (Christchurch: Caxton Press, 1936)
Blackwell, Basil (ed.), *The Book World* (London: Thomas Nelson & Sons, 1935)
Bolitho, Hector, *My Restless Years* (London: Parrish, 1962)
Burton, Ormond Edward, *The New Zealand Division* (Auckland: Clark & Matheson, 1936)
Butler, Samuel, *A First Year in Canterbury Settlement* (London: Longman, Green, 1863)

Cadey, Prudence, *Broken Pattern* (London: Fenland Press, 1933)

Courage, James, *The Call Home* (London: Jonathan Cape, 1956)

Davin, Dan, *Cliffs of Fall* (London: Nicholson & Watson, 1945)

——, *The Sullen Bell* (London: M. Joseph, 1956)

Devanny, Jean, *Point of Departure* (St Lucia, Qld: University of Queensland Press, 1986)

——, *The Butcher Shop* (Auckland: Auckland University Press, 1981)

Domett, Alfred, *Ranolf and Amohia: A south sea day-dream* (London: Smith, Elder, 1872)

Duggan, Eileen, *New Zealand Bird Songs* (Wellington: Harry T. Tombs, 1929)

——, *Poems* (London: Allen & Unwin, 1937)

——, *More Poems* (London: Allen & Unwin, 1951)

Fairburn, A.R.D., and Edmond, Lauris (eds), *The Letters of A.R.D. Fairburn* (Auckland: Oxford University Press, 1981)

Glover, Denis, *The Arraignment of Paris* (Christchurch: Caxton Press, 1937)

——, *Hot Water Sailor; & Landlubber Ho!* (Auckland: Collins, 1981)

Grossmann, Edith Searle, *Hermione: A knight of the Holy Ghost* (London: Watts, 1908)

——, *The Heart of the Bush* (London: Sands, 1910)

Hellier, F., *Colonials in Khaki* (London: Murray & Evenden, 1916)

Hoggard, Noel, *The Inky Way* (Wellington: Handcraft Press, 1940)

Holcroft, Monte, *The Way of a Writer* (Whatamongo Bay: Cape Catley, 1984)

Hyde, Robin, *Journalese* (Auckland: National Printing Company, 1934)

——, *The Godwits Fly* (London: Hurst & Blackett, 1938)

Kenny, Alice A., *The Rebel* (Sydney: Macquarie Head Press, 1934)

Lawlor, Pat, *Confessions of a Journalist* (Auckland: Whitcombe & Tombs, 1935)

The Lyceum Club, *London: A prospectus* (London, 1903), Bodleian Library Bookstack

Lynn, David, *Love and Hunger* (London: Kangaroo Books, 1944)

Lyttleton, Edith, *Promenade* (London: John Lane, 1938)

Mackay, Jessie, *The Spirit of the Rangatira and Other Ballads* (Melbourne: Robertson, 1889)

——, *From the Maori Sea* (Christchurch, Whitcombe & Tombs, 1908)

——, *Vigil* (Auckland: Whitcombe & Tombs, 1935)

Mander, Jane, *The Story of a New Zealand River* (London: Bodley Head, 1920)

——, *The Passionate Puritan* (London: John Lane, 1922)

——, *The Strange Attraction* (London: Bodley Head, 1923)

Mansfield, Katherine, *Journal of Katherine Mansfield* (Auckland: Hutchinson, 1984)

Marsh, Ngaio, *Black Beech and Honeydew* (London: Collins, 1981)

Mulgan, Alan, *Home: A New Zealander's adventure* (London: Longmans, Green, 1927)

——, *The Making of a New Zealander* (Wellington: Reed, 1958)

Peacocke, Isabel Maud, *The Guardian* (London: Ward, Lock, 1920)

——, *London Called Them* (London: Ward, Lock, 1946)

Richardson, Henry Handel, *The Fortunes of Richard Mahoney* (Melbourne: Text Publishing, 2012, first published in a single volume by Heinemann, 1930)

Sargeson, Frank, *Sargeson* (Auckland: Penguin, 1981), reprint of *Once is Enough* (first published Wellington: Reed, 1973), *More than Enough* (1975), and *Never Enough* (1978)

Satchell, William, *The Land of the Lost* (London: Methuen, 1902)

Scanlan, Nelle, *Ambition's Harvest* (London: Jarrold, 1935)

——, *Road to Pencarrow* (London: Robert Hale, 1963)

Scott, Mary, *The Unwritten Book* (Wellington: Reed, 1957)

——, *Days that Have Been* (Auckland: Blackwood & J. Paul, 1966)

Smyth, Walter, *Jean of the Tussock Country* (London: Mills & Boon, 1928)

Trollope, Anthony, *Australia and New Zealand*, Vol. 2 (London: Chapman & Hall, 1873)

Vogel, Harry, *A Maori Maid* (London: Macmillan, 1898)

Wall, Arnold, *London Lost and Other Poems* (Auckland: Whitcombe & Tombs, 1922)

Wilcox, Dora, *Verses from Maoriland* (London: George Allen, 1905)

Winks, Robin, *These New Zealanders* (Christchurch: Whitcombe & Tombs, 1954)

SECONDARY SOURCES

Books, articles and theses

Alomes, Stephen, *When London Calls: The expatriation of Australian creative artists to Britain* (Cambridge: Cambridge University Press, 1999)

Alpers, Anthony, *The Life of Katherine Mansfield* (Oxford: Oxford University Press, 1982)

Andersen, Johannes (ed.), *Annals of New Zealand Literature* (Wellington: New Zealand Authors' Week Committee, 1936)

——, 'Early Printing in New Zealand', in R.A. Mackay (ed.), *A History of Printing in New Zealand, 1830–1940* (Wellington: Wellington Club of Printing House Craftsmen, 1940)

Anderson, Benedict, *Imagined Communities* (London; New York: Verso, 2006)

Arnold, John, 'Australian books, publishers and writers in England, 1900–1940', in Carl Bridge, Robert Crawford and David Dunstan (eds), *Australians in Britain: The twentieth-century experience* (Clayton, Vic: Monash University Press, 2009)

Ashcroft, Bill, 'Australian transnation', in David Brooks and Elizabeth MacMahon (eds), *Modern Mobilities: Australian-transnational writing* (Blackheath, NSW: Brandl & Schlesinger, 2011), pp. 18–40

Aston, Elaine and Clarke, Ian, 'The dangerous woman of Melvillean melodrama', *New Theatre Quarterly*, vol. XII, no. 45, 1996, pp. 30–42

Baird, Rosemary, 'Across the Tasman: Narratives of New Zealand migrants to and from Australia, 1965–95', PhD thesis (University of Canterbury, 2012)

Ballantyne, Tony, 'On place, space and mobility in nineteenth-century New Zealand', *New Zealand Journal of History*, vol. 45, no. 1, 2011, pp. 50–70

——, *Webs of Empire: Locating New Zealand's colonial past* (Wellington: Bridget Williams Books, 2012)

——, 'Mobility, empire, colonisation', *History Australia*, vol. 11, no. 2, 2014, pp. 7–37

Barnicoat, Constance A., 'The reading of the colonial girl', *Nineteenth Century and After: A monthly review*, vol. 60, no. 358, 1906, pp. 939–50

Barnes, Felicity, 'New Zealand's London: The metropolis and New Zealand's culture, 1890–1940', PhD thesis (University of Auckland, 2008)

——, *New Zealand's London: A colony and its metropolis* (Auckland: Auckland University Press, 2012)

Barnes, John, *The Writer in Australia* (Melbourne: Oxford University Press, 1969)

——, '"Heaven forbid that I should think of treating with an English publisher": The

dilemma of literary nationalists in federated Australia', in Simon Eliot, Andrew
Nash and Ian Willison (eds), *Literary Cultures and the Material Book* (London:
British Library, 2007), pp. 319–413

Barrowman, Rachel, *Mason: The life of R.A.K. Mason* (Wellington: Victoria University
Press, 2003)

Baughen, G.A.K., 'C.N. Baeyertz and The Triad 1893–1915', BA (Hons) thesis
(University of Otago, 1980)

Belich, James, *Making Peoples: A history of the New Zealanders from Polynesian
settlement to the end of the nineteenth century* (Auckland: Penguin, 1996)

——, *Paradise Reforged: A history of the New Zealanders from the 1880s to the year
2000* (Auckland: Penguin, 2001)

——, *Replenishing the Earth* (Oxford: Oxford University Press, 2011)

Bennett, Bruce and Pender, Anne, *From a Distant Shore: Australian writers in Britain
1820–2012* (Clayton, Vic: Monash University Press, 2013)

Bertram, James, 'Poetry comes of age', in Ray Knox (ed.), *New Zealand's Heritage*
(Wellington: Paul Hamlyn, 1971–73)

——, *Dan Davin* (Auckland: Oxford University Press, 1983)

——, *Flight of the Phoenix: Critical notes on New Zealand writers* (Wellington:
Victoria University Press, 1985)

Bevan, David, *Literature and Exile* (Amsterdam; Atlanta, GA: Rodopi, 1990)

Binney, Judith, *Mihaia: The prophet Rua Kenana and his community at Maungapohatu*
(Wellington: Oxford University Press, 1979)

Birns, Nicholas and McNeer, Rebecca (eds), *A Companion to Australian Literature
since 1900* (Rochester, NY: Camden House, 2007)

Bishop, Catherine, 'Women on the move: Gender, money-making and mobility
in mid-nineteenth century Australasia', *History Australia*, vol. 11, no. 2, 2014,
pp. 38–59

Bones, Helen, 'A dual exile? New Zealand and the colonial writing world, 1890–1945.'
PhD thesis (University of Canterbury, 2011): http://hdl.handle.net/10092/5618

——, 'New Zealand and the Tasman writing world, 1890–1945', *History Australia*, vol.
10, no. 3, 2013, pp. 129–48

Bourdieu, Pierre, *The field of cultural production: Essays on art and literature*
(Cambridge: Polity Press, 1993)

Bradbury, Malcolm, 'Second countries: The expatriate tradition in American writing',
The Yearbook of English Studies, no. 8 (1978), pp. 15–39

Brantlinger, Patrick, *Rule of Darkness: British literature and imperialism, 1830–1914*
(Ithaca, NY: Cornell University Press, 1988)

Broughton, W.S., *A.R.D. Fairburn* (Wellington: Reed, 1968)

Buckridge, Patrick, 'A kind of exile: Godfrey Blunden – an Australian in Paris', *Journal
of Australian Studies*, vol. 26, no. 73, 2002, pp. 111–18

Burns, Rebecca, 'Snapshot of a life reassessed: Edith Searle Grossmann', *Kōtare: New
Zealand Notes and Queries* (Wellington: Victoria University Press, 2009)

Byrnes, Giselle (ed.), *The New Oxford History of New Zealand* (Melbourne: Oxford
University Press, 2009)

Calder, Alex, 'Introduction', *The Writing of New Zealand* (Auckland: Reed, 1993)

——, *The Settler's Plot: How stories take place in New Zealand* (Auckland: Auckland University Press, 2013)

Carter, David, 'Good readers and good citizens: Literature, media and the nation', *Australian Literary Studies*, vol. 19, no. 2, 1999, pp. 136–51

——, 'Structures, networks, institutions: The new empiricism, book history and literary history', in Katherine Bode and Robert Dixon (eds), *Resourceful Reading: The new empiricism, eresearch and Australian literary culture* (Sydney: Sydney University Press, 2009), pp. 31–52

Challis, Derek and Rawlinson, Gloria, *The Book of Iris* (Auckland: Auckland University Press, 2002)

Chapman, Robert, 'Fiction and the social pattern', *Landfall*, vol. 7, no. 1, March 1953, pp. 26–58

Coney, Sandra, 'Riemke Ensing on women writers', *Broadsheet*, no. 22, 1974, p. 12

Connolly, C.N., 'Class, birthplaces, loyalty: Australian attitudes to the Boer War', *Historical Studies*, vol. 18, no. 11, 1978

Craven, Peter, 'No success like failure', Introduction to Henry Handel Richardson, *The Fortunes of Richard Mahoney* (Melbourne: Text Publishing Company, 2012), pp. vii–xvii

Curnow, Allen, 'Introduction', *A Book of New Zealand Verse 1923–1945* (Christchurch: Caxton Press, 1945), pp. 13–55

——, 'Modern Australian poetry', *Landfall*, vol. 1, no. 2, 1947, pp. 142–50

——, (ed.), *Penguin Book of New Zealand Verse* (Harmondsworth: Penguin, 1960)

Daley, Caroline, *Leisure and Pleasure: Reshaping and revealing the New Zealand body 1900–1960* (Auckland: Auckland University Press, 2003)

Dalziel, Raewyn, 'The colonial helpmeet: Women's role and the vote in nineteenth century New Zealand', *New Zealand Journal of History*, vol. 11, no. 2, 1977, pp. 112–23

——, 'Presenting the enfranchisement of New Zealand women abroad', in Caroline Daley and Melanie Nolan (eds), *Suffrage and Beyond: International feminist perspectives* (Auckland: Auckland University Press, 1994), pp. 42–64

Davidoff, Leonore, *The Best Circles: Society etiquette and the season* (London: Cresset Library, 1986)

de la Mare, Frederick, *G.B. Lancaster 1873–1945: A tribute* (Hamilton: Waikato Times, 1945)

de Montalk, Stephanie, *Unquiet World* (Wellington: Victoria University Press, 2001)

den Hartog, Dirk, 'Australian male writers', in Samuel Louis Goldberg and Francis Barrymore Smith (eds), *Australian Cultural History* (Cambridge: Cambridge University Press, 1988)

Dixon, Robert, *Writing the Colonial Adventure: Race, gender, and nation in Anglo-Australian popular fiction, 1875–1914* (Cambridge: Cambridge University Press, 1995)

Dougherty, Ian, *Books and Boots: The story of New Zealand publisher, writer and long distance walker, Alfred Hamish Reed* (Dunedin: University of Otago Press, 2005)

Eddy, John and Schreuder, Deryck, *The Rise of Colonial Nationalism: Australia, New Zealand, Canada and South Africa first assert their identities* (Sydney: Allen & Unwin, 1988)

Eder, Doris L., *Three Writers in Exile: Pound, Eliot and Joyce* (Troy, NY: Whitston, 1984)

Eggert, Paul, *Biography of a Book: Henry Lawson's While the Billy Boils* (Sydney: Sydney University Press, 2013)

Elder, Charlotte, 'An annotated edition of the correspondence between Ursula Bethell and John Schroder', MA thesis (Victoria University, 1999)

Ensor, Jason D., 'Places of publication and the Australian book trade: A study of Angus & Robertson's London Office, 1938–1970', PhD thesis (Murdoch University, Australia, 2010)

Eriksson, Sofia. 'Observing the birth of a nation: British travel writing on Australia, 1870–1939', PhD thesis (Macquarie University, Australia, 2011)

Evans, Patrick, *Penguin History of New Zealand Literature* (Auckland: Penguin, 1990)

——, *The Long Forgetting* (Christchurch: Canterbury University Press, 2007)

Fairburn, Miles, *The Ideal Society and its Enemies: The foundations of modern New Zealand society* (Auckland: Auckland University Press, 1989)

——, 'Is there a good case for New Zealand exceptionalism?', *Thesis Eleven*, no. 92, 2008, pp. 29–49

Feather, John, *A History of British Publishing* (London; New York: Routledge, 1988)

French, Anne, 'Georgians and New Zealand Georgians: A study of Eileen Duggan and R.A.K. Mason, and New Zealand poetry of the twenties and thirties in the context of Georgian poetry in England', MA thesis (Victoria University, 1979)

Garner, Jean, *By His Own Merits* (Hororata: Dryden Press, 1995)

Gąsiorek, Andrzej, *A History of Modernist Literature* (Chichester, West Sussex: Wiley Blackwell, 2015)

Gibbons, Peter, 'The far side of the search for identity', *New Zealand Journal of History*, vol. 37, no. 1, 2003, pp. 38–49

Glover, Denis, 'Pointers to Parnassus: A consideration of the morepork and the muse', *Tomorrow*, no. 2, 1935

Goldberg, Samuel Louis and Smith, Francis Barrymore, *Australian Cultural History* (Cambridge: Cambridge University Press, 1988)

Gonley, Winnie, 'New Zealand life in contemporary literature', MA thesis (University of New Zealand, 1932)

Griffith, Penny, Harvey, Ross and Maslen, Keith (eds), *Book and Print in New Zealand: A guide to print culture in Aotearoa* (Wellington: Victoria University Press, 1997)

Griffith, Penny, Hughes, Peter, and Loney, Alan (eds), *A Book in the Hand: Essays on the history of the book in New Zealand* (Auckland: Auckland University Press, 2000)

Gurr, Andrew, *Writers in Exile: The identity of home in modern literature* (Brighton: Harvester Press, 1981)

Hamilton, Stephen, 'New Zealand English language periodicals of literary interest active 1920s–1960s', PhD thesis (University of Auckland, 1995)

Hankin, Cherry (ed.), *Life in a Young Colony: Selections from early New Zealand writing* (Christchurch: Whitcoulls, 1981).

Hawke, G.R., *The Making of New Zealand: An economic history* (Cambridge: Cambridge University Press, 1985)

Hempenstall, Peter, Mein Smith, Philippa, and Goldfinch, Shaun, *Remaking the Tasman World* (Christchurch: Canterbury University Press, 2008).

Hilliard, Chris, 'Island stories', MA thesis (University of Auckland, 1997)

———, 'Colonial culture and the province of cultural history', *New Zealand Journal of History*, vol. 36, no. 1, 2002

———, *The Bookmen's Dominion: Cultural life in New Zealand 1920-1950* (Auckland: Auckland University Press, 2006)

Holcroft, Monte, *The Deepening Stream* (Christchurch: Caxton Press, 1940)

———, *Discovered Isles: A trilogy* (Christchurch: Caxton Press, 1950)

———, 'A professional expatriate', in Ray Knox (ed.), *New Zealand's Heritage 6* (Wellington: Paul Hamlyn, 1973), p. 2210

———, *Mary Ursula Bethell* (Wellington; New York: Oxford University Press, 1975)

Hurst, Maurice, *Music and the Stage: A century of entertainment 1840-1943* (Charles Begg: Auckland, 1944)

Jensen, Kai, *Whole Men* (Auckland: Auckland University Press, 1996)

Johanson, Graeme, *Colonial Editions in Australia, 1843-1972* (Wellington: Elibank Press, 2000)

Jones, Lawrence, *Picking Up the Traces: The making of a New Zealand literary culture 1932-1945* (Wellington: Victoria University Press, 2003)

Kalliney, Peter, *Modernism in a Global Context* (London; New York: Bloomsbury Academic, 2016)

Karim, Karim H., *The Definition of Visible Minority: A historical and cultural analysis* (Ottawa: Department of Canadian Heritage, 1996)

Kavolis, Vytautas, 'Women writers in exile', *World Literature Today*, vol. 66, no. 1, 1992, pp. 43-46

Keesing, Nancy, *Australian Writers and Their Work: Douglas Stewart* (Sydney: Lansdowne Press, 1965)

Kemp, Sandra, Mitchell, Charlotte and Trotter, David, *The Oxford Companion to Edwardian Fiction* (Oxford; New York: Oxford University Press, c. 1997)

Kirkpatrick, Peter, *The Sea Coast of Bohemia: Literary life in Sydney's roaring twenties* (Perth: API Network, 2007)

Lambert, David and Lester, Alan (eds), *Colonial Lives across the British Empire: Imperial careering in the long nineteenth century* (Cambridge: Cambridge University Press, 2006)

Lawson, Bertha, *My Henry Lawson* (Frank Johnson: Sydney, 1943)

Lee, John, '"A private history": towards a biography of James Courage, expatriate New Zealand writer', MA thesis (Victoria University, 2001)

Lee, Robert, *Transport: An Australian history* (Sydney: University of New South Wales Press, 2010)

Leggott, Michele, 'Opening the archive: Robin Hyde, Eileen Duggan and the persistence of record', *Hecate*, vol. 20, no. 2, 1994, pp. 266-93

Lester, Alan, 'Historical geographies of British colonisation: New South Wales, New Zealand and the Cape in the early nineteenth century', in Simon Potter (ed.),

Imperial Communication: Australia, Britain and the British Empire 1830–1850
(London: Menzies Centre, 2005)

Louis, W.M. Roger, 'Introduction', *The Oxford History of the British Empire: Volume IV: The twentieth century* (Oxford: Oxford University Press, 1999)

Loveridge, Steven, 'The "other" on the other side of the ditch? The conception of New Zealand's disassociation from Australia', *Journal of Imperial and Commonwealth History*, vol. 44, no. 1, 2016, pp. 70–94

Lyons, Martyn and Arnold, John (eds), *A History of the Book in Australia 1891–1945: A national culture in a colonised market* (St Lucia, Qsld: University of Queensland Press, 2001)

Macdonald, Peter D., *British Literary Culture and Publishing Practice, 1880–1914* (Cambridge; New York: Cambridge University Press, 1997)

Mackay, F.M., *New Zealand Writers and their Work: Eileen Duggan* (Wellington: Oxford University Press, 1977)

Magner, Brigid, 'Trans-Tasman Impostures', *Journal of the Association for the Study of Australian Literature*, January 2013, pp. 174–80

Mantz, Ruth, *The Life of Katherine Mansfield* (London: Constable, 1933)

Mao, Douglas and Walkowitz, Rebecca, 'The new modernist studies', *Publications of the Modern Language Association of America*, vol. 123, no. 3, 2008, pp. 737–48

Marshall, Theresia, 'New Zealand literature in the Sydney *Bulletin*' (PhD thesis, University of Auckland, 1995)

Maurois, Andre, *Points of View: From Kipling to Graham Greene* (London: Frederick Muller, 1969)

McCormick, Eric, *Letters and Art in New Zealand* (Wellington: Dept. of Internal Affairs, 1940)

——, *The Expatriate: A study of Frances Hodgkins* (Wellington: New Zealand University Press, 1954)

McEldowney, W.J., *The New Zealand Library Association 1910–1960 and its Part in New Zealand Library Development* (Wellington: New Zealand Library Association, 1962)

McGregor, Rae, *The Story of a New Zealand Writer: Jane Mander* (Dunedin: University of Otago Press, 1998).

McKay, Frank, *Eileen Duggan* (Wellington: Oxford University Press, 1977)

McLaren, Ian F., *Whitcombe's Story Books: A trans-Tasman survey* (Parkville: University of Melbourne Library, 1984)

McLean, Denis, Review of *Dance of the Peacocks*, *New Zealand International Review* 29 (2004)

McLeod, Aorewa, 'A home in this world: Why New Zealand women stopped writing', *Women's Studies Journal*, vol. 14, no. 2, 1998, pp. 61–76.

McNaughton, Howard, *New Zealand Drama* (Boston: Twayne Publishers, 1981)

McNeish, James, *Dance of the Peacocks: New Zealanders in exile at the time of Hitler and Mao Tse-tung* (Auckland: Vintage, 2003)

Mein Smith, Philippa, 'Mapping Australasia', *History Compass*, no. 7, 2009, pp. 1–24

Meinig, David, *The Shaping of America* (New Haven: Yale University Press, 1986)

Milbauer, Asher Z., *Transcending Exile: Conrad, Nabokov, I.B. Singer* (Miami: Florida International University Press, 1985)

Millar, Paul, *No Fretful Sleeper: A life of Bill Pearson* (Auckland: Auckland University Press, 2010)

Miller, E. Morris, *Australian Literature: A bibliography to 1938, extended to 1950* (Sydney: Angus and Robertson, 1956)

Modjeska, Drusilla, *Exiles at Home: Australian women writers 1925–1945* (London: Sirius Books, 1981)

Moretti, Franco, *Graphs, Maps and Trees: Abstract models for a literary history* (London, Verso, 2005)

Morrisson, Mark, Review of *Locations of Literary Modernism: Region and nation in British and American modernist poetry* (edited by Alex Davis and Lee M. Jenkins), *Comparative Literature Studies*, vol. 39, no. 1, 2002, pp. 82–87

Morton, Peter, *Lusting for London: Australian expatriate writers at the hub of empire, 1870–1950* (New York: Palgrave Macmillan, 2011)

Mulgan, Alan, *Literature and Authorship in New Zealand* (London: George Allen & Unwin, 1943)

Murray, Heather, 'Celebrating our writers: 1936, 1951', *Journal of New Zealand Literature*, no. 10, 1992, pp. 99–114

Murray, Stuart, *Never a Soul at Home: New Zealand literary nationalism and the 1930s* (Wellington: Victoria University Press, 1998).

——, Review of *Story of a New Zealand Writer*, *Landfall*, no. 197, 1999, p. 156

Nash, Andrew, 'Literary culture and literary publishing in inter-war Britain: A view from Chatto & Windus', in Simon Eliot, Andrew Nash and Ian Willison (eds), *Literary Cultures and the Material Book* (London: British Library, 2007), pp. 323–41

Needham-Gillespie, Dulcie, 'The colonial and his books: A study of reading in nineteenth century New Zealand', PhD thesis (Victoria University, 1971)

Nesbitt, Bruce, 'Aspects of literary nationalism in Australia and New Zealand with special reference to the *Bulletin*, 1880–1900', PhD thesis (Australian National University, 1968)

New Zealand Department of Censuses and Statistics, *General Report, Population Census* (Wellington: Department of Censuses and Statistics, 1926 and 1936).

New Zealand Department of Censuses and Statistics, *The New Zealand Official Yearbook, 1934* (Wellington: Government Printer, 1933)

Newton, John, 'Colonialism above the snowline', *Journal of Commonwealth Literature*, vol. 34, no. 85, 1999, pp. 85–96

O'Neill, Reginald, *The Press, 1861–1961: The story of a newspaper* (Christchurch: Christchurch Press, 1963)

O'Sullivan, Vincent, '"Finding the pattern, solving the problem": Katherine Mansfield the New Zealand European', in Roger Robinson (ed.), *Katherine Mansfield: In from the margin* (Baton Rouge: Louisiana State University Press, 1994), pp. 9–24

——, 'Katherine Mansfield: The exile of the mind', in Anne Luyat and Francine Tolron (eds), *Flight from Certainty: The dilemma of identity and exile* (Amsterdam: Rodopi, 2001), pp. 134–39

————, *Long Journey to the Border* (Auckland: Penguin, 2003)

Ogilvie, Gordon, *Denis Glover: His life* (Auckland: Godwit, 1999).

Ovenden, Keith, *A Fighting Withdrawal: The life of Dan Davin* (Oxford: Oxford University Press, 1996)

Pearson, Bill, *Henry Lawson Among Maoris* (Wellington: Reed, 1968)

Phillips, A.A., 'The cultural cringe', *Meanjin*, no. 4, 1950, pp. 299–300

Phillips, Jock, 'Musings in Maoriland – or was there a *Bulletin* school in New Zealand?', *Historical Studies*, vol. 20, no. 81, 1983, pp. 520–35

————, *A Man's Country? The image of the Pakeha male, a history* (Auckland: Penguin, 1987)

————, 'Of verandahs and fish and chips and footie on Saturday afternoon', *New Zealand Journal of History*, vol. 24, no. 2, 1990, pp. 118–34

Pierce, Peter (ed.), *The Cambridge History of Australian Literature* (Cambridge: Cambridge University Press, 2009)

Plumridge, Elizabeth, 'The negotiation of circumstance: New Zealand women artists c. 1890–1914', PhD thesis (Australian National University, 1985).

Pocock, J.G.A., *The Discovery of Islands: Essays in British history* (Cambridge, UK: Cambridge University Press, 2005)

Prickett, Nigel, 'Trans-Tasman stories: Australian Aborigines in New Zealand sealing and shore whaling', in Geoffrey Clark, Sue O'Connor and Bryan Leach (eds), *Islands of Inquiry: Colonisation, seafaring and the archaeology of maritime landscapes (Volume 29 of Terra Australis)* (Canberra: Australian National University EPress, 2008), pp. 351–66

Ramazani, Jahan, 'A transnational poetics', *American Literary History*, vol. 18, no. 2, 2006, pp. 332–59

Reeves, William Pember, *The Long White Cloud* (London: Horace Marshall & Son, 1898).

Rhodes, Winston, *New Zealand Novels* (Wellington: New Zealand University Press, 1969)

Rice, Geoffrey (ed.), *The Oxford History of New Zealand* (Auckland: Oxford University Press, 1992)

Robinson, Howard, *A History of the Post Office in New Zealand* (Wellington: Government Printer, 1964)

Robinson, Roger and Wattie, Nelson (eds), *The Oxford Companion to New Zealand Literature* (Oxford: Oxford University Press, 1998)

Rochester, Maxine, *The Revolution in New Zealand Librarianship: American influence as facilitated by the Carnegie Corporation of New York in the 1930s*, Occasional Papers Series 50 (Halifax, Nova Scotia: Dalhousie University, School of Library and Information Studies, 1990)

Rogers, Anna and Rogers, Max, *Turning the Pages: The story of bookselling in New Zealand* (Auckland: Reed, 1993)

Ronnie, Mary, *Books to the People: A history of regional library services in New Zealand* (Wellington: New Zealand Library Association, 1993)

Rushdie, Salman, *Imaginary Homelands* (London: Viking, 1991)

Russell, Roslyn, *Literary Links: Celebrating the literary relationship between Australia and Britain* (St. Leonards, NSW: Allen & Unwin, 1997)

Scholefield, Guy H., *Newspapers in New Zealand* (Wellington: Reed, 1958)

Serle, Geoffrey, *From Deserts the Prophets Come: The creative spirit in Australia 1788–1972* (Melbourne: Heinemann, 1973)

Seyhan, Azade, *Writing Outside the Nation* (Princeton: Princeton University Press, 2001)

Shep, Sydney J., 'The printers' web: New tools to crack old chestnuts', in Paul Longley Arthur and Katherine Bode (eds), *Advancing Digital Humanities: Research, methods, theories* (Basingstoke: Palgrave Macmillan, 2014), pp. 68–82

Simpson, Peter, *Bloomsbury South: The arts in Christchurch 1933–1953* (Auckland: Auckland University Press, 2016)

Sinclair, Keith, *A History of New Zealand* (Harmondsworth, Middlesex: Penguin, 1959)

——, (ed.), *Distance Looks Our Way* (Auckland: Paul's Book Arcade, 1961)

Smith, Angela, *Katherine Mansfield and Virginia Woolf: A public of two* (New York; Oxford: Clarendon Press, 1999)

Smithies, James, 'Modernism or exile: E.H. McCormick and letters and art in New Zealand', *Journal of Commonwealth Literature*, vol. 39, no. 3, 2004, pp. 93–106

Sobocinska, Agnieszka and White, Richard, 'Travel and connections', in Alison Bashford and Stuart Macintyre (eds), *Cambridge History of Australia: Volume 2 – The Australian Commonwealth* (Melbourne: Cambridge University Press, 2013, pp. 472–93

Stafford, Jane, 'Fashioned intimacies: Maoriland and colonial modernity', *Journal of Commonwealth Literature*, vol. 37, no. 31, 2002, pp. 31–48

Stafford, Jane and Williams, Mark, *Maoriland: New Zealand literature 1872–1914* (Wellington: Victoria University Press, 2006)

Stevens, Joan, *The New Zealand Novel 1860–1965* (Wellington: Reed, 1966)

Sturm, Terry, 'Introduction', in Frank Anthony, *Follow the Call* (Auckland: Auckland University Press, 1975)

——, 'The neglected middle distance: Towards a history of TransTasman literary relations', *Ariel*, vol. 16, no. 4, 1985, pp. 29–46

——, (ed.), *Oxford History of New Zealand Literature* (Oxford: Oxford University Press, 1998)

——, *An Unsettled Spirit: The life and frontier fiction of Edith Lyttleton (G.B. Lancaster)* (Auckland: Auckland University Press, 2003)

Sullivan, Alvin, *British Literary Magazines, V3: The Victorian and Edwardian age, 1837–1913* (Westport, Conn: Greenwood Press, 1983–1986)

Sutch, W.B., 'Libraries for all', *Tomorrow*, vol. 2, no. 1, 1935, p. 5.

Tasker, Meg, '"When London calls" and Fleet Street beckons: Daley's poem, Reg's diary – what happens when it all goes "bung"?', in David Brooks and Elizabeth MacMahon (eds), *Modern Mobilities: Australian-transnational writing* (Blackheath, NSW: Brandl & Schlesinger, 2011), pp. 107–26

Trainor, Luke, 'British publishers and cultural imperialism: History and ethnography in Australasia 1870–1930', *Bibliographical Society of Australia and New Zealand Bulletin*, vol. 20, no. 2, 1996, pp. 99–106

——, 'Imperialism, commerce and copyright: Australia and New Zealand, 1870–1930', *Bibliographical Society of Australia and New Zealand Bulletin*, vol. 21, no. 4, 1997, pp. 199–206

——, 'New Zealand writers seeking overseas publishers, 1870–1914: Some issues of nation and empire', *Script & Print*, vol. 29, no. 1–4, 2005, pp. 311–22

Traue, J.E., 'The public library explosion in colonial New Zealand', *Libraries and the Cultural Record*, vol. 42, no. 2, 2007, pp. 151–64.

——, 'Submerged below the codex line: New Zealand's neglected nineteenth century serial novels', *Journal of New Zealand Studies*, no. 20, 2015, pp. 2–9

Trevelyan, Jill, '"Perfectly fairy-godmotherish": The friendship of Toss Woollaston and Ursula Bethell', *Kōtare*, vol. 4, no. 1, 2001

Trussell, Denys, *Fairburn* (Auckland: Auckland University Press, 1984)

Turner, Dorothea, *Jane Mander* (New York: Twayne, 1972)

Vincent, David, *Literacy and Popular Culture: England 1750–1914* (Cambridge [England]; New York: Cambridge University Press, 1989)

Waite, Noel, *Adventure and Art: The Caxton Press* (Wellington: National Library of New Zealand, 1998)

Waller, Philip, *Writers, Readers and Reputations: Literary life in Britain, 1870–1918* (Oxford; New York: Oxford University Press, 2006)

Wedde, Ian, 'Introduction', *The Penguin Book of New Zealand Verse* (Auckland: Penguin, 1985), pp. 23–52.

Wevers, Lydia, 'Books: Are New Zealand and Australia part of the same literary community?', in Bruce Brown (ed.), *New Zealand and Australia: Where are we going?* Papers presented at the seminar arranged by the New Zealand Institute of International Affairs at Victoria University, Wellington on 4 July 2001 (Wellington: New Zealand Institute of International Affairs, 2001)

——, *Reading on the Farm: Victorian fiction and the colonial world* (Wellington: Victoria University Press, 2010)

——, 'First, build your hut', *Pacific Highways. Griffith Review*, no. 43, 2013, p. 267

Willcox, Walter F. and Ferenczi, Imre, *International Migrations VI* (New York: Gordon and Breach, 1969)

Williams, Mark, 'Repetitious beginnings: New Zealand literary history in the late 1980s', *Journal of New Zealand Literature*, no. 7, 1989, pp. 65–86

Wilson, Janet, 'Constructing the metropolitan homeland: The literatures of the white settler societies of New Zealand and Australia', in Michelle Keown, David Murphy and James Procter (eds), *Comparing Postcolonial Diasporas* (Basingstoke: Palgrave Macmillan, 2009), pp. 125–48

Wilson, Phillip, *William Satchell* (New York: Twayne Publishing, 1968)

Wild, Judith, 'The literary periodical in New Zealand', MA thesis (Victoria University College, 1951)

Woolf, Virginia, *A Room of One's Own* (Oxford: Oxford University Press, 1992)

Woollacott, Angela, *To Try Her Fortune in London: Australian women, colonialism and modernity* (Oxford: Oxford University Press, 2001)

——, *Settler Society in the Australian Colonies* (Oxford: Oxford University Press, 2015)

Woollaston, Toss, *Sage Tea* (Wellington: Te Papa Press, 2001)
Wright, F.W. Neilsen, *Theories of Style in the Schroder-Marris School of Poets in Aotearoa: An essay in formal stylistics with particular reference to the poets Eileen Duggan, Robin Hyde and Ruth Gilbert* (Wellington: Cultural and Political Booklets, 2001)
Young, David, 'Courage in exile', *New Zealand Listener*, vol. 101, no. 2211, 1982, p. 24

Internet sources

Australian Bureau of Statistics: 'Population and vital statistics bulletin, 1920': www.abs.gov.au/AUSSTATS/abs@.nsf/DetailsPage/3141.01920
Australian Dictionary of Biography (ADB): http://adb.anu.edu.au
Bartle, Rhonda, 'John Brodie – New Plymouth's neglected author', Puke Ariki: http://pukeariki.com/Learning-Research/Taranaki-Research-Centre/Taranaki-Stories/Taranaki-Story/id/105/title/john-brodie-new-plymouths-neglected-author
Dictionary of New Zealand Biography (DNZB): www.teara.govt.nz/en/biographies
An Encyclopaedia of New Zealand, 1966: www.teara.govt.nz/en/1966
Glass, Hayden and Choy, Wai Kin, 'Brain drain or brain exchange?', Treasury Working Paper 01/22: www.treasury.govt.nz/publications/research-policy/wp/2001/01-22/twp01-22.pdf
Encyclopedia Britannica: www.britannica.com
History of Cable Bay Station, Cable Bay Holiday Park: www.cablebayfarm.co.nz/history2.html
Kōtare: New Zealand Notes and Queries, Victoria University of Wellington: www.nzetc.org/tm/scholarly/tei-corpus-kotare.html
Labour and Immigration Research Centre, 'Permanent and long term migration: The big picture', Ministry of Business, Innovation and Employment: www.mbie.govt.nz/publications-research/research/migration/plt-migration.pdf
'The "Lost Generation" – American literature in Europe 1850–1950', British Library: www.bl.uk/onlinegallery/features/amliteuro/lostgen.html
New Zealand Book Council: www.bookcouncil.org.nz
New Zealand Electronic Poetry Centre: www.nzepc.auckland.ac.nz
New Zealand Electronic Text Centre: http://nzetc.victoria.ac.nz
New Zealand History Online, Ministry for Culture and Heritage: www.nzhistory.net.nz
Oxford English Dictionary Online: http://oed.com
'Register of New Zealand Presbyterian church ministers, deaconesses & missionaries from 1840', Presbyterian Church of Aotearoa New Zealand Archives Research Centre: www.presbyterian.org.nz/archives/Page159.htm
Statistics New Zealand: www.stats.govt.nz
Te Ara – the Encyclopedia of New Zealand: www.teara.govt.nz
US Census Bureau: 'Population, housing units, area measurements, and density: 1790 to 1990': www.census.gov/population

Index

Cluett, Isabel *see* Peacocke, Isabel Maud
Clyde, Constance 92
Colenso, William 31
colonial editions of books 35–37, 64, 77
'colonial exotic' 89–90, 171
colonial romance genre 91, 92, 93
colonial stereotypes 23–24, 52
colonial writing world and networks 10,
    11, 12, 16–20, 21, 52, 61, 73–94, 103,
    104, 105, 166–68; access to up-to-
    date literature 39; commercial and
    political connections 32, 80–81;
    communication 82–83, 173–74;
    importance in the creation of
    New Zealand literature 55, 72,
    120, 132, 162–64, 176, 180–81,
    182–83; modernity, multiplicity of
    connections and mobility 117–23,
    133; personal connections 83–84,
    111; role of bookmen 55; and
    'unhousedness' 101, 121, 122, 180,
    184; *see also* British Empire; literary
    expatriates, New Zealand, in Britain;
    publishing, Britain; Tasman literary
    connections
Columbia Press 84
competitions, literary 42, 50, 146, 150,
    167
Conrad, Joseph 14, 109, 151, 157
Cooke, Ella 169
Cosmopolitan 80
Courage, James 124, 126, 131, 141, 154,
    171, 176, 178; *The Call Home* 135;
    The Fifth Child 101
Cresswell, D'Arcy 43, 49, 50, 76, 116, 126,
    131, 133, 149–50, 157, 158, 163, 165–
    66, 171, 182; *Lyttelton Harbour* 179
Crisp, Percy 43–44
cultural cringe 97, 100, 113
cultural nationalism, New Zealand 12,
    24, 25, 42, 51, 52–53, 54, 182;
    British models 19; and colonial
    writing world 55, 74, 182–83;
    ignored international influences on
    New Zealand writing 19, 26, 37,
    38–39, 53, 55, 105, 182–83, 184;
    and literary expatriates 10, 15,
    96–97, 102–06, 122, 154, 174–75,
    180–81; marginalisation of women
    writers 54–55, 181–82; and

publishing 18–19, 55, 76, 97, 102–03,
    106–07, 179–80; and trans-Tasman
    links 59–60, 70–72
culture and society, New Zealand: colonial
    culture 24, 25, 26–27, 28–33, 34,
    37, 52, 118; influences of British
    culture 24, 25, 27, 29, 31, 32–38, 39,
    51, 53, 103, 168, 182; mobility and
    'world connectedness' 17, 117, 118–
    20, 121, 122, 125; New Zealanders as
    superior Britons 37–38; the product
    of outside influences 39, 97–98;
    rigidity and conformity 127–29,
    130, 131–32; state of never feeling at
    home 121–22; twentieth century 25,
    117; views of NZ as cultural
    wasteland 11–12, 23–24, 110–11,
    127–29, 138; *see also* literary culture,
    New Zealand
Curnow, Allen 52, 53, 54, 60, 72, 105, 106,
    107, 121–22, 182, 183; introduction
    to *A Book of New Zealand Verse* 18,
    103

Daley, Caroline 128
Daley, Victor 105, 174, 183
Dalziel, Raewyn 92, 128
Dannevirke 50
Davin, Dan 112, 126, 133, 143, 170, 171,
    176; *Cliffs of Fall* 84, 95, 96, 101; *The
    Sullen Bell* 140, 165; 'The Vigil' 152
Davin, Winnie 84, 152, 171
de la Mare, Walter 82
de Montalk, Geoffrey 42, 44, 49, 78, 84,
    129, 131, 138, 140, 142–43, 172–73,
    174; 'Return to London' 173; *Wild
    Oats* 129
Deamer, Dulcie 88, 128
Dent, Hugh 76
Devanny, Jean 66, 76, 92, 101–02;
    'Bushman Burke' 102; *The Butcher
    Shop* 66, 101
Dixon, Robert 90
Domett, Alfred, *Ranolf and Amohia* 90
Donnelly, Ian 82, 129
Douglas, Lord Alfred 51
Dowling, Basil 125
drama and theatre, New Zealand 26–27
Drew, John 47, 125
Duckworth, Gerald 139

atmosphere 141; productivity of New
Zealand writers 162–63; reception
of New Zealand writers 161–62;
successful New Zealand writers 99–
100, 153, 157, 162–63; *see also*
publishing, Britain
Lone Hand 61
'Lost Generation' 9
Lowry, Bob 47, 179
Lyceum Club, London 78, 144–45, 167;
New Zealand Circle 167, 178
Lynn, David, *Love and Hunger* 141–42
Lyons, Martyn 35–36, 77
Lyttelton 30
Lyttleton, Edith (pseud. G.B. Lancaster) 10,
20–21, 69, 99, 112, 123, 131, 134,
175; 'Dominion' novels 71; *The
Law-Bringers* 80; in London 139–
40, 157–58, 161, 163, 165, 167,
178; *Pageant* 71, 74, 83, 86, 145;
participation in colonial writing
world 71, 75; Pinker as agent 82–83,
157–58; *Promenade* 38, 90; *Sons o'
Men* 83, 160; *A Spur to Smite* 83,
160; successful writer while in New
Zealand 50, 140; travel in Canada 80;
use of pseudonym 10, 160; *The World
is Yours* 80; writing published in
magazines and newspapers 58, 61, 79,
80, 140, 161

Mackay, Charles 131
Mackay, Jessie 42, 49, 51–52, 53, 62, 63,
64, 66, 76, 123, 131, 167, 178, 181;
Poems 63; Scottish poetry 79, 121;
*The Spirit of Rangatira and Other
Ballads* 181; *Vigil* 121
Macky, Edna Graham 50
Macmillan publishers 85–86
Macmillan's Colonial Library 36, 82
Macquarie Head Press 63
Mactier, Susie 92
magazines *see* periodicals, international;
periodicals, New Zealand
Magner, Brigid 119
'man alone' figure 54
Manchester Guardian 73
Mander, Jane 11–12, 43, 45, 46, 49, 89, 92,
111, 130, 131, 132, 175; agent 157;
Allen Adair 115; Columbia School

of Journalism and New York 80,
115, 126, 157, 170; compared
to Mansfield 115, 134; letter
writing 173; letters to Holcroft 83,
93–94, 98; in London 76, 77, 86, 98,
110, 142, 144, 145, 149, 154, 157, 161,
163, 164–65, 167, 170, 171, 173, 174,
179; in Paris 153; *The Passionate
Puritan* 120, 129; *The Story of a New
Zealand River* 23, 39, 76, 101, 128–29;
The Strange Attraction 154
Mansfield, Katherine 12, 15, 82, 96,
134–35, 170, 182; agents 157; in
England and Europe 11, 24, 97, 98,
108, 110, 111–12, 115–16, 134, 148,
163, 165, 167; identification with New
Zealand 116, 174, 176, 178–79; sense
of exile 108, 110; stories published in
Australian newspaper 61, 63
Mantz, Ruth 116
Māori: appropriation of cultural elements
in New Zealand nationalism 38;
connections to Britain 33;
descriptions of life and culture
by writers 89–90; tradition 105;
writers 90
'Maoriland' school of writing 25, 90
marriage, and writing 130–31
Marris, Charles 44, 51, 182
Marsh, Ngaio 27, 43, 88, 131, 133–34,
154, 157, 163; 'A new Canterbury
pilgrim' series of articles 173; *Colour
Scheme* 88; *Died in the Wool* 88;
Vintage Murder 88
Marshall, Theresia 50, 58, 61, 72
Martindale, C.C. 82
Mason, R.A.K. 24, 49, 53, 86, 93, 129,
140, 141, 150, 155, 168, 177, 182; *The
Beggar* 41, 86
Mayhew, Arthur 84
McClelland, David (pseud. David
Lynn) 162
McClure Newspaper Syndicate 34
McCormick, Eric 15, 25, 30, 50, 55, 59,
96, 97, 98, 99, 103, 107–08, 116, 123,
125, 134
McEldowney, Dennis 30–31, 44, 45;
'Publishing, patronage and literary
magazines' 75–76
McLean, Denis 125

in Australia 62–63, 74, 76, 83, 156;
published in Britain 73–74, 75, 76,
77, 84, 86–87, 89, 90, 91, 92–93, 99,
156; published in New Zealand 74,
75, 156; published in the United
States 74, 156; search for 'great New
Zealand novel' 25, 47, 55; serialised
in newspapers and magazines 47

Observer 79
O'Neill, Reginald 43
Orwell, George 157
Osmond, Sophie, Ponga Bay 93
O'Sullivan, Vincent 108, 117, 135
Otago Daily Times 69
Otago Witness 46, 62, 173
Ould, Herman 170
Oxford History of New Zealand
    Literature 9, 23–24, 75–76
Oxford University Press 133, 170

Pall Mall 79
Palmer, Nettie 11, 42, 49, 62, 63–64, 66,
    83, 104, 145
Palmer, Vance 63–64, 104, 164
Paris 9, 14, 20, 23, 137, 143, 153, 154
Park, Ruth 127
Paterson, A.B. (Banjo) 57, 104
Peacocke, Isabel Maud 13, 50, 79, 89,
    99, 100, 101–02, 123, 144, 162;
    The Guardian 91; London Called
    Them 143–44, 145–46, 171; Songs of
    the Happy Isles 43, 62
Pearn, Nancy 84, 152
Pearson, Bill 46, 102, 126
Pelorus Press 47
PEN (Poets, Essayists, Novelists) 144, 153,
    170; New Zealand Centre 17
Pender, Anne, From a Distant Shore 13
Penguin Classics library 151
Penguin History of New Zealand
    Literature 182
periodicals, international: Australia 61–
    62, 70, 78, 85; Britain 79, 85, 145,
    150, 152, 159, 171; New Zealand
    contributors 78, 79–80, 85, 152, 153,
    159, 164, 171; United States 79–80
periodicals, New Zealand 33, 34, 38;
    Australian writers 62; children's
    pages 46; publishing opportunities
    for writers 11, 12, 44–46, 55, 75,

153, 158; see also newspapers, New
    Zealand; and titles of individual
    periodicals
'peripheral survival' 32
Phillips, A.A. 100, 127, 164
Phillips, Jock 37, 38, 57
Phoenix 47, 180
Phoenix group 52–53, 54, 106, 107,
    180–81
piano sales 27
Pierce, Peter, Cambridge History of
    Australian Literature 13
Pinker, J.B. 82–83, 157, 158
pioneers, New Zealand see settlers, New
    Zealand
Plumridge, Elizabeth 27, 166, 169
Pocock, J.G.A. 120, 121
poetry, New Zealand 49, 51–52, 70, 87,
    90, 149–50; British models 51, 106;
    cultural nationalism 54, 103; dislike
    of free verse 51, 53; New Zealand
    content 51–52, 93, 171; published
    in Australia 11, 61, 62–63, 74, 79;
    published in Britain 11, 73–74, 78,
    79, 83, 84–85, 171; published in New
    Zealand 41–42, 43, 44, 45, 46, 47,
    74, 75, 156; published in the United
    States 11, 74, 79; see also names of
    individual poets
postal communication 34, 48–49, 82
Pound, Ezra 9, 45, 109
Powys, T.F., Mr Weston's Good Wine 151
Press (Christchurch) 43, 44, 88, 168, 173,
    174
printing, New Zealand 30–31, 35, 42
publishing, Britain: Australasian
    market 35, 58, 64–65, 81, 99;
    Australian attitudes to 98, 103–04;
    and Australian writers 13–14; 'Book
    of the Month' 145, 146; books
    by innovative writers 150–51;
    contracts 146, 158; distribution
    arrangements 99, 162;
    dominance 35; and New Zealand
    writers 47, 73–74, 75–78, 79, 80–94,
    97–99, 115, 139–40, 143–44, 145, 146,
    154, 155, 156, 158–61, 170; published
    books by location of author 155,
    156; writers' techniques to achieve
    publication 158–60